PURE GOLD

PURE GOLD

BY

O. E. RÖLVAAG

ENGLISH TEXT BY SIVERT ERDAHL
AND THE AUTHOR

GREENWOOD PRESS, PUBLISHERS
WESTPORT, CONNECTICUT

Library of Congress Cataloging in Publication Data

Rølvaag, Ole Edvart, 1876-1931.
  Pure gold.

  Reprint of the ed. published by Harper & Bros.,
New York.
  A considerably rev. English ed. of the author's
To tullinger, et billede fra idag.
  CONTENTS: The days of the honeymoon.--Pure gold.
--On the mount of temptation. [etc.]
  I. Title.
PZ3.R6275Pu10 [PT9150.R55]   839.8'2'372
ISBN 0-8371-7070-2   73-11846

Originally published in 1930 by Harper & Brothers, New York

Copyright 1930 by Harper & Brothers

Reprinted with the permission of Harper & Row, Publishers, Inc.

Reprinted in 1973 by Greenwood Press
A division of Congressional Information Service
88 Post Road West, Westport, Connecticut 06881

Library of Congress Catalog Card Number 73-11846

ISBN 0-8371-7070-2

Printed in the United States of America

10 9 8 7 6 5 4 3 2

*"But God said unto him,
  Thou fool, this night thy soul
  Shall be required of thee: then
  Whose shall those things be,
  Which thou hast provided?"*

—LUKE XII, 20

CONTENTS

PURE GOLD

I. The Days of the Honeymoon

THE threshers had just arrived at Tom Öien's.
Midway between the granary and the barns stood
several settings of grain stacks, waiting for the
threshing.

It was already late afternoon; the day beautiful;
the loveliest autumn weather imaginable; clear skies—
the whole firmament only lazy, indolent blueness
domed over a drowsing earth.

The crew worked swiftly and with a sure grasp to
get the machine in readiness for starting up. Some
were setting the separator; others were working at
the horsepower. Two men drove down stakes; the thud
of the sledge-hammers beat heavily across the yard,
and even into the kitchen where doors and windows
had been opened wide because of the oppressive heat.
Now and then came the sound of laughter and ripping
words of command from hale men, conscious of their
own strength.

Lizzie Öien, Tom's only child, already well past
twenty-five, flew to and fro, now to the pump for a
pail of water, now to the cellar for milk and cream
and fresh butter. The jellies, the plum jam, and the
beet pickles she must not forget. She had better hurry!
Supper-time was fast nearing, and there were twelve

hungry men to feed besides father and mother and herself. Hungry threshers could do away with a lot of food . . . that Lizzie knew from many former seasons—it wasn't the first time she had been responsible for the inner wants of a crew like this.

Whenever Lizzie was outside she had to give a hurried look in the direction of the men at work. Each time her eyes singled out the same figure, the man who tended the horsepower. Once, just as she had come in and closed the screen door behind her, she had to turn around and look again, fascinated by what she saw: The man, shoving aside a youngster trying to drive a stake, seized the sledge, made some kind of remark—evidently a witty one because the bystanders laughed uproariously—and swung the sledge-hammer himself. Through the screen door Lizzie watched him. Heaving the heavy sledge above his head, his muscular body bending gracefully under the weight, he struck the peg squarely every time. As she watched, the rhythmic motion of his body and the sound of the impact changed into music. Never had Lizzie witnessed anything so beautiful. She remained at the door until the stake had been sunk to the proper depth, then turned and placed the cream pitcher on the table, her face flushed and hot, her hand trembling. She hurried to the open window and fanned herself with her apron.

When the rig had been fully set in order the hour was close on six. A couple of the neighbours who had chores to do after they reached home in the evening, hinted that now it was time to call it a day and quit.

They grumbled as they saw Lars Houglum beginning
to hitch the teams to the horsepower. The two owners
of the machine, Jens Haugen and Lars Houglum, paid
no particular attention to the mutterings of the men.
Jens merely observed that the weather was fine and
the grain dry, and the time to get some good threshing
done was right now; they had come to do a day's work
and would have to stay until sundown—after that they
could go home and fool with their wives all they
damned pleased. . . . Hell—the idea of quitting now
. . . scarcely dinner-time yet!

Shortly, Jens called out from the top of the
separator:

"All right. Get 'em going, Lars!"

In one mighty leap Lars was standing on the platform of the horsepower. Swinging the long whip over
his head, he cracked it in the air with sharp reports like
pistol-shots. The horses strained forward and pulled
hard; slowly the separator gained motion and began to
hum, coughing up a fine dust, almost like smoke; the
feeder took his accustomed place on the platform, and,
on each side of him, a bundle-cutter; the pitchers
scrambled on top of the stacks. In a moment the work
was in full swing.

Like a deep, sonorous voice the droning of the machine floated through the soft, silken air of the still
evening. Enthroned upon his horsepower, an absolute
monarch, Lars sat, swinging his great whip, intently
watching his subjects and the work. The separator
hummed lustily. At intervals the rumbling of a wagon

cut in upon the undulating sing-song of the machine, loud and hollow when approaching, dull and heavy when leaving with a full load. Each man bent to his job. The whole yard was enveloped by a cloud of dust, of chaff, and of chopped-up straw. Floating a while in the still air, the fog at last sank, a fine yellow powder settling on the ground and near-by buildings.

From the kitchen came pleasant odours of savoury food; the men hauling grain sniffed and reported their findings to the rest of the crew, who gave a shouting cheer—tonight they'd do full justice to Mrs. Öien's good cooking. . . . Let's get done, boys, doggone it! No loitering there, you rascals!

Not until the last bundle of the four stacks, which constituted the first setting, had been sent through the separator, did Lars Houglum call out his ringing, "Whoa-boys!" About time, too, some of the men thought; the sun had set quite awhile ago, now only a deep glow marking the place in the western sky.

But nothing more was said about working overtime. Hurriedly the teams were being unhitched, each man taking care of his own. Though tired after the long day's work, the men cracked jokes and bandied good-naturedly with one another; among the younger members of the crew there was loud talk and much laughter.

As soon as the men had cared for the horses they hurried up to the house. On a wooden bench, standing alongside the porch, there were four wash-bowls, and by the side of each a bar of soap and clean towels. The threshers not being too fastidious, two men washed in the same bowl. No time to waste now—this was no Fourth of July celebration!

Lars Houglum did not come up with the others. He had two teams to look after. It was often said of Lars that he took better care of his horses than he did of himself, which might be true, too. Because of this habit he was always late for meals; the rest of the crew joked him about it, and taunted him by saying that if he had paid half as much attention to the girls as to his old plugs, he would have been married long ago, and by now would have had his own bundle-cutters! Lars only grinned sheepishly whenever he was teased about the girls.

Tonight he took extra care with his scrubbing. One washing didn't satisfy him. Having been to the pump for another pail of water, he rolled his shirt collar as far down as it would go and began washing in real earnest.

In the kitchen the meal was almost over. With glowing cheeks Lizzie had fluttered about the room, from cupboard to table, from table to stove, and back again to the table, her mother directing the work. But now that the rush was over, Lizzie stepped out on the porch for a breath of cool air.

When she came out, Lars, for the second time, was vigorously dipping into the wash-basin. Hearing some one come, he squinted up, getting one eye sufficiently open to see who it was. "Glad to see you, Lizzie; this job is too much for one man!"

"Is it? You need some one to help you?"

"Uh-huh!" agreed Lars, again bending over the bowl. "You better call the rest of the crew!"

Lizzie had come a little closer and was leaning against a post, with her left arm around it. The sight of Lars' nut-brown neck, arched over the bowl, caught her attention; she leaned forward. To one with an eye for colour that neck was really a study. Close to the nape, the skin was burnt dark brown; downward it gradually shaded off into lighter tones, till between the shoulder blades it became white and soft.

"You aren't using enough water," laughed Lizzie, teasingly.

"Who said so?" For a moment Lars blinked up at her through the soapy froth, and then went on scrubbing.

Lizzie did not answer his taunt. Bending down quickly, she snatched a towel, dipped it into the pail, and slammed it down his neck; the water splashed as the towel struck. "There now!" she laughed in a low, liquid voice.

Lars jumped, gasping for breath. "You crazy kid!" he choked and shook himself like a dog just coming out of the water. Then he straightened himself up. For a moment, motionless, he stared at her, uncertain, hesitating. What happened next he himself did not quite realize until it was over because it came so suddenly. In two leaps he was standing on the porch beside Lizzie; before she had time to stir, his arm was around her neck. . . . "Guess I better pay you for that . . . now, come along!"

Sounds of the scuffle penetrated into the kitchen. Some of the men were through eating and came rushing out to see what was happening, their shouts and laughter bringing the others. Soon there was not a soul left in the kitchen. The men, bantering and guffawing, cheered on now one and now the other of the two combatants.

When Lizzie realized what Lars had in mind she held on to the post till her fingers whitened—not for all the world would she give in! Lars was just as determined; his left arm held her like a vise, his right hand working frantically to get both of her hands loose at the same moment in order to pull her away from the post. But Lizzie was quick as a cat; no sooner had he succeeded in wrenching one hand loose, than the other would catch hold. Her strength and her agility were equally marvellous.

Finally he got her left arm under his own left, and, by bearing down on it, prevented her from reaching the post. The rest was comparatively easy; he was, after all, the stronger of the two. For a second he stood irresolute, holding her in a tight clasp. Had it not been for the presence of the others and their verbal mix-up in the affair, he might have let her go. Now he could not; he felt instantly that it would not do. But it looked silly to stand here embracing Lizzie—just holding her in his arms. And so Lars, picking her up bodily and carrying her down the steps to the nearest wash-bowl, doused her face properly while the crew cheered wildly.

Throughout the tussle neither of the two had uttered

a syllable, only short, hot pantings. The minute he released her she flashed around the corner and was gone.

Lars looked at the corner around which she had vanished so suddenly, and grinned. How still the air was tonight! . . . Fine weather for threshing tomorrow! . . . He found nothing to say . . . could not have spoken now if he had to. Strange emotions were astir within him, feelings that made him want to be alone and to sing. It would have been pleasant to sing. An odd bashfulness had overtaken him; yet he was not ashamed of himself. What should he be ashamed of? He and Lizzie had only had a little fun! . . . In a soft, queer joy he stepped up on the porch and stood among the men. . . . Perhaps he better comb his hair before going in? Where were the comb and the looking-glass? The glass had been hanging there on the wall. Couldn't he see tonight? What was the matter with him?

The others made up for his silence. Svend Skarstad and John Hove, generally acknowledged to be the two worst clowns in the whole settlement, wouldn't let him alone. Svend insisted to the others that from now on it would not be safe to let Lars run loose; either they'd have to fence him in or tie him up. Safest, perhaps, to do both. Gosh almighty! How he had hugged that girl! Terrible when a fellow got as hard up as all that. . . .

"You're right, you're right," nodded John Hove, gravely. "Suppose he should get into his head to kiss anything wearing skirts? What would there be left for the rest of you boys?" John waved his hand dramatically.

"That's right, too," rejoined Svend. "I didn't think of that. Who would want a girl that Lars had kissed?"

Lars was oblivious to the jibes of the men; he had combed his hair and was standing with his hands in his pockets, wondering whether he ought to go in and get something to eat. . . . Lizzie could hardly have eaten yet, either?

As he swung the screen door open to enter the kitchen, admonitions hailed about his ears: "Now be careful, Lars." "Don't do anything rash." "Some of us better go in and keep an eye on him." One volunteered to fetch the minister; another suggested the sheriff. "No, boys," broke in John Hove, decisively, "you get *both*—this is nothing to fool with!"

Not until Lars was almost through eating—and to-night he took plenty of time—did Lizzie come in. She had changed her dress, he noticed. This one was of a dark-blue colour, which made her flushed, strong face seem still healthier. Her hair, too, must have been combed over. . . . Lars ate more slowly.

Lizzie did not look in the direction of the table, but went directly to the stove, lifted a cover, and put in some more wood, then refilled the teakettle.

"It's a fine man that takes to wrestling with a woman!" She had some trouble in getting the cover adjusted properly.

Lars sipped his coffee slowly. When he spoke there

was unfeigned admiration in his voice; the words carried a soft tenderness:

"It beats all how strong you are!"

She glanced over quickly, and turned to face him. They were alone in the room; the twilight was fast deepening into darkness. . . . Perhaps she ought to light the lamp? One couldn't hear oneself talk in here.

"Is that so?" she answered, mockingly.

"Yes, sir, and no mistake about it. It was just like wrestling with a man!"

At that Lizzie laughed a little, and a queer laugh it was, as though she were embarrassed. "You oughtn't be so rough—not with a girl!"

"Guess that's right. Threshers don't know nothing about girls. Tough life, all right. . . . I don't suppose you could spare me another drop of coffee; I'm all tuckered out after that tussle."

Lizzie hesitated a moment. "If you'll wait till I get the lamp lit."

She set the lighted lamp down in the centre of the table, got the coffee-pot, and filled his cup. Lars couldn't take his eyes off her. She felt the persistence of his gaze, and the colour in her face deepened.

"There," she said, handing him the cup.

"You ain't angry with me, Lizzie?" Lars was reaching for the cream and did not dare to look up.

Lizzie laughed softly; a melodious song in her laugh. "Oh, I don't think so; anyway, not so bad that I won't get over it." Again her eyes sought his in a swift glance; there was a sly twinkle in them.

Lars caught that glance, and a pleasant dizziness overtook him; his eyes blurred; he laughed giddily, got up and stretched himself . . . now he could easily wrestle some more! He searched for something to say, something really nice that would make her laugh again, but he was interrupted by Mrs. Öien who came in, carrying two full milk-pails. She began setting up the cream separator, which stood in the corner by the table. Lars recovered with a start. What was he thinking of, fooling away his time in here? He had his horses to tend for the night; it was pitch dark already. . . . What had he done with his hat?

II

The next day, in spite of a steady run, the threshers had all they could do to finish the job at Tom Öien's. When they were through it was too late to move on, and so they had to stay one more night at Tom's. In the days of the horsepower the rig did not furnish its own complete crew. The two owners and the feeder, McLaughlin, an old Irishman, were the only permanent fixtures. The remainder of the crew the farmers themselves supplied by hiring and by exchanging work with one another.

Jens Haugen, who was married and had a big farm of his own to look after, drove home evenings, if the distance were not too great. Thus it came about that

Lars and McLaughlin were the only two men to remain at Öien's that night.

During supper McLaughlin had received many serious warnings to take good care of Lars, now that the poor fellow would be left to his sole charge. By this time he knew how impossible Lars would act up whenever the spells seized him. . . . Poor Lars, he really wasn't responsible, with girls around; they all knew that. . . . What a pity that he never could get himself married! . . . There must be some defect or other about him since the girls hated him so. Had he ever consulted a doctor, they wondered? . . . Strange, too, when one came to think about it. Lars wasn't worse than many other fools, not much worse, anyway. And as for looks, well, many a scarecrow had succeeded in getting a girl, though the Lord knew Lars was no Madonna! . . . Perhaps the crew ought to act in his behalf? That had been done in olden times. . . .

Lars was well seasoned and met the thrusts good-naturedly. Usually he would defend himself, but to-night he just laughed with the rest. Throughout the meal he maintained an unruffled calm. . . . If only Lizzie hadn't been in the room! And tonight she looked still more handsome.

In reality, it was Lizzie who had to run the gauntlet. Lars understood that much. Though she pretended not to hear what the men were saying, still she could not help joining in the laugh at some of the sallies, the remarks were so irresistibly funny.

The climax came when John Hove took her hand to

say good-bye. Now she must be strictly on her guard, John admonished. No danger as far as McLaughlin was concerned, because he was innocent, as a lamb almost. Besides, he had a wife of his own down in Kansas. No, the man to look out for was Lars. Poor, poor boy! John Hove suddenly found it difficult to restrain his tears and would not let her hand go.

"Isn't that just what I have been saying?" added Svend, with a solemn nod. "Yes, sir, it's still pretty early in the season, but to my own personal knowledge Lars so far has proposed to no less than fifteen girls and had a flat *no* every doggone time. I know it, because the girls have told me themselves. Now the man is down-right desperate. You see"—Svend became confidential—"the trouble is this: Every time a girl turns him down he takes it so confounded hard—he hasn't any sense."

"Don't we all know that?" chimed in John. "I shall never forget last summer, the time he went to work and popped the question to that Irish girl out West here. You remember, Svend, how you and I the next morning found his overalls hanging in the straw-carrier? A sorry sight, I tell you; Lars himself was sleeping peacefully in the straw pile, with no more clothes on his body than *that*. It took up until Thanksgiving to convince him that he wasn't dead and buried. . . . It's just awful when Lars takes to acting that way! . . . Well, good night! I'd like to stay and look after him myself."

The last belated member of the crew had taken his

leave; the rumbling of the wagon came at intervals, a distant dying sound far away out in the darkness.

Lars was enjoying delectably sweet peace over his corncob pipe. He and Tom Öien, leaning comfortably back in their chairs, were engaged in small talk. Tom was in a most excellent humour; now that he had his crop safely in the granary, a sense of quiet satisfaction possessed him.

The talk died down between them, each busy with his own thoughts. Tom fell to thinking about the man sitting beside him—much nonsense had been spoken at the supper table tonight. The girl would have to marry, sometime. . . . Lars was saving and sober, a steady worker; no fooling of any kind. The prairie needed just such men . . . such always made headway. . . . Yet Lars didn't seem to be getting there very fast. . . . Tom turned the problem in his mind. . . . The share in the threshing rig must be all he owned? And threshing was a poor business, in the long run. . . . The other thing he had heard said about Lars, that he was slow with books and such matters, would not make so much difference. One could get along all right without knowing much about books—Tom knew that. . . . Enough sin and wickedness in the world; no need to go to books and newspapers after more. What mattered was honesty, and willingness to work, and ambition to get ahead. . . . Tom knocked the ashes out of his pipe and got up, remarking that he supposed it was time to crawl in. With a friendly good night he left Lars to himself.

Lars intended to follow him presently. But first he had to make a trip to the barn to look after his horses. McLaughlin was already deep in the sweet slumber of the righteous; there were regularly recurring trumpet-blasts coming out of an upstairs window.

Lars took plenty of time with the horses. No hurry. He didn't feel like going to bed yet. There were certain things he ought to figure out. . . . The boys had been a little rough tonight, and Lizzie had had to listen to it all. Wonder how much she believed? A damned sensible girl—how gloriously she had fought! . . . Lars walked out of the barn. Midway up to the house he stopped to listen. Even down here he could hear McLaughlin. Just wait, old fellow; I'll soon put a stop to that racket! . . . Lars had a certain trick with McLaughlin, one that he had invented himself: a short decisive pinch in the ribs, like a quick cut with a pair of scissors, then a twist, and immediately McLaughlin would roll over on the other side. The pause which followed would last long enough for Lars to drop off to sleep.

Lars sauntered over to the pump for a drink of water. Downstairs the house was all dark. As he was standing there, some one opened the kitchen door quietly, came out and sat on the porch. Lars felt his hand tremble; to steady his nerves and gain time he pumped another cupful, which he drank slowly. He waited a minute before he strolled over to the house.

His "good evening" sounded as solemn as though it had been spoken in church. Lizzie's answer was not much louder, but it had a friendly sound. The other chair was standing where it had stood only a minute ago, and so he sat down. The wind was slow and cool; no moon; the stars looked calmly through the darkness; the night was full of a mysterious quiet, alive and listening.

"Fine evening." Lizzie spoke first.

"A nice day for threshing tomorrow." Lars looked up and studied the sky. "The grass is heavy with dew."

"Is that a sign of clear weather?"

"Uh-huh. That's what the old-timers say."

A long pause; both were at a loss for more to say, and felt far apart.

Again Lizzie spoke first: "I wouldn't care to be a thresher."

Lars, taken aback, looked at her. "Why not? . . . Because they are so rough?" he added with a dry laugh.

Lizzie didn't join in. "Not that so much. . . . It's better to be a farmer. The farm is certain and, well, dependable . . . you can get ahead on the farm."

"That's all true enough," Lars admitted; "but what's the fellow going to do who hasn't got a farm?"

"Get one, of course!" There was a note of raillery in her deep voice. "Joe Lunde's farm is for sale, I hear. Pretty good buildings on it, too."

"Talk is cheap; it takes money to buy whisky. Joe is asking eight thousand dollars . . . not that I haven't had it in mind," Lars added, soberly.

"That shouldn't be much for a man like you . . . especially if you got a little help!"

Lars' mind was suddenly thrown into chaos. Shooting stars flickered before his eyes. The strong man who could drive stakes so lustily that the mere sight of him was good to behold, sat there helpless. For two years he had had his eye on Lizzie, but had never dared to come near her—had seen her both when he was awake and in his dreams, at times wanting her beyond madness. And now, here she sat right by his side, taunting him about a thing that was clearly impossible! Disconcerted, befuddled, he fumbled in his pocket for his Battle-Ax plug, fished it out, and bit off a big piece.

"If I got help?" he echoed, dejectedly.

Lizzie was humming a tune, quietly, all to herself. The rocker dipped back and forth ever so little, her right foot softly tapping the rhythm of the tune. Suddenly she faced him:

"How much money have you?"

"Not a great deal, I tell you! Figuring the machine and horses and everything, I suppose I could scrape together about two thousand. . . . That wouldn't go very far on a farm like Joe's."

When Lizzie spoke again her words were barely audible and she made brief pauses: "I suppose Father could help a little . . . a thousand or two, perhaps. . . . And a team . . . a few cows, maybe . . . a little something to start with, at any rate."

Lars spat furiously, the way he did when the machine was humming the liveliest and every man of the crew was working away for dear life, and sprang up.

"Gosh, Lizzie—then you, too, would have to move

over to Joe's farm!" He stopped, terror-stricken because of what he had said.

"Oh, do you really think so?" Her little laugh added
music to her words, soft, unutterably sweet music, and
made Lars shake as if in an attack of ague. Then in
the same tone, Lizzie added, "We could agree on that
later, couldn't we?" Suddenly she got up. "I am cold!"
she said. . . . "I can't be staying out any longer!"
There was a shiver in her voice as though she were in
a chill. She held out her hand to him: "Good night,
Lars!"

Lars grasped her hand; it was long and slender; the
body of it disappeared entirely within his huge fist . . .
lay there warm and tender. He made an effort to speak:
. . . "You certainly aren't playing with me, Lizzie?"
His voice was hoarse and strained from pent-up emotion. Then more pleadingly, almost in tears, "I can depend on you, can't I?"

"Oh, you silly boy!" She laughed softly, close to his
face. "You will have to ask Father, I guess." Dis-
engaging her hand she stepped inside quickly and disappeared into the darkness of the room.

Lars waited until he heard her door close upstairs.
Still less now than earlier in the evening did he feel inclined to join McLaughlin. How could he sleep? His
heart was thumping wildly in tumultuous, reckless
joy. . . . He began strolling back and forth in the
yard, to the barn first, once more looking in upon his
horses, then to the machine, assuring himself that everything was in readiness for the morrow. . . . He'd

show the men how to work! . . . When he sauntered to the barn for the last time, there was nothing left of the Battle-Ax plug. . . . Wrapping himself in a heavy horse blanket, Lars made his bed that night in the straw pile.

III

Shortly before Christmas Lars bought the Lunde farm. Though he paid a high price, he made a good bargain because Joe Lunde included so much in the deal: several pieces of furniture, all the machinery, considerable stock, and one horse.

His engagement to Lizzie Öien caused much comment among the young people in the neighbourhood, for not many things happened those days, and all news was welcome. Lizzie did not bother about the talk, little heeding the scraps that came to her ears—there were other matters to think of now! Always before she had been living on the outskirts of life; now it was opening its gates wide; soon she would be entering the very mystery of it. She felt herself singled out from her unmarried friends, blessed, set apart as it were. Her vague longings, all her uneasy stirrings, the sweet discontent she had felt so often, had suddenly been stilled. In her steps had come a new certainty; she worked with a sure grasp on things, for now she knew what was to become of her. She would recall the story of the Virgin

Mary and smile secretively. Life was beautiful, and hers to enjoy. She and Lars were the only two people that really existed; as for the others—well, who cared about the others?

Already she had drawn a mental picture, detailed and carefully worked out, of how she would arrange her new home after the wedding. The upholstered rocker she would place in the coziest corner of the living-room . . . it might be pleasant to rest there after a hard day's work . . . and Lars wouldn't mind having her on his lap . . . then she would be good to him! Whenever she thought of his great strength she shivered in pleasant excitement.

. . . The round table she would leave in the centre of the parlour floor, but the big sofa she would move into the living-room between the window and the front door—she had measured the distance the last time she was over. Everything about the place was going to be neat and attractive . . . she would show the women of the neighbourhood that she knew how to keep house!

Throughout the winter Lizzie lived in the future; at times her face would have an absent look. . . . If only Lars could manage his end of it! Not that she didn't intend to help him with the outside work, too. But Lars wasn't very strong on planning and such like— no one is perfect in everything, anyway. . . . She would have to stand by him and help think things out and decide. The first year they would have to get along without a hired man . . . perhaps the next, too . . .

that way they'd save enough to pay all the interest on the mortgage, and save they must.

. . . Another advantage, too, in not having a stranger around the house: she could have her strong, big husband all to herself . . . morning, noon, and night, only the two of them! They would have the farm as a world they ruled over . . . only the two of them in their own universe!

Her mind was constantly building pictures. There was the problem of the poultry; by tending the poultry well she could make enough to pay for the groceries she and Lars needed . . . perhaps buy their clothes also. Mentally, she was selecting the hens she intended to take with her when she moved. . . . Now that she was to set up in life for herself, it was only proper that Father and Mother should help her get established. And they could afford it; Father had considerable money put aside . . . moreover, he and Mother had their lives behind them, while she and Lars were about to begin theirs.

. . . To be sure they would make things go. On an occasional Sunday she would ask the old folks over for dinner . . . at Christmas she might even invite the minister . . . then people would get something else to talk about than this old foolishness about her never getting married! 'Twould serve 'em right, too. That Minnie Dahl, for instance, and Jennie Haugan . . . both of them the same age as she. Never would they get a man like Lars . . . no one in sight yet for any of them. . . . Oh no! If you wanted to get anywhere, you had to bestir yourself—nothing like making good use of an opportunity. . . . What a dear that Lars was! . . . so strong and innocent, and so slow! Lizzie smiled to herself.

. . . Of course, they would have to be careful not to spend money needlessly. No cheap thing to entertain a lot of company . . . then, too, one could waste a lot of time that way . . . and since Lars was going to do all the work alone, she would have to be his hired man . . . for a while. . . . Later there would be other things to look after!

Best of all she loved to let her heart play with Lars and how wonderfully good she would be to him once she had him all to herself. The finest man on the whole Green Prairie she would make him; when he walked into church the congregation would have to look! . . . First of all she'd touch up his name. Lars sounded so foreign; it wasn't a bit nice, either; she'd call him *Louis;* that was American. Now listen to this: Mrs. Louis Houglum—Mrs. Lizzie M. Houglum, oh, there was a name to feel proud of! And other things, too, she'd do with him; Lars was so strong and helpless, just like a little boy who hadn't had any care for a long time. . . . So Lizzie planned happily, blissfully, like a child playing with precious toys.

During the winter Lars and Lizzie had had few opportunities to be together alone, but, now that spring was in the air, conditions changed.

Early and late during the week Lars toiled on the

farm. Under the incentive which love gives, he did the work of two men. . . . Hire help? Oh, no, not with that mortgage on the place! That mortgage was the only cloud in an otherwise clear sky. And he could easily do the work alone. From sunup to sundown he was on the job. A pity that he had to work his horses so hard. . . . In the evening, to compensate for it, he took care of them as a fond mother would look after her children.

Every Sunday Lars came to Öien's around noon, ate dinner there, and then, in the afternoon, brought Lizzie over to her new home. On these visits she always helped him tidy up the house; in the evening she cooked the supper; afterward they went out to the barns to gather eggs, while Lars marvelled at her quickness in finding the nests, and told her so. On these rounds she taught him many useful things about the fowls and told him what kinds she meant to have later. If the evenings were not too chilly, they moved their chairs out on the porch. When the twilight had deepened sufficiently, one chair was enough. Then both felt deeply that greater bliss no human being had any right to expect. What would it not be after they were married? Both grew silent; the thought made them dizzy.

It was on one of these Sunday evenings that Lizzie, just for fun, began calling him Louis. From now on, she said, her left hand playing with his hair, her right holding his chin, she would call him by that name because Louis was ever so much prettier than Lars. . . . Couldn't he hear how much nicer it sounded? . . . As if there was no doubt about the truth of it, she bent over and kissed him.

Lars met the proposal with silence; he was in so happy a mood that he didn't pay much attention to her words; nor could he get his voice up for articulate speech; but when she repeated the name, he felt a touch of displeasure. Perhaps it wasn't displeasure, just a shudder in the cold air—the nights were chilly so early in the spring. Rousing himself, he said recklessly that if she preferred his name that way, it was all the same to him . . . most likely she was not far wrong . . . a more wonderful girl ——! To give greater emphasis to his words he hugged her closer, burying his face in her bosom. And when she responded willingly Lars murmured dizzily that she might call him anything she pleased. To quiet that odd sensation he told himself that Louis did sound a good deal better, at least the way she pronounced the name.

"That's the boy. . . . Now *there!*" crooned Lizzie, softly, kissing him again and petting his cheek. "Now I want you to call me Maggie!"

At that Lars sat bolt upright and removed her hand. "Nonsense, Lizzie! Call you *Maggie!* What are you talking about? Why, that's the name of my old horse!" Lars was so disturbed that he felt in his pocket for his Battle-Ax plug but checked himself in time. "No, that I'll never do!"

Lizzie's suggestion came about naturally enough: In baptism she had been christened Lisbeth Marie but when she entered school the teacher had changed the first name to Lizzie because that seemed easier, and more genteel for an American girl. By the time she was in the eighth grade she had begun to read a few story books—not many were to be found in the neighbourhood—but from Minnie Dahl she borrowed a love novel in which figured a girl by the name of Maggie. Lizzie fell in love with that name. It was so round and plump and lovely, so soft and velvety-like; one could almost caress it; and it had a deep, mysterious sound—it could never be spoken harshly. One evening Lizzie remained after school to help the teacher tidy up the room, and asked her if the Norwegian *Marie* wasn't the same as *Maggie* in English. The young teacher confessed her ignorance, but assured her that it made no difference, for if she liked Maggie better, she had a perfect right to take it. America was a free country, and this custom of having ignorant parents fasten upon an innocent child a name which she detested was nothing but a remnant of barbarism. What right did a parent have thus to embitter a child's life? Lizzie was very happy that night but at home she met with an indignant rebuff. Her father told her plainly enough that unless she got such silly notions out of her head he would thrash them out of her!

And now the suggestion did not meet with Lars' favour, either. She folded her hands in her lap and sat silent. To soothe her, Lars called her Maggie all through the evening—that is, unless he forgot himself. Thus good feeling was partly restored. But during the week, the more he thought of the proposal the more he made up his mind to talk the idea out of her. And, oddly enough, on the following Sunday, when he spoke his mind to Lizzie—not angrily but in clear words of reason—she at once agreed that he was right. This simply showed how foolish she was and what good sense he had, and really, it made no difference . . . she had only mentioned it for fun . . . she had been thinking of something else. At that Lizzie blushed bashfully and added that perhaps they'd have use for that other name, some day. Who could tell? Lars listened, his eyes sparkling; in his heart sang a great joy.

Thus it came about that his name was changed to Louis and hers remained Lizzie. After the wedding, which took place just before corn-planting time, they turned their thoughts and efforts to matters more important.

II. Pure Gold

SUMMER and fall were gone, and most of the winter. Past the middle of February already.

Day had almost disappeared; a purple twilight, fast growing and making the western sky more and more unreal, would soon change into complete darkness. During the long afternoon a bright sun had been flooding the prairies with yellow warm light, working havoc with the fine sleighing; even late in the day it was still thawing; from the roofs big drops of water struck the ground with loud splashes. A day or two more of sunshine like this and the snow would be all gone.

Dressed in an old duck coat of her husband's, a woollen scarf she had knitted this winter bundled around her head, and an empty milk-pail in each hand, Mrs. Lizzie Houglum was standing on the front porch, listening down the road. She breathed deeply; in the quiet air she detected an unmistakable odour of spring. Just so the mild weather would last for a while! . . . A good thing, she mused, that Louis today had hauled out the last load of corn—from now on there wouldn't be much sleighing.

This was the second time during the last half hour that she was looking for her husband, now a bit uneasy because of his long absence. . . . Today he is taking his time, all right. Oh well, she concluded as she started down the steps, he had many things to attend to before he could leave town . . . there was the settlement for all the grain he had hauled since Christmas . . . just so the town sharpers didn't cheat him—he couldn't think fast, that man of hers, that was certain!

While walking across the yard she listened intently down the road. No sign of him yet. Resolutely she opened the barn door, which made a harsh, screeching noise, and went in. . . . By hurrying, perhaps she could finish the milking before he returned; then he would be so pleased and brag of her, and they'd have a long, cozy evening before she put him to bed.

The barn was warm and full of pleasant sounds; the cows, crunching their hay and softly swishing their tails, gave an air of deep contentment. Soon Lizzie's uneasiness vanished; streams of milk squirted and splashed into the pail, forming a high covering of foam; resting her forehead against the creature's flank, she pulled long, full tugs. . . . Good fun to milk!

Lizzie milked the three cows, and sat stripping the last—just fooling with the tits. . . . Too bad they had so few cows! More cows would mean more butter to take to town . . . bigger due bills with which to buy necessities for the house . . . more calves, too, and more hogs . . . in fact, more of everything. Not being able to extract another drop, she got up and put the stool away. . . . Next Sunday the folks were coming over for dinner; then she would mention to Mother that she could easily manage one cow more . . . Louis, with no parents to help him, had bought two, she only one . . . she'd tell Mother about it, because it wasn't quite right. And Mother had more than enough work, anyway, now that she wasn't there to help her. . . . Father ought to help them a bit more . . . he could at least lend them a cow for a year or two . . . it would only be helping Mother. Lizzie smiled as she closed the door to the barn.

In the yard she stopped twice to listen. Almost dark now. On the porch she put the pails down in order to open the door. Again she listened, holding her breath. A sound caught her ear—a faint sound of splashing hoofs and of runners pulled over bare ground. There he was! She hurried in, got the lamp lit, her barn clothes off, and her hands washed; the next moment she was bending over the stove, preparing supper. . . . He must be hungry, poor man, not having had a bit to eat since breakfast!

Awhile later she heard his familiar steps on the porch; a toe tapped on the door, a deep voice boomed out, "Open for me, please! . . . Good evening, Mrs. Houglum!" he greeted her pompously as he came in, kicking the door shut behind him; in his arms he carried a load of bundles and packages of various sizes. "If it pleases the madam, will she please rid me of some of these many blessings?"

Lizzie smiled up at him. "What a long day you've made of it! Aren't you starved to death?" She spoke with motherly concern.

"I'm as empty as seven lean years; my innards have

been hollering bloody murder all the way home! Never saw such crowds in town; every store packed; you couldn't get a clerk to wait on you if you paid him for it." Louis hung up his coat and cap in the corner by the door. "And you've done the milking already. Gosh almighty, what a smart wife I've got!"

"Don't brag too much," she warned him as she stood by the stove stirring a pan of potatoes. "Unless your hired man gets a raise in wages pretty soon, he will go on strike—you just see if he won't!"

"Is that so?" he drawled out, affecting an air of profound contempt. "Just let him try it, and I'll take him across my little knee and spank him—like *this!*" Louis slapped his big hands together, took a chair, and sat up to the table.

Lizzie, having brought the food on, sat down opposite him. "The corn hadn't gone down any today, had it?"

Louis had begun to eat, which made talk for him difficult. "No . . .got twenty cents today . . . yes, sir, twenty."

"What? Gone up two cents overnight? Great Scott, how they are robbing us poor farmers. Why didn't you get that yesterday?—How could it have gone up during the middle of the night—when people are asleep? Isn't there any law against such tricks?"

"Perhaps you think I didn't tell 'em! 'Why don't I get the same price for the load I brought in yesterday?' I said. But this here—what's his name?—Curran, said,

'Business ain't done that way,' he said; that's how much good it did."

"Scoundrels the whole pack of 'em!" Her face flushed with indignation.

For a while nothing more was said. The good supper and Lizzie's presence dispelled the troubles he had suffered during the day. With his first appetite appeased, Louis looked across the table and asked whether she had felt lonely while he was gone.

—No, she answered, absent-mindedly, still thinking of the corn and that he had given up too easily—not so bad today, not bad at all; she had had callers, twice, mind you, one in the forenoon, the other just after dinner; and no lady friends, either of them—Lizzie threw her head back challengingly . . . after this he had better not spend too much time away from home . . . hard to tell what might happen!

"Gosh almighty—the nerve of some fellows! Who can be mean enough to angle for my innocent wife the minute I leave the house?"

Lizzie gave him a swift look, greatly pleased because of the concern he pretended. Oh, well, there was no immediate danger, she laughed, though she wouldn't answer for what might happen in the future. . . . The first one was that old, sly fox, Torstein Hegg, who was out collecting money for the minister's salary; the other——"

Louis interrupted her: "How much did you put us down for?"

"I paid him cash . . . thought we might as well be done with it."

"How much?"

"Only three dollars."

"Three dollars!" Louis dropped his hands on the table. "Nothing small about you, I must say. That's more than two dollars too much. . . . We won't be needing the minister, not for a while yet!"

"I know," she admitted, her tone serious. "But Father was down for ten, so what could I do?"

"That's all right for him. The old man has plenty. When you and I have farmed as long as he has, we'll give twenty and never wink an eye. . . . And what about the second thief?"

"Just another beggar."

"You scare me, Lizzie!"

"He was a travelling man collecting subscriptions for *Skandinaven*[1] . . . really a nice fellow . . . he praised our farm. I told him you always looked after money matters yourself, and that he'd have to come some other time. He wasn't so terribly insistent. . . . Don't you think you might discontinue the paper? We would save a dollar and a half that way." Lizzie seemed concerned about the matter of stopping the paper.

"Don't worry, Lizzie," Louis consoled her. "We'll cross the bridge when we come to it; the time isn't up for a month or two yet. . . . Father took that paper as long as he lived."

---

[1] A Norwegian newspaper published in Chicago.

Lizzie changed the subject. "Did you pay off any on the mortgage?"

Louis had finished eating and pushed his chair back. "Bet your boots I did! Six hundred and fifty dollars —not so worse in less than a year's time?" He threw his head back, his eyes full of pride as over some great achievement.

Lizzie took the news calmly. "Next year we'll slice off a full thousand," she said, getting up and clearing the table.

"Darned right we will, and no mistake about it, either!"

While she washed up the dishes, Louis indulged in his evening smoke. He felt tired and drowsy after the long ride; his old corncob pipe was sour and wheezy but he didn't have energy enough left to get up and clean it. As soon as Lizzie had put the dishes away she devoted her attention to the packages he had brought home, opening one after another and storing away the contents of each in the proper place; her husband, too lazy even for talk, observed her in silence. Seeing her sniff into one package and grimace disgustedly, he came to with a start.

"Hey there! that's mine. Throw it here!"

"Huh! Did you really have to buy tobacco now again? Just the other day you came home with a big package! How much is this luxury costing us a year? . . . It isn't a bit nice, either," she added, poutingly.

"Well, we need steam to make things hum!" Louis gave a chuckle which was a bit forced.

"Yes, *steam!*" she mocked, contemptuously. "What have we women got?"

"*Us,* and that ought to be enough!"

"And you aren't worth having!" Her laugh was more natural than his.

The silence which fell between them made Louis feel wider awake. His pipe empty, he put it away on the window sill, and yawned, once, then a second time; he arose, got a drink of water, came back to the table, and sat down again; stretching out a leg, he hooked a chair which he pulled up beside him. "Now be a good girl, Lizzie, and come and sit down. I'd like to show you what I picked up in town."

Having finished her work, Lizzie accepted the invitation, but rather indifferently. She pulled the chair close to the table, leaning both elbows on the top, her thumbs forming a resting-place for her chin, her fingers knit. Her angular profile made a strong picture. Clumsily Louis patted her on the cheek, telling her that she was the prettiest girl in twenty-four counties; then he fetched out his pocketbook and opened it with much deliberation:

"Here is the receipt for the payment on the mortgage—safest that you take care of it. And here"—Louis unfolded a brand-new bank note—"are ten plunks in return for the three you gave Torstein Hegg . . . now don't you devil me about this!" Louis pointed to the package of tobacco. There was a note of mock finality in his voice. Not waiting for her to answer, he fished out of the pocketbook a ten-dollar gold piece, first holding it up to the light, then dropping it on the table to let her hear the deep clang of it. "See, Lizzie, this is pure gold!" His voice had dropped low, in his eyes was a fascinated look.

Without a word Lizzie picked up the piece and examined it; she turned it about in her hand, weighed it, stared unbelievingly. . . . Was it possible? How could this little thing be so heavy? As she studied it more closely her brows knit; finally she burst out in a gasp: "Did you ever! It can't be worth ten dollars—this little thing?" The coin was the first gold piece she had seen and now she refused to believe her own eyes. Again she weighed it; first in one hand, then, shifting it, in the other; she held it closer to the light. The yellowish gleam of the metal shone secretively, with a dull, mysterious light, softly, yet deep and strong. To Lizzie it seemed to be hiding a thousand secrets. Her indifference had been swept away; her eyes sparkled; a strange eagerness had come upon her; she spoke softly, in an awed voice, as if under a spell.

"Doesn't it beat all?" Louis marvelled, lovingly; he felt happy, and proud of himself because of what he had done. "Just think of the value in that one small piece! I once saw a twenty-dollar piece . . . it wasn't much bigger but must have been considerable heavier. . . . Let me feel of it again!" He laughed quietly, to himself. "It almost makes a person feel spooky, doesn't it?" In Louis' face was boyish excitement. "If we had a few hundred fellows like this tucked away in our stockings, we could let the rest of the world do the worrying. . . . Now I'll tell you something," he went on, chummily. "You take him and hide him where he is absolutely safe! . . . I might have planked him, too, on the mortgage, but I just couldn't do it. I said to myself, 'you take that fellow home and give him to Lizzie'—yes, sir, that's what I said! It makes you feel secure to have a lay-by at home, something reliable that the neighbours don't know about, and that the assessor can't tax you for. . . . By and by we'll try to add a few more . . . it won't be many until that darned mortgage is in the stove, but I'll try to rope one now and then. What do you say, Lizzie?"

At first Lizzie never answered a word. She wrapped the gold piece in her apron; the act seemed to be done unconsciously. But as he talked on she turned her face toward him; her eyes were half closed, almost hidden by the lashes; her angular features had softened to warm tenderness; in them lay an expression he had not seen there since those first nights after they were married, when she would pull the shades of the bedroom window down low before she began to undress, and he had sensed a mysterious force emanating from her that made him tremble. Now it was upon her again. . . . Gosh almighty, what a girl!

At last she spoke, quietly, only a few words, "You aren't so foolish, sometimes . . . I don't mind telling you!" Her hand worked nervously with the knot in the apron.

Louis broke into a loud laugh: "That I've suspected for some time! Anything else you'd like to tell me?"

The spell was broken. And now they settled down to a chummy discussion about the spring work which soon would be coming on, about crops and harvest, and how best to utilize each field. Their most fertile acres they must, of course, use for the wheat, they were fully agreed on that, because the wheat was Omnipotence itself; it might bless them with riches, or, for years to come, keep them in poverty. Louis brought up other problems, grave questions that he had been wrestling with all through the winter. He must try to get himself another team of horses. He could easily work the farm alone if he only had plenty of horses. Never again would he run to his father-in-law the way he had had to do last year. One's independence was worth something, too!

Lizzie listened to his argument, but kept her thoughts to herself. She would see about that, though. . . . Father was not a poor man . . . she was the only child . . . he had more than enough already, and——

It was late that night before they retired.

II

Only the ticking of the clock punctured the stillness in the room. For an interminably long time Lizzie lay awake, listening to it. Sleep nowhere in sight, as wide awake now as if she had just got up from the breakfast table. Occasionally she would stretch herself, feel-

ing good and enjoying being alive and little by little
becoming more wakeful. In her contentment had been
kindled a tiny spark of uneasiness . . . only a shadow
of unrest, just enough to keep sleep away. Ideas, popping up in her consciousness, linked themselves together
into chains of thought; always there were new ones;
they fell in line with the others . . . passed by slowly
. . . turned and came back bolder and more insistent,
never giving her sufficient time to drop off—not that
it mattered much, for she wasn't a bit sleepy.

An innocent full moon, slowly mounting a deep sky,
was the cause of it all. Soon after they had retired,
Louis was breathing quietly, with the measured regu-
larity of sound sleep. Somnolent and satisfied, she had
turned away from him, prepared to follow his example.
For the last time she opened her eyes in order to close
them in peaceful sleep, and then it happened: there
was the moon, big, round, aglow, standing in the window. Before she realized it she was studying it, trying
hard to recall something she must have forgotten . . .
the colour of it? What was the exact colour of the
moon, anyway? Opening her eyes wider, she smiled,
pleased as a child that has found its toy: a gold piece
of the same size, how much might that be worth? . . .
Gracious! but that would weigh a lot, for the thickness
must be proportionate to the width. She tried to estimate the value . . . perhaps one thousand? . . .
Two? Oh no—three, at least . . . maybe four? . . .
Must be more than that, even . . . five—ten? . . . It
might easily be worth ten thousand, she decided quite

awestricken, since that little tiny speck of a thing Louis had brought home was worth ten!

The idea of ten thousand dollars in gold swept the last traces of sleep out of her being. . . . Would they ever have so much money? It looked impossible, preposterous. . . . Let's see, how many ten-dollar pieces would that make? . . . Yes, how many would that require? Lizzie did problems in mental arithmetic until she became restless, had to turn over on the other side to find peace, and then she worked all the harder . . . ten in each hundred . . . fifty in every five hundred . . . five hundred would make? No, that was too difficult—she better count by hundreds . . . one hundred to the thousand, that's it, one hundred to each thousand, that would require one whole thousand. Lizzie gasped at the sum. . . . Mercy me! one thousand ten-dollar gold pieces! Impossible . . . they could never save that much! Had she figured right? Let's see once more. . . . She figured the problem again and got the same result, which turned her thoughts into another channel. . . . One whole thousand of them! After one year of hard work and careful saving they had only one—just one! Lizzie lay dejected and miserable.

. . . Still, today he had paid six hundred and fifty on the mortgage . . . that would have made sixty-five pieces, so it would . . . and he had brought one home . . . yes, and one bill—sixty-seven in all, which wasn't so far from a hundred! . . . In ten years more—if it weren't for that mortgage! . . . This year Louis was determined to cut it down one thousand. He was an able farmer, Louis was. . . . Wonder if they couldn't stretch it a bit more? She would help him plan, and get better bargains—he gave in too easily. . . . How could the corn be worth two cents more today than yesterday? Next time he settled up she'd be with him herself!

In the course of the next few days the ten-dollar gold coin, emitting a drowsy glow and resting snugly in the soft folds of her best handkerchief tucked away in the innermost corner of the top drawer of the bedroom bureau, was scarcely out of Lizzie's mind. By contrast, the new bill received scant attention; that she kept in a small toy box which Louis had given her for Christmas, among hairpins, bracelets, and other keepsakes; the box was standing on top of the bureau, in plain sight of anybody who might chance to come into the room. In order to get at the other she had to pull the drawer clear out; and that was inconvenient, because often the coin would not leave her in peace till she had been to the bedroom to look at it. This would happen frequently, but never when Louis was in the house.

Saturday afternoon, when she was standing by the kitchen table, baking cookies, her fancy played her a funny trick: The batter was of the proper consistency; the stove baked nicely; she felt much pleased with herself—she had never turned out finer cookies . . . so crisp and rich and yellow. After cooling the trays in the window, she laid the round delicacies in a crock, arranging them in piles neatly stacked up. She put down the last cake and gave a pleasant chuckle: the cookies were ten-dollar pieces . . . the crock was almost full! . . . How many might there be? Immediately the idea absorbed her. Having lifted the piles from the crock to the table, she counted each one carefully, half aloud . . . one hundred and forty-eight—that's a lot of money! . . . Too bad she hadn't mixed a little more batter . . . an even two hundred would have been nicer. . . . No, she better not . . .this was Saturday . . . she had much to do . . . besides, this baking would last her a long time.

Lizzie was preoccupied these days. At times she would show temper, would grow taciturn and moody; or again, she would joke with her husband, grow hilarious, and laugh until he had to join in; but it happened, too, that he might ask her a question and never get a word from her.

Louis watched his wife closely and wondered what could be the matter with her. She wasn't a bit like her old self; he felt distressed and worried. . . . Perhaps . . . no, he didn't want to think of *that*. It would, of course, have to happen, sometime, though just now, with the spring work coming on, it certainly would be devilish inconvenient. He had figured on her running the pulverizer and doing the dragging while he got some plowing done. . . . She ought to wait another year . . . plenty of time . . . they were young yet. His awkward questionings made him feel all the more uneasy, for she would only laugh slyly and give queer answers: What did he know about such things, he who only snored all night long? He better be minding his own business. . . . Sick? No—she had more important matters to think about than being sick!

With a warm light in her eye, she left him to his worries. But during the day she worked as hard as ever, now and then lending him a hand whenever she could spare the time. Alone in the house, she occasionally would steal into the bedroom to have a look at the little fellow sleeping in the bureau drawer. . . . Yes, there he lay, the sleepy-head . . . so alone and abandoned, with nobody to look after him . . . poor little dear! . . . Such a smart fellow, too. When she held him up to the light he seemed to awaken, smile, and beam at her; there was a twinkle for every turn. Of course he was lonesome . . . no one to talk to . . . nobody to play with. . . . Don't worry, little man— there'll be company, all right, just you wait!

One morning—it was already past the middle of March—Louis came in from the chores, announcing that today he'd have to make a trip to town; spring work would be upon them almost any day; after that they'd be too busy to look up. Did she have any errands for him?

—No, she smiled, in great spirits over the prospects of a trip to town. Today she'd go with him herself; she had some cases of eggs saved up, much to get for the house—a lot of things, in fact . . . she'd be ready in no time.

Presently they were sitting in the wagon, jogging

across the prairie, Lizzie in high spirits and bubbling over with good talk. In all she said there was not the slightest hint of danger. Louis felt greatly relieved. Of course she was too clever a girl to let anything like that happen to her just now! . . . The long, tedious journey, which he always hated to make, came to an end before they had got properly started, it seemed to him. Tying up the horses, he whistled a merry tune.

While he was at the blacksmith shop to have a plow-share sharpened Lizzie slipped into the bank. No sooner had she come inside the door than her confidence left her. She hesitated, uncertain of how to proceed. The room was divided into two compartments by a heavy iron fence. At the desk back of the fence stood a young man in fine attire, counting bills, his hands full of them. It was so still in here; the bills crackled between his fingers. A feeling of awe came upon her. Stepping up to the window in the iron fence she asked timidly in a low voice if she might exchange a ten-dollar bill for the equivalent amount in gold . . . it was a new bill, she added, crest-fallen, realizing that she was asking a preposterous thing. How could she have been so foolish—gold must be worth much more than paper? She could hear the pounding of her own heart and felt a pallor mounting into her face. But the young man only looked at her with cold, indifferent eyes; taking the bill he scrutinized it closely, then handed her the gold piece in return. Never a word did he say during the transaction. Lizzie hurried out of the bank, her hand clasping the coin tightly. . . . The fellow was only a boy—he might not know much about money; but there had been no one else in the bank, no one that could have seen them. As she hurried on down the street her face grew hot and flushed, her courage reviving. . . . Just let that strip of a fellow come after her gold piece!

Never once looking back, Lizzie made straight for the store, Jenkins' Drygoods & Groceries, where her family had done their trading as far back as she could remember. She was well acquainted, and once inside, she felt at home and at her ease. Stepping up to the counter, she inquired about the price of eggs.

"Two forty in trade," the clerk answered, promptly, in a business-like manner. There was an air about these townspeople that she didn't quite like—one couldn't talk to them.

"What about cash?"

"Two dollars."

"Two dollars!" Lizzie looked the man straight in the eye . . . the nerve of that fellow! But the clerk never flinched. She pondered for a minute. Must she make him a present of eighty cents? There were several people in the store, all the clerks running between counter and shelves, and no time to fool away.

Resolutely she turned around, went out, and brought in her three cases. She would have cash for two of them, she explained, the third she'd take out in trade. She was in a hurry; she gave her orders sharply and definitely; every now and then she cast a glance at the door. A good while before Louis returned from the blacksmith's Lizzie had received her money, done her trading, and carried the empty cases back to the wagon. She was waiting for him, uneasy because it took him so long.

But on the way home Lizzie was only sunshine. Occasionally her hand went down into the pocket of her coat. She felt of her precious possession, remembered how well she had executed her plans. . . . Pretty soon there'd be more, for now she knew the way . . . only three cases more and there would be another one. Louis would have to jump if he intended to keep up with her!

Safely out of town, she began to unfold to him some of the plans that lately had taken definite shape:

—He meant to have her as his hired man, this coming summer, also, didn't he?

—Oh, certainly . . . provided she was available?

—That all depended . . .

—On what? Louis looked at her, deadly serious.

—He would have to pay her fair wages; nobody worked for nothing these days.

—Sure, he'd pay! Louis felt so relieved that he put his arm around her and squeezed her.

But then she turned sober:

"That kind of pay won't do—I tell you frankly." The toe of her right foot tapped against the wagon box. "I'll work this summer, too, and that'll save you a hired man, but you'll have to pay me for it. . . . That money we're going to lay aside, you understand; when the mortgage is paid up we won't have to begin

all over again . . . see? . . . Then we'll have a start
. . . be well on the way. Don't you think that's smart?"

"Gosh! yes—of course it is," Louis scratched his
forehead with the butt end of the whip. "But—well—
don't you see that the more we pay on the mortgage
each year the sooner we can burn the damned thing—
and begin saving in real earnest?"

"Oh, you lubber—don't I know that much?" Lizzie
nudged his ribs, roguishly looking at him through the
corner of her eye. "Suppose you listen to me." Lizzie
laid before him a plan she had worked out, and concluded by saying that it wasn't more than right that
her father helped them a bit.

"Not by a jugful!" Louis shook his head. "We don't
do our threshing that way."

"Will you please listen to me?" Lizzie rebuked him in
a motherly tone, "and keep still till I get through talking! I am nearly thirty years old—I don't mind telling
you. All these years I've worked for Father, yes—until
last year you came along. . . . Behave yourself and
shut up! . . . He gave me no pay except my clothes,
and now and then a few cents. . . . Do you think I
was satisfied? Well, I was not. . . . I wanted to go to
business college and learn something about money and
such things . . . be something that counted. . . . I've
always liked business. . . . Father wouldn't hear of it;
he'd rather have me become a deaconess . . . go out
to the heathens as a missionary. . . . Me going to the
heathens? No, sir—then I'd rather milk cows!". . .
Her lips closing tightly after each sentence gave great

emphasis to the pauses. Louis did not dare to interrupt her. "I've promised myself that some day Father would pay for his stubbornness—for never letting me get anywhere—and he's going to pay, but that's my business, I'm just telling you! . . . I happen to know that he has money saved up, considerable of it; that money he is going to lend us—only lend it, you understand, and we'll pay it on the mortgage. In that way I'll collect my wages and we'll save a lot of interest. . . . What does he need more money for? He only wastes it, on missions and orphan homes and such foolishness. . . . I know him! I tell you, Louis, we'll do him a kindness by taking the money, for then it will be safe." Lizzie talked with a quiet earnestness; in her voice there was a peculiar tenseness.

"That's true, all right," Louis agreed, thoughtfully, "but we can't ask him to loan us the money—it's just out of the question . . . why, gosh darn it! he has given us fifteen hundred dollars already!"

"You silly boy! Who said we were going to ask him? What I mean is—if he comes and offers us the money of his own accord. I am positive that when he stops to think about it, he will offer it to us of his own free will. But I'm going to talk it over with Mother. . . . She knows what I have been doing at home and how I wanted to get away."

"Course, that'd be a different thing." Louis was still thinking hard. "I'd rather be owing him than anybody else, but that you can't mention either to him or to her!"

"Course not," she assured him. "But this is my business; Father isn't owing you anything. . . . You keep your hands off . . . I am settling with Father!"

There was a long silence between them. Louis' brown face puckered in thought.

Lizzie broke the silence first; her voice was amiable and teasing:

"My boss will pay me wages, won't he?"

Louis came to with a start. "Well, gosh darn it! I have to have somebody—at least part of the time. How much do you want?"

"That all depends on how many months you want me," she said, shrewdly, tilting her head to one side.

"For how many months?" he ejaculated. "So, that's it? If you don't beat all when it comes to driving a bargain!" Louis laughed, a spiritless, woebegone laugh. "Suppose we say from May first?"

"From May first? What about April? Father always hires in March in order to get the man he wants."

"Make it April first then and be done with it!"

Louis flicked the off horse with the line and drove fast; the rumbling of the wagon made talk impossible. As soon as the horses slowed down Lizzie asked, "How many months do you hire your man for?"

"How many months?" There was a foolish grin on his face; he was caught in a trap and couldn't get out. "As long as I need him, and not a day longer."

"Oh, no, thank you! None of your foxy thresher's tricks! What'll it be, to October or to November?"

"To October, and not a day longer!" Louis was disgusted and didn't care who knew it.

With both hands Lizzie took hold of his arm and leaned toward him. "And what wages are you paying this year?"

"Name them yourself; you'll have it your own way, anyway."

"Since I'm only a woman and have all the housework to do besides, the cooking and everything, I don't suppose I can ask more than ten a month?"

"I suppose not. Let's see—that's six months . . . sixty dollars. . . . That's a hell of a lot of money, if you want to know it!"

Lizzie looked surprised, quite shocked. "Is it really as much as all that?"

Not until they were ready to go to bed in the evening did she show him the new ten-dollar gold piece and tell him the story of how she had obtained it. And then both of them lost themselves, as two children over a fairy tale. They weighed the piece in their hands . . . tried the sound of the metal . . . studied the imprint . . . fell to wondering about the mysterious life in it; it changed illusively according to the way you held it. . . . But wasn't it smaller than the other? Louis insisted that it was, and so Lizzie went to the bedroom and got the other. Placing it beside the newcomer, she chuckled happily, "Now see him wake up, will you! He has been lonesome, poor thing; he is so glad to get company."

She sat down close by her husband, and told him what she intended to use the wages for. Afterward she entreated him earnestly to use his wits so that they could earn a little extra—yes, and save a dollar now and then because it took only ten of them . . . only ten, remember!

As Louis turned to the wall to settle down to sleep he was convinced beyond any possible doubt that a more sensible woman than Lizzie never existed. She was unbeatable. . . . She might be unreasonable at times, but what of it? A woman with her brains had a right to be!

In a blissful state of mind and full to bursting with good sleep, he put his hand behind him, patting the covers. "Now you go to sleep, girl . . . go to sleep, I say!"

She held his hand and squeezed it, held it to her and would not let it go; but Louis had already entered the Land of Nowhere.

III

Louis could not think as fast as Lizzie; with him ideas germinated slowly, as the corn in a cold season; but once planted, the idea would lie there and, perhaps by and by, develop into long series of thought.

The matter revolving in his mind these days was the proposal of Lizzie's that he also, occasionally, find

some way of earning an extra dollar or two. . . . Not
so easy—the way he was fixed. Where would he find
the money? Nevertheless, the idea refused to leave
him. It was present in whatever he worked at. He
pondered and kept turning it in his mind until his
eyes grew small and took on a piercing stare, and he
grew tired from vexation. . . . He couldn't hire out
to anyone, with all the work at home. . . . The produce
of the farm was Lizzie's as much as his . . . and the
few pennies from the eggs and the butter she took care
of herself. Doggone the luck! He couldn't go out and
steal . . . no money to pick from the trees! And nothing yet, at any rate, to sell. Truth to tell, he was more
in need of buying than selling. He ought to get more
horses, not to speak of cows and hogs. Where the hell
would he get the money? And here she came telling
him that he must find some way of laying by an extra
dollar! . . . No, nothing to do about it, that he could
see . . . he was no magician that could pluck money
out of people's ears and noses!

As far as that was concerned, this thing that Lizzie
was up to was really no economy at all when you came
to look at it; he might with equally good reason demand pay from her . . . or from himself; the case
would be just the same. . . . Not that he didn't like
her plan; he rejoiced in it fully as much as she did,
only he couldn't work that way.

Louis could not get the thought out of his mind.
One day at the dinner table he talked to Lizzie about
it; he was gloomy and depressed.

Lizzie met him understandingly; she saw the problem clearly—it certainly wasn't easy. Of course, she didn't want him to rob anyone, or commit murder. How silly he talked! . . . No easy task for poor people to lay by anything. But why worry about it? He would find a scheme some day . . . she wasn't expecting to get rich right away! . . . Lizzie was in high spirits and full of good courage. "You must remember, Louis," she concluded in a motherly voice, "that we're just beginning!"

Louis said nothing; but the meal over, he lit his corncob pipe and stretched himself on the floor, using his duck coat for a pillow. Every day he would take a few winks at noon, in order to rest his horses before hitching them up for the long afternoon's work. And he was fond of these minutes; lying here enjoying his pipe, he would watch Lizzie do the dishes and discuss things with her. Today he was silent.

Contrary to her custom, Lizzie let her dishes stand. She came and sat beside him on the floor. Putting her hand under his neck she asked lovingly what he might be thinking about so hard.

Louis turned his head away:

—Oh, nothing. Just wind and weather, that's all.

—Now did you ever! Was he looking after the weather, too? Didn't he have enough with her and a two-hundred-acre farm? she asked, teasingly, and petted him.

Louis puffed on in silence, blowing thick clouds of smoke.

"Poof!—that pipe of yours is awful; it stinks like a manure pile . . . not a bit of fun to come near you!"

A grunt escaped Louis. "Yep, she's in no better humour than I am myself."

"Shame on you, Louis!" Fanning the smoke away with her apron, she drew nearer and took hold of his chin. "How much did you pay for the package you brought home the other day?"

"My tobacco, you mean?"

"Yes."

"Don't remember . . . dollar and a half, I guess," he said, indifferently.

"How long does a supply like that last you?"

"How long does it last? What you want to know for?"

"I'm just asking. You needn't get so cross!"

"Cross, nothing!"

"Tell me, then!"

"That all depends on what kind of work I'm doing," Louis admitted, grudgingly.

"Does that make any difference?"

"Certainly it does! But womenfolks don't understand such things." Louis turned on his back, staring into vacancy. "This time of the year a package like that lasts a whole month, maybe longer, but not when I'm threshing."

Lizzie was running her finger through his hair, for a while saying nothing; then, bending over and looking down into his face, she spoke softly, convincingly:

"But that makes fifteen to twenty dollars a year! That would make two brand-new ten-dollar pieces to put aside by Christmas time."

"Ah-hm," assented Louis, "so it would!"

"And it won't hurt you a bit to give up the nasty stuff."

"No, you are right on that," he said, thoughtfully, "for it would only kill me!"

"Now listen to the silly boy!" Lizzie slapped his cheek reproachfully and pouted.

"Guess I know who is silly—talk is cheap! It ain't your funeral, this ain't." Louis raised himself into a sitting position and tried to look cross and forbidding. "You simply don't know what you're talking about. You can believe it or not, but when I am out of tobacco, I don't do the work of half a man. Gosh almighty—I might as well try to run the farm without horses!" He slapped his knee and yawned hard.

Patting his cheek once more, without response from him, she got up and went to the stove. "You'll have to do as you please about it," she sighed. "I am not going to kill anybody; I just wanted to show you how easily you could save us a nice sum of money." Putting dish after dish into the pan, she continued analyzing the problem, and now in a firmer voice: "It's nice to have a bit laid by for a rainy day. . . . There aren't many farmers having chunks of pure gold hidden around the house. . . . Anyhow, I'd try, if I were you." Suddenly a bright idea struck her and she came halfway across the floor toward him, the towel over her arm. "I tell you what I'll do: if you will quit when this supply is gone, I myself will have two more ten-dollar pieces by Christmas, and I'll give them to you. Now, isn't that a bargain for you?" Lizzie's cheeks flushed with excitement. . . . "What do you say?"

Louis rose heavily, yawned and stretched himself, then went to the door, paused, and smiled, a little sheepishly. "What do I say? Blamed funny that a good girl like you can be so foolish, that's what I say!" Stopping long enough on the porch to light his pipe once more, he strode across the yard.

Somehow, no matter how desperately hard he tried, Louis could not rid himself of Lizzie's suggestion. The idea hovered in his consciousness like a threatening cloud on a near horizon; as soon as he looked up it was there.

During the afternoon he frequently took the plug out of his pocket and looked at it, studied it judiciously, estimating how long he might make it last; but he always denied himself. Each time he became more firmly convinced of how utterly impossible this nonsense of Lizzie's was. Giving the horses a brief breathing-spell just before starting to make the last rounds, he was overcome by the desire to have a taste. Deliberately opening his jackknife he cut off a little piece, a tiny piece, it was—he could at least economize! Getting the full taste of the juicy tobacco, he immediately felt refreshed and strengthened. He wouldn't mind doing another half-day's work right now . . . he might easily go without supper! . . . Louis trudged vigorously, clucking to the horses and telling them to move—blame it, couldn't they get a move on? . . . No use talking, in spite of her cleverness, there were things that Lizzie could not understand. If he had taken this little snippet earlier in the day, he'd have had more plowing done. . . . Talk about penny wise and pound foolish. . . . Get up there, I tell you!

After supper Louis merely dry-smoked his pipe. But in his left cheek he held the tiniest speck of a quid, just enough to give him a fair taste. Thus he managed very well throughout the whole evening. Lizzie looked at him now and then, talked pleasantly all the time, never hinting at what they had discussed at noon. Nothing but peace and bliss in all she had to say. Louis mellowed; he just couldn't help himself. When they went to bed he had practically made up his mind to break himself of the habit; he would take it gradually, by easy stages; she would never know what he was up to . . . this trick of having his pipe in his mouth would fool her. Luxuriously satisfied with himself, Louis turned over to go to sleep . . . women couldn't see very far, could they?

The next morning, contrary to his custom upon getting up from the breakfast table, Louis did not light his pipe in the house. But to be on the safe side, he stuffed it plumb full, packing the tobacco hard. Placing the pipe carefully in the pocket of his jacket and saying a brief good-bye, he hurried out to the barn, got the horses ready, and was in the field in no time. Having hitched the team to the plow, he stopped a moment to allow himself a niggardly cut of the plug, really not much more than a mere imitation of an ordinary chew. Now, that would have to do him through the forenoon! Louis adjusted the reins over his right shoulder and under his left arm . . . now, he might leave the pipe for the afternoon, or perhaps, until after supper. If he got along as nicely as he had done last night, maybe he could save the pipe for breakfast—even make it last the whole forenoon. . . . Now geddap, you lazy plugs! . . . Louis spoke loudly and sharply to his horses.

For a while the work went briskly, one furrow after another of rich, black soil, glistening in the sun, curved down upon the other, little by little widening the plowed field into a big black patch on the prairie. As the day wore on, the flood of yellow light increased in intensity, drenching meadow and fields with quivering streams. Before long, the horses, sleek and shiny with sweat and puffing hard, needed frequent breathing-spells. During one of these Louis felt impelled to see how the contents of his pipe was faring. Discovering that half of the tobacco had fallen out, he swore softly between his teeth. . . . Now doggone it, that's what a man gets for stinting himself! . . . He removed his jacket and sat down on the beam of the plow, carefully turning the pocket inside out and emptying the contents into the hollow of his hand. . . . Not all pure tobacco, this, but one better save what he could.

Striking a match, Louis sucked hard. The pipe hissed

and sputtered and wouldn't burn; it tasted of burnt straw and manure. His face wrinkled in dismay; had he had the package at hand, he'd have emptied the pipe for a real smoke just to spite himself. Come sunshine or hailstorms, this would never do! Replacing the pipe in his pocket, he fetched out the plug and cut off a decent piece. After giving it a few turns, he spat meditatively. . . . No, if he wanted to get his work done, he'd have to drop this darned foolishness! Such crazy notions! With ordinary firing he'd gladly do the work of two men . . . and wouldn't that be saving money? Women oughtn't meddle in matters they didn't know anything about! Louis got up and spat furiously. . . . Geddap there. What are you hanging your heads for?

At noon Louis smoked his pipe as though no thought of giving it up had ever entered his mind. But he denied himself his customary nap; having lit his after-dinner pipe he immediately hastened off to the barn.

During the next two days Louis, to all appearances, behaved as usual; whenever he felt the need he would cut a piece from the plug that was fast diminishing; he smoked his pipe both during the noon hour and after supper, but at noon, either in the barn or in the granary. Yet he did not find the enjoyment in it that he should have found. The pipe didn't taste right; the smoke had no savoury odour in it. Though Lizzie never hinted at the matter again, he could not help feeling how earnestly she wanted him to quit. And somehow, deep down at the bottom of his heart a voice was say-

ing loudly that she was right . . . blame it all if she
wasn't! Here she pinched every penny in order to lay
aside a little nest egg while he was spoiling the whole
plan—he spat away money and sent it up in smoke.
Fine provider he was! And she meant it all for his
own good, too. . . . No, he was hardly doing the right
thing by her. . . . If he only could have hit upon some
other scheme of making a few cents! He trudged
doggedly behind the plow, with the problem constantly
on his mind. He could see it on the handles of the
plow. . . . Suppose he buried his pipe when the supply
had run out? . . . or burnt it? Then he'd have to quit
—wouldn't he? Well, he'd soon have to face it. No getting to town, either, until after the corn-planting, which
would mean not before a week or two. . . . No, he
better not burn it—just dig it down. Thus, in case he
ever started up again, Lizzie would know nothing about
the experiment . . . she was so easy and innocent, she
was!

Louis ran short of both chewing and smoking tobacco simultaneously. A trip to town now, with all
the work hanging over him, was simply out of the
question, and to borrow from the neighbours he refused to do—he could at least wait awhile. . . . The
result would, of course, be the same whether he burnt
the pipe or simply stuck it away out of sight. At all
events, nothing could be worse than this insufferable
dry-smoking. . . . Safest to burn all bridges behind
him. If Lizzie was able to save up twenty dollars be-

tween now and Christmas, he'd be worse than a black
Indian unless he made a real attempt.

Two days later the larder was empty—absolutely
cleaned. Louis had saved the last bit of the plug until
about eleven o'clock, but then he put it into his left
cheek, soberly assuring himself that now the game was
up; from now on there would be hell to pay. He cursed
his horses roundly and worked them hard until dinner-
time.

And he had no sooner eaten than he left the house
hurriedly. Lizzie came out on the porch and called to
him. What was the matter with him? He wasn't going
to kill himself working? Had he got tired of his little
girl? He seemed to detect a catch in her voice.

"Never mind me," he waved back at her, and tried
to laugh. "It's only an old harness that needs mending!"

In the granary he took out his jackknife and scraped
the bowl of the pipe to the very bone. Lighting a
match, he sucked hard, holding the bowl horizontally,
and actually succeeded in getting a few puffs. But
that was all; the bowl did not even get hot. Thrusting
the pipe into his pocket he went out of the granary
and began to look for the spade. . . . Where had he
left the spade, anyway? It must be standing behind
the chicken-coop where he had been grubbing trees
the other evening. Stepping around the corner of the
coop, he threw a furtive glance at the house—she wasn't
watching him, was she? An excited, feverish hurry
was upon Louis; he grabbed the spade and, turning over

the loose mould, he dropped the pipe into the wedge-shaped hole. Quickly he removed the spade and straightened, an air of defiance and finality about him—so there now, that job was done! . . . During the afternoon he urged on his horses mercilessly, having apparently lost all compassion for the poor beasts.

Three whole days passed. To Louis they seemed so many dreary eternities. He was low-spirited and restless, and so touchy that he did not dare remain in the house. One evening he walked behind the chicken-coop and looked darkly at the spot, his face a cloud of gloom. No—no use . . . done was done . . . he was no baby . . . if she wanted to kill him, he'd show her that it did not matter to him!

At noon the third day, as soon as he had finished his meal, he went into the bedroom, closing the door after him, and hunted through the pockets of his Sunday clothes. In the corner of the vest pocket he found a few pieces of chewing tobacco; they were dry and must have lain there for a long time. Louis handled them carefully as if they were nuggets of gold. That afternoon he treated his horses kindly and did a great deal of work.

In the evening, shortly after chore-time, Jens Haugen and his wife came to call on the Houglums. The sight of his former threshing partner revived Louis' spirits and made him forget his troubles. Lizzie and Mrs. Haugen were old acquaintances; soon the talk flowed easily, merrily; the two threshers, both in high spirits, fell to recalling experiences; the talk between them grew so good-natured and jolly that the women had to listen, and then join in. As he finished a good yarn over which all four laughed uproariously, Jens Haugen brought out his pipe and the smoking tobacco; filling his own pipe first, he tossed the package to Louis, "Let's get the steam up!"

Louis jumped up excitedly, running his hands through his pockets, and colouring furiously. "Doggone the luck! I'll just bet I've left my pipe in the barn?" Instantly he made for the door. "I'll be back in a minute!"

The spade was standing where he had left it the other day. Knowing every inch of ground perfectly, he was not long in recovering the pipe. On his way back to the house he blew out the stem and rubbed the bowl on his trousers leg. Seated by the table again and partly turning his back to his wife, he filled the pipe with great care; but instead of tossing the package back to Jens, he left it in the centre of the table within easy reach of both of them.

"Isn't it awful," remarked Lizzie, laughingly, to the other woman, "how these boys of ours have taken to bad habits? How do you suppose we can cure them?"

"Try the Keeley Cure, I guess. I've just about given up hopes of reforming mine."

"That's right!" Louis chimed in, laughing boisterously. "But leave us in peace until I have all my corn cribbed!"

Jens Haugen joined in the laugh but otherwise paying no attention; he scratched the stubble on his chin while he waited for them to get through laughing. He had come over on a serious errand; now he brought it up: He wanted to hire Louis for the threshing this fall; he just had to have him—no two ways about that! Last season everything had gone wrong because he had got a man who didn't understand his business; should he run into another fall like that, he'd be living next door to bankruptcy. Jens Haugen was speaking quietly —the two women had stopped their chattering to hear what the men were saying. What he needed, continued Jens, was an expert, a real thresher; the rig was old and so damned particular that unless he got a good man with him, he might as well sell the whole outfit. And Louis was the man—why, he knew that machine as he knew his Catechism! If Louis would join him with three horses, he'd pay him five dollars a day; that was more money than he had ever paid a man, but he considered Louis worth it. He had figured that they'd thresh their own grain first and get done at home before starting on the regular run; that is to say, they'd shock-thresh; in that way they'd save the work of stacking, which was only foolishness, anyway. Jens refilled his pipe and threw the package at Louis.

Like a well-trained old cavalry horse raising its ears at the beat of a drum, Louis felt a thrill of joy at the idea of once more running the horsepower; it meant freedom and hustle and great fun, the song of the machine rising above the dust and the rumbling and the rattle of wagons—easy work, only play so to speak, and Christmas fare whenever he sat down to a table! Louis could not utter a word; his eyes sparkled and danced; his throat felt dry. . . . Five dollars a day, and on such conditions. . . . No foolish nagging, either, on account of an innocent pipe! Unconsciously his head rose, his whole figure erect and determined.

During Jens' speech Lizzie had looked at her husband, once, twice. Suddenly she got up and went to the water-pail, where she drank from the dipper; her hand shook a bit. Coming back again, she threw a swift glance at Louis. His brown, irregular features were transfigured with the light emanating from them; her own face was cold and expressionless, showing no interest.

But she was the first to comment on the proposal. From the way she talked one couldn't be sure whether she was for or against Louis' accepting the job. . . . They better think this over, she said. . . . If Louis were to be gone all fall, she didn't see how she could manage alone, and it would cost money to hire help . . . there was the fall plowing that had to be done, and the corn? How would they get the corn picked? Not that they wouldn't like to help out if they could, but they would have to think it over.

As she analyzed the proposition, Louis' head fell perceptibly; what she said was the plain truth—though as for the corn-husking . . . he could pick every Sunday; with big money in sight, one better not be too finicky about working on Sundays. . . . He might get a little help from his father-in-law; the old man had a good hired man this year. . . . By Thanksgiving they'd be through threshing . . . much corn had been husked after that time. . . . He might even hire a man to do some plowing. . . . Good God—five dollars a day!

Jens Haugen had listened attentively to Lizzie's objections. He had prepared himself to meet more strenuous opposition, and felt considerably relieved. As for the plowing, he assured them, addressing himself to Lizzie, they need not worry; he had solved that difficulty already: next spring, any time they said the word, he'd guarantee to lend them a man and a team for a whole week's plowing; Louis might pay him back during threshing a year from now. And if they finished the season early this fall, he himself would be glad to come over and help with the corn-picking. He simply had to have Louis with him—no ifs about it; if necessary he'd dynamite him loose to get him!

There was much talk back and forth without any decision being reached. Before leaving, Mrs. Haugen invited the Houglums to drive over for dinner two weeks from the next Sunday. By that time they would have slept on the proposition and would have their minds made up.

Louis saw Jens down to the buggy, the two women coming arm in arm a little way behind.

"Say," Louis whispered, hurriedly, "you aren't fixed so that you could loan me some tobacco?"

"Sure. You take the plug—here, take the package too; I've plenty at home."

Before going to bed Louis and Lizzie held a long conference over what answer to give Jens Haugen, Louis doing most of the talking. Having lit another pipe and put his feet on a chair, he asked Lizzie what she thought of the proposal.

"I don't see how I can, Lizzie," he ventured, judiciously.

"Of course you take it!" She seemed sober and thoughtful.

"Do you really think I ought?" Louis did not look at her.

"I certainly do; but not on the conditions he offered tonight."

"What do you mean?"

"For one thing, you can't take more than two horses; I will be needing the other two for the plowing. And you are not to hire out by the day." Lizzie took hold of the table. "If we get a rainy fall, you see where you'll be at . . . you hire out by the week . . . and for ten weeks!" Her lips closed tightly after each statement.

Louis gazed speechlessly at his wife. . . . "If you aren't a marvel, Lizzie, I'd like to know!"

His admiration sounded so unfeigned that she looked up at him, but her face never altered an expression.

"What wages should I ask, do you think?"

"For yourself and two horses, thirty dollars a week," she said in a quiet, even tone.

"He won't pay that; why, doggone it! he can't afford it—it would ruin him!"

"If you are as good a man as he claims, he'll pay it, all right. And another thing: he is to furnish tobacco for both of you!"

Louis' face coloured to deep brown. "For the love of Mike, Lizzie, let's not be unreasonable!"

"Just let him refuse; it's his move, not ours . . . you aren't asking for the job." Lizzie spoke coldly; there was not a trace of emotion in her voice.

Louis was too excited to sit still; he got up, walked the floor, rubbing his hands. Pinching off a tiny piece from the plug, he smuggled it into his mouth. Presently he was talking, more to himself than to her. . . . "It's this way, you see, that horsepower has to be run just so . . . she is as particular as an old woman given to fits; she gets 'em, too, let me tell you. If she's run a little too slow or just a trifle too fast, she kicks and coughs and splutters—well, she just won't work, that's all! But properly tended, she spins like a top from morning till night . . . there is no end to the amount of grain you can shove through her." . . . Louis grew more self-confident the longer he talked. "I want to tell you that it isn't everybody that knows how to set a horsepower decently—no, you bet not . . . and Jens knows that I can deliver the goods. . . . Thirty dollars a week, that makes three little fellows . . . we'll have many of them by Thanksgiving." He came across the floor and patted her cheeks. "Won't we, Lizzie?"

"I hope so," she said, coolly, getting up to go to bed.

IV

The years ran their course over the prairies, one after another, with little variation; only this noticeable difference: each hurried faster than the one gone before.

Off and on much talk was heard about Louis and Lizzie Houglum. Gossip had it that they had plucked old Tom Öien clean of practically everything he possessed, save the farm.

And it was next to impossible, at least so it was said, for any solicitor to obtain contributions from the Houglums except perhaps a few cents now and then to Foreign Missions. Although members of St. Paul's Norwegian Lutheran Congregation of Greenfield, they refused to contribute either to the support of the local congregation or to the synodical treasury. For two years running, Tostein Hegg, who possessed unusual talents for raising money, had failed utterly.

Tostein took the matter as a personal affront; his good name and reputation had suffered; some of his fellow-members taunted him about it. Being a shrewd man, he began to study the problem seriously. He had been beaten twice, yet he did not feel himself defeated

—some way must be found to get even with them, and so he decided to try strategy. Calling on the minister one day, he suggested innocently that they drive over to the Houglums; Louis was not paying his dues as an honest man should; something must be done about it, and now he'd like to have Louis turn him down in the presence of the minister. "You see," explained old Tostein, judiciously, "it will be less trouble for you to go with me on this errand than to have to oust them from the congregation. You need not say a blessed word; just listen while I do the talking." Old pastor Christensen was such a kind soul that he did whatever was asked of him as long as it might help the cause of the church. And that was how it happened that Tostein got his revenge, and that the minister came to Louis and Lizzie for two years in succession asking them to contribute a little something toward his own salary. Each time as soon as the visitors had stepped into the house, Tostein spoke up, "If you want your own pastor to starve to death, I'd just as soon have you tell him so yourself instead of asking me to do it for you!"

With the minister himself present—oh, well, who could say *no* under such circumstances? Besides, he had both baptized and confirmed Lizzie, and married her, too. Lizzie and Louis were so polite, seemed so anxious to contribute, that Reverend Christensen was quite captivated by their goodness of heart. After a long conference in the kitchen between husband and wife, Louis came into the parlour, bringing three silver dollars which he handed the minister—Tostein he never as much as noticed. The minister turned the money over in his hand, apparently at a loss how to proceed, then asked timidly if Louis couldn't increase the amount to five, because that was what the assessment committee thought he ought to pay. No, Louis said—and he was as sober as the minister—now they had scraped the bottom! But Lizzie spoke up quickly, her voice choking with emotion: How could the neighbours be so spiteful? Would they like to see them driven from house and home? . . . Six years ago she and Louis had gone into debt for the farm, without a penny to their name . . . they were still so poor that they couldn't afford decent clothes. . . . Their little gift today must not be taken as an indication of unwilling hearts—she hoped the pastor had more sense than to listen to the slanderous gossip of evil-minded tongues! Reverend Christensen was moved to such pity that if Tostein Hegg had not sat there listening, he might have given her back the three dollars.

That was how it had gone for two years. But the third—the pastor was alone this time, because Tostein was busy elsewhere—he found no one at home. He thought this queer, for it was a week day and just before dinner-time; but for all he hunted and called, not a soul was to be seen. On his way home he went by the field where the Houglum hired man was working, and stopped to ask him. The man, grinning maliciously up into the minister's face, admitted that it was queer —it was damn queer, for it couldn't be more than half an hour since he with his own eyes had seen Lizzie going across the yard to the house; but you could never figure them fellows out!

The incident soon became a choice bit of gossip; the whole neighbourhood talked about it. According to the most popular version, Louis and Lizzie had lain flat on the upstairs floor, each peeping through a corner of the window while Reverend Christensen was prowling about the yard, shouting Louis' name. But as tongues always are bound to wiggle and wag, one should make proper allowance for embellishment.

Though only a common country woman, Lizzie was remarkably competent in business dealings. As the years elapsed she and Louis acquired a number of interests: their stock increased; fall and spring there was much to sell; and it often fell to her to make deals and close bargains, especially when Louis was away. Frequently a buyer of hogs or cattle would come to the farm, looking for trade. If Louis happened to be away or if he were working in the field, it fell to her to do the bargaining.

Not that she was a bit easier to deal with than he. Rather the other way around. She knew to a dot how much Louis wanted for this or that bunch of cattle, even for every hog and steer individually. If they wished to buy, she assured them, they might as well make the bargain with her and save themselves another trip—the price would be the same when Louis came home!

Strictly speaking, Lizzie was a little wide of the mark

in making this statement. In the evenings, after the hired man had gone upstairs, husband and wife would often sit up late, discussing the value of every creature on the farm, and agree on prices. But Lizzie had formed the habit of adding a little to the price when the buyer showed up, allowing for the fact that the beast would be growing and fattening all the time; Louis, however, always stood by the agreement. The buyers did not like her any too well; they swore that no one in the settlements where they did their trading could demand such exorbitant prices as that darned Norwegian woman out in the Greenfield neighbourhood—she was simply impossible! Every time they made an offer, she would shake her head and say, calmly, "Too little money!" At that she would walk away from them, as though taking it for granted that there would be no deal. According to one version of the story, it had actually happened once or twice that she had come down on the price. But when they finally had got her down to the figure she and Louis had agreed upon in the silent hours of the night, it did not matter to her in the least how much they argued and fumed; Lizzie with an expression of utter innocence was as immovable as the Rocky Mountains.

In the course of years Lizzie acquired a certain fame for her business talent. She was known in all the small towns round about, but not by her real name: among the Yankees she was never called anything but "Too little money." It might happen that cattle-buyers, standing by the bar over a friendly drink, would fly into a rage at the mention of her name and pound the counter so that the glasses rattled, for there was hardly one among them whom she, at one time or another, had not taken by the nose. Oh, yes, that devil of a hussy could throw a trick or two! they would say, and much more. But one had better not take too much stock in the talk of tipsy cattle-buyers carousing in a small-town saloon!

Strange how well the Houglums got along together. Peace and harmony in that home. That, too, the neighbours talked about. Apparently they never disagreed. When, for example, Louis, in a merry gathering, good-naturedly held forth about how he as a mere stripling, during winters down in Iowa, had hauled wheat to McGregor, the oxen moving so slowly that they went backward instead of forward, with the cold so intense that their breaths stuck in the air like huge icicles—it was like driving through a forest, almost—Lizzie would listen to him in unfeigned admiration; she might add, affirmingly, "That's the gospel's own truth you're telling; I can remember it myself!" At first the neighbours had had a lot of fun with them, for they knew that Louis could spin a yarn as good as any of them, and, also, that Lizzie had never once set foot on Iowa's soil. But her saying, "That's the gospel's own truth, Louis," she repeated until it became a habit with her, and finally, a proverb in the settlement.

Once this habit of hers got her into a serious difficulty: Their hired man, who had been with them for several years, was a cantankerous fellow, a Cain upon earth—unmarried and well along in years, so crabbed and quarrelsome that nobody would have put up with him except the Houglums. Indeed, had he not been a good worker, and had they not hired him so cheaply, Lizzie would have insisted upon getting rid of him.

That summer a temperance speaker found his way into the settlement, remaining there a considerable length of time. On week days he drove around the neighbourhood, trying to enlist members in a temperance society he was organizing; on Sunday afternoons he held meetings in the schoolhouses. A great orator the man was, Demosthenes himself come to life again. People flocked to hear him, even confirmed topers, who would gladly walk miles to share in a pony keg of undrinkable beer. One Sunday he delivered a furious attack against all ministers who had the brazen effrontery to teach, and even proclaim from the pulpit, that the wine our dear Saviour used at the Wedding Feast in Cana was intoxicating. Talk about ungodliness! When such were the shepherds, what could be expected of the flock? Instead of leading people to heaven, they led them straight to hell. Here were wolves in the innocent garb of sheep! For more than an hour the speaker thundered against the clergy; by the time he had finished, the preachers left aboveground were few and far between.

The Houglum hired man considered the speech a masterpiece. Not at any time had he been too fond of men wearing the black cloth. For this ingrown dislike he had good reasons. One of them had humiliated him beyond endurance, had marked him for life; the minister in Norway had compelled him to study two years for confirmation instead of the customary one, which decree, whenever it was pronounced, was considered a great disgrace. The insufferable treatment had enraged the man so that the year he obtained confirmation he had struck out for the Land of Freedom. Who could amount to anything in the old country, having to begin life with such a millstone about his neck? Ever since that day he had been nourishing a hot hatred for all ecclesiastics. No wonder that the speech did him much good—he could not remember ever having received so much blessing from any sermon! That was his own testimony.

That evening there was a dispute at Houglum's. At the supper table sat the hired man, repeating bits from the speech, now and then adding an opinion of his own. Unfortunately, Louis had been brought up in an orthodox congregation, belonging to the Norwegian Lutheran Synod, which held strictly to the old, uncontaminated teaching concerning the wine used at the famous wedding feast. Although Louis seldom mixed up in any serious discussion, on this particular occasion he felt it to be his Christian duty to reason sense into his hired man, and so he pointed out to him, that since the Scriptures stated in plain words that it was wine, it must have been *wine* . . . if it had been only grape juice and such swill, it couldn't very well have been called wine; and the Scriptures, he added, admonishingly, were inspired . . . in this particular case God

Himself and the leaders of the Synod agreed . . . it ill behooved an ignorant farm-hand to hold an opinion to the contrary! This reasoning was so logical and clear that no man, no matter how perverse, could deny the truth of it.

And Lizzie, who had been listening to the men, was of the same opinion. "Grape juice!" she exclaimed. "Good gracious! was that any miracle?" Why, she could make that kind of wine by the barrel!

At this unforeseen opposition the man grew furious. Laying down his knife and fork, and wildly gesticulating with both hands, he demanded to know if Louis was so maggoty-headed as to believe that the Lord went about on the earth fooling innocent people into getting drunk? Was that the kind of Christianity they lived on in America? What? The man broke into a derisive laugh.

Lizzie was so put out with him that she told him to shut up, asserting heatedly that Louis was right, indeed he was. In her great eagerness the words came to her lips before she realized what she was saying: "Shame on you, the way you talk! What Louis says is true . . . I can well remember the time myself—yes, sir, I can!"

At that, according to Lizzie's own account later, a demon must have taken possession of the hired man; he had turned vicious, downright insulting: Aha, ship ahoy! he yelled in her face. She remembered that wedding, did she? . . . Well, siree! . . . So she was present that time? Had she been the cook? or perhaps one of the bridesmaids? Or maybe it was her own wedding the Gospel told about? And all this time he'd been living under the same roof with her and didn't know it—by God, that was funny!

There had been a terrible time; Lizzie wept when she told her mother about it. Louis and Lizzie were on the point of kicking the fellow out of the house, but agreed to let him stay on; the cutting would begin the next day, and to get a new man for the same pay this time of the year would be next to impossible.

But from that day on the hired man never referred to Lizzie by any other name than the Bride of Cana. And without doubt he was the source of much of the talk drifting about the neighbourhood concerning the Houglums.

V

They lived happily together, these two human beings—at least tolerably so. Both were strong, in the best of health; they slept well at night, and their savings increased from year to year. Louis saved in his way, Lizzie in hers; together they invented many schemes by which they might save more. They worked early and late, never hiring help oftener than absolutely necessary, and always thinking twice before making the smallest expenditures. Slowly but steadily their savings grew; bank notes as well as coin multiplied. Whenever the pile reached one hundred dollars—not an infrequent occurrence—they rejoiced like little children before a richly decorated Christmas tree. Their happiness was very real and their satisfaction thoroughly genuine. Each year their feeling of snug security increased.

No children came to the Houglums; for that they could only be thankful, Lizzie would say if the subject were mentioned in her presence. . . . What should they want children for—yes, why should they? The way young people behaved nowadays, anyone who didn't have them certainly ought to consider himself lucky. At such times there was an unusual harshness in her voice.

One day old Reverend Christensen came to see them on a queer errand; he had just returned from a visit to the Orphans' Home, of which governing board he was a member. The institution was filled to overflowing with hungry, thin-faced, shabbily dressed children of all ages—the sight was enough to make a good man sick. And there were more requests for admission than they could take care of. On the way home it had occurred to him that the Houglums could easily afford to give a home to one of these unfortunates—maybe even to two, and be glad for the chance. Now he was here to lay the matter before them.

Finding Louis in the barn, he broached the subject to him, speaking with a quiet earnestness. Louis scratched his head and grinned uncomfortably, it might mean either yes or no; he hemmed and stuttered, then broke into a laugh. Having regained sufficient composure, he told the minister to go in and discuss the

proposition with Lizzie . . . for, after all, a matter of
this nature concerned her more than it did him—no
harm in finding out what she thought about it.

Louis went into the kitchen with the minister . . . it
might be interesting to hear what she had to say. Lizzie,
with sleeves rolled up above her elbows, was bending
over a tub, washing clothes, her face flushed and per-
spiring. Before Reverend Christensen was through
talking she gave him a flat refusal; seemingly, she took
the proposal as a personal insult. Bending over the
washboard and scrubbing so that the suds flew, she
talked indignantly, in a loud voice: Nonsense and silly
talk . . . menfolks with nothing to do could think up
queer things! . . . If the Lord had wanted her to have
children, He'd have seen to it that she got them! Or
didn't the pastor believe that Providence took care of
that, too? . . . No, thank you, she'd have nothing to
do with other folks' brats . . . those who had gotten
them into the world had better take care of them!

"Yes, yes," assented the minister, meekly, "but—
well—suppose now, that this is His way of giving you
a child?"

"His way!" Lizzie slammed the shirt into the tub,
"I guess not . . . not unless He has changed His way
lately! . . . You might go carry in a pail of water for
me, Louis." Her face was so cold and forbidding that
the minister shuddered.

For many days after the visit Lizzie was hard to get
along with; she nagged Louis, and sneered at everything he had to say.

To all men is portioned out a fair share of adversity. There is only this difference: some get more than others and some stand up bravely under it; others are broken utterly, and are swept away like chips upon a swift current. But mountain peaks crumble and high hills are worn low, so why should the poor earthlings crawling upon them complain?

On the Houglums, too, troubles descended, and, as usual in such visitations, from a source least expected and in ways that made the burdens harder to bear:

It had taken them about five years to pay up the mortgage on the farm. From Tom Öien they had borrowed all he had to lend them; thus they saved a neat sum of interest. Let it be said in all fairness to them that they paid back every cent of the loan—Louis had insisted on that.

By the time their indebtedness was lifted, the Houglums had considerable money hid away at home; with no more debt to worry about, and with hard work and assiduous saving, they saw their treasures growing surprisingly fast.

At last a question presented itself, a problem which seemed silly, for really, it should not be a problem at all: but what should they do with the money they laid by? Neither of them cared for more land than the two hundred acres they already had. . . . No pleasure in owning a lot of land, and land was expensive—very expensive unless farmed efficiently . . . it might easily become a liability instead of an asset. Money thus invested was out of one's reach . . . one couldn't even look at it. . . . . And they got such fun out of seeing the money come in and the piles grow; they played with bank notes and silver dollars and their precious gold coins as youngsters do with fine toys. With them it was a game. By and by they had money in small bags, stuck away here and there in all kinds of improbable hiding-places. In the evenings as they sat there all alone, or on Sunday afternoons—it was seldom that anyone called—they would bring out the bags, take out the money, play with it, fondle it caressingly; then, after having counted it with much care, they would hide the bags in their secret places. What could be more interesting? To make the bags swell—now, there was something worth striving for!

In time they had hoarded in the house two thousand dollars, hidden in various places—some silver in a crock, four wads of bills, and an even one thousand in pure gold, exactly one hundred ten-dollar pieces. Both bills and silver were dear to them, but most precious of all was the heap of gold—on that point they agreed thoroughly. The small, round coins of heavy metal cast a spell, a faintly burning splendour coming out of their warm hearts. . . . There they lay, somnolent, yet solid and dependable . . . just feel of them! They represented security itself, the basis of all that was safe in life, the very rock-bottom of dependableness. And they had other qualities, too, equally remarkable: in them life lay asleep . . . no, not exactly asleep, just a bit heavy-eyed and lazy; Fortune Herself it was, not caring to stir! One need only to shake them about to see the radiance. . . . Let them sleep, poor things, no need of their being active . . . not yet, anyway. . . . Lizzie loved to let them slip from one hand into the other, to jostle them about enough to give her a smile. The weight of them would frighten her . . . what could they be made of? Pure gold, yes, that was it— pure gold!

Gold Louis would ask for whenever he received settlement for some deal, and whenever he cashed in his grain checks.

And now they had a whole thousand! Lizzie had made a neat, cozy nest for the little fellows, a leather bag which lay hidden in a most unthinkable place. That the trick was clever she knew because she had tested it out on Louis. The bag rested right by her head in the mattress which they slept on every night; lying in bed, she could easily reach it with her hand—that she had tried on nights when she could not sleep. From an old mattress of the same pattern of cloth she had made a small pocket; with great skill of workmanship she had stitched the pocket to the mattress on three sides; the top of the pocket she fastened to the mattress with small hooks and eyes, well concealed under the edge; so neatly was the job executed that the mattress did not even bulge out where the pocket sat.

After hiding the bag of gold there she was anxious to test the fool-proof safety of her invention; one day she asked Louis to carry out the mattress and sweep it thoroughly, particularly along the seams, and while he was dusting she stood beside him, watching with secret delight, nagging him wickedly because of his slovenly work. When the mattress had been brought in again and she had revealed the secret to him, both laughed heartily, first at her incomparable cunning and next at his stupidity—here he had had one thousand dollars in pure gold right under his very nose and hadn't even smelt it! The other thousand was hidden elsewhere, but not more than two hundred in any one place.

In the course of years, with the piles growing about the house, Louis and Lizzie invented a secret vocabulary, a code-language, intelligible only to themselves. The gold pieces they called *babies,* the bank notes *brats,* while the clumsy, big silver dollars were termed *shillings.* Whenever Louis had been marketing cattle or hogs, or had received settlement for grain, Lizzie would be sure to meet him in the yard on his return, eager to learn how he had fared. "All right," she might ask, "how did you make out today?" If he then could answer, "Fine, I tell you!" or, "Lots of babies today!" she would glow with a radiant joy. On such evenings they pulled the shades low, and then counted the money, sorting it and playing with it, happy as two lovers, until far into the night.

But one night a grave disaster struck near by: fire broke out in the house of a neighbour, an old bachelor, and before help could reach his place, the house had been utterly destroyed; the man barely escaped with his life.

The accident gave the Houglums a terrible fright.

But it was not the destruction of the neighbour's home that worried them; to that part they never gave a thought. The story soon leaked out that the man had had six hundred dollars in paper money lying about the house, and how all of it was lost, all had vanished as the smoke from the burnt-down house had mingled with the very elements. Not a trace, not a sign left! . . . God have mercy—could it be possible? . . . Simply uncanny to think of . . . there was some kind of doom in it . . . no power on earth could restore that money to the owner, nor could he go to anyone to demand it back—to whom should he go? . . . Was money, too, a staff which broke when you leaned upon it? To the Houglums the ground they walked on had begun to sway under their feet.

On the night following the catastrophe neither of them got much sleep; like a ghostly spectre the thought of the fire hovered before their eyes—it might happen to anyone. . . . Suppose now (this was Louis) that a spark lay smouldering somewhere, glowing redder, and ready to burst into flames at any minute! . . . He fell to thinking about how carelessly he threw matches away after lighting his pipe, never looking whether the flame had gone out or anything . . . simply dropped them . . . here, there, anywhere, everywhere. This very evening he had thrown burning matches into the wood-box . . . Lizzie usually kept dry corncobs in the box! Louis strained his ears, listening for crackling sounds.

Lizzie's thoughts ran in the same narrow lane; she

couldn't get her mind off the stove . . . that scorched spot on the wall, back of the oven . . . many times that must have been near to catching fire . . . often big sparks flew when she opened the door to put in more wood! Without realizing what she did, she lay sniffing the air—she would, of course, smell the smoke!

But their neighbour did not know how the fire could possibly have started; he awoke in the middle of the night, with flames roaring about him, almost suffocated by smoke. Lizzie thought of it until her body was wet with cold perspiration. . . . With the babies there could be no possible danger, she assured herself . . . nor with the shillings, either—they would stand it all right. She saw the very spot in the ashes where she would stick her hand down and pick out the babies— clear as day, she saw it. . . . But the poor brats, they'd be gone with the first whiff . . . all eight hundred of them, God have mercy! . . . Suddenly she sat bolt up in bed and grabbed her husband's shoulder. "Louis," she whispered, hoarsely, "get your pants on and put the brats in your pockets. . . . Hurry now. You know where they are . . . the last twenty-five you brought home are lying in the south corner of the lower bureau drawer . . . if anything should happen, we'll have most of it safe!" She was greatly agitated; in her hoarse whisper was a frantic note.

Without a word Louis got out of bed and into his overalls—for sure, there Lizzie had a fine idea . . . it would have to be pretty bad if the clothes burnt off his body before he got himself out of the house! When he got into bed again he had his overalls on and the $800 stuck safely in his pockets. Both fell asleep with the same problem in mind: they would have to find a safe place for the money!

VI

It was the worry over the safety of the paper money that forced the Houglums seriously to consider the bank. Perhaps they'd better do as many other people did: place their money on deposit so as to have it safe.

Time and again they had thought of such a course; they had talked about it, had discussed it from many angles; but they had always come back to the same conclusion: they'd keep the money at home and have some enjoyment out of it. Once they put it into the bank they'd not see it again until they drew it out, couldn't even touch it; it was gone, almost; just a plain certificate—that's all they'd have. And what fun was there in that stiff, old piece of paper made out by the fellows at the bank? Once they had seen one at Öien's and had exchanged knowing smiles—some folks didn't get much fun for their money! On the way home they had talked about how foolish the old folks were. . . . But now the worry would let them have no peace; they must do something about the money. Every night Louis slept in his overalls with the money in his pockets, a measure of precaution that was all right for the night; yet

no one could tell what might happen during the day
. . . there were tramps prowling along the roads, and
Louis couldn't carry all that money on him wherever he
went.

One night in bed, after lying awake for a long time
discussing the problem, they decided to put some of
the money in the bank, they saw no other way out. The
next day Louis must make a trip to a couple of neighbouring towns to see if he couldn't change some of the
paper, perhaps some silver, too, into gold. . . . Gold
did not take much room . . . it did not burn . . .
easy to hide . . . besides, well—neither of them cared
to part with the babies. . . . But if they put some of
the money into the bank, there would be interest to get
and it would be safe against both fire and theft.

Returning late the next evening, Louis had one hundred dollars more in gold and exactly that much less
in bills. The same week he took seven hundred in paper
and one hundred in silver to the First National Bank of
Greenfield, which he deposited on a savings account at
five per cent interest.

But that they ought not to have done it, both soon
realized; for now there followed a long period of dull,
drab days, with no fun at all. Louis went about his
work, silent and out of sorts, having no ambition for
anything. Lizzie seemed to take it harder still; the
house was cold and lonely after the brats had been
taken away from her . . . what of it if they were resting in a safe place?—she couldn't see them, anyway!
But with Louis it was precisely the question of their

safety that worried him. He felt less secure now than before. He remembered only too well how terribly recklessly the fellow in the bank had thrown the money around . . . with no more respect than if he had been spreading manure on a field—awful to look at! The bills which he and Lizzie had handled with so great tenderness, that snot of a clerk had sorted indifferently and tossed onto piles—the fives onto one, the tens onto another, and the twenties, with no more concern than if they had been two-cent stamps. . . . They weren't even allowed to be all together! . . . In sorting them, the man wickedly thumbed and stretched and scrutinized each one as though they had been criminals caught in the very act. . . . But Louis never mentioned his worries to Lizzie.

That was considerate of him, because she had enough as it was. She actually felt lost after her dear ones had been taken away, lost and disturbed. Heavy of heart she would go into the bedroom, take out the certificate of deposit, and absent-mindedly glance at the official piece of paper. In small figures was written the sum, $800, and in words also, but the writing was so scrawly that she could hardly make it out. She would put down the certificate, shake her head in disgust, and give a pent-up sigh. What did this insignificant piece of paper with some figures and letters scribbled upon it by a young snip amount to in comparison with the real little brats? Nothing! . . . When they came of age and had been tamed properly they yielded to the slightest touch . . . laid against your cheek they felt warm and downy as the softest silk . . . you could feel how the life in them caressed you! . . . And they had pretty pictures printed on them, figures that were alive just so you took time to look at them. . . . Not until they had been taken away from her did she realize fully how fond she had grown of the brats; had it not been that they were so difficult to look after and care for, she often told her husband, she'd just as soon have them at home as the babies. . . . The babies—oh well, that was another story. Lizzie's face would light up; going to the bed she would stick her hand down into the pocket and take out the bag, open it and stir with her finger . . . nothing wrong with them, thank goodness! Why should there be? They could stay at home and just lazy themselves! Much comforted, she would put the bag into its hiding-place and go back to her work.

As the bitterest grief bv and by changed to a dull, aching, pain, the thought of the interest became a source of real comfort to them both. In these times of unreasonably high prices, forty dollars a year, got for nothing, was not to be sneered at. One evening after supper, when they were both sitting by the table in the kitchen, he smoking and doing nothing, she bent over her mending, silent and downcast, Louis, to cheer her up, spoke of the interest they were earning, pointing out how much it would amount to at the end of the year. Over her face came a curious smile, as on an elder's who hears a child's innocent prattle. "I s'pose," she answered, meditatively, "now they've left us to go out into the world to start up by themselves, they feel they must do a little something for us . . . we've certainly slaved hard enough to get them!"

Two years later came the shock; first the crash; then the shock. One fine day the First National Bank of Greenfield went bankrupt. The blow struck like a bolt of lightning out of a clear sky, suddenly, unexpectedly, blinding everybody, leaving utter darkness behind. A government official from St. Paul came down, turned the key, and the key—so it was said—he took with him when he left. In the Greenfield country a number of people were hit by the failure, some only lightly, while others were as good as ruined. But none felt the crushing force of the catastrophe more than Lizzie and Louis Houglum.

One hot July day while Lizzie washed the dishes, Louis was taking his usual noonday nap on the kitchen floor. To protect his face from the pestering flies, he had covered it with last week's *Greenfield County Courier*. He was only half asleep. His thoughts moved faintly and on a far-away sky line, at times barely visible. . . . The hogs? . . . How many of them ought he to market in the fall? . . . He had to keep a number for spring breeding—that was certain and settled. . . . Prices were high now . . . would most likely stay up until fall. . . . Probably no hurry about selling yet . . . this time of the year they fattened without feeding . . . it had paid him fine to fence in that hog pasture. . . . The price might go higher yet. . . . If he waited until late fall, then marketed as many as he could spare, he'd have both brats and babies to bring home to Lizzie . . . more than any year before! . . . By the looks of things the wheat crop this year would break all records. . . . Louis lay enwrapped in a feeling of quiet contentment . . . if he didn't get up pretty soon, he'd drop right off to sleep . . . perhaps he ought to lift a corner of the paper to see how far along she was with her work?

Just then Lizzie called him. She was hanging up her apron in the corner by the stove. . . . They better stir now if they were going to get all that millet cocked before supper. . . . What had he done with the water-jug?

Arousing himself with an effort, he sat up on the floor; the paper dropped from his face and lay across his knees. Every muscle in his body felt stiff and sore from having tugged at the millet during the forenoon. As he sat there yawning, his blurred sight caught some words on the page before him—some big, awful words, telling an incredible story: FIRST NATIONAL BANK FAILS. LOCAL INSTITUTION CLOSED. Wide awake, the soreness all gone, Louis sat staring as though he had been in the presence of a ghost. Without stirring, he read the item clear through—in a paper that was over a week old!

He remained sitting so long that Lizzie lost all patience and began to nag him: Did he intend to sit there all day? . . . With all the millet waiting, he better get busy . . . better not depend too much on her . . . she had the housework and the chores. . . . They couldn't afford a man before harvest—they would make a few cents that way, too . . . and maybe they could even get along during harvest . . . might exchange work with a neighbour who needed help during threshing. . . . Would he never get himself ready?

Louis sat motionless, not a sound crossing his lips. But finally he got up quickly and came across the floor. Spreading the paper on the table, he called, hoarsely, as a man in pain, "Come here!" Pointing to the headlines, he added in a choked, quivering voice:

"Can you understand this?"

Lizzie looked at the paper and began to read, slowly, laboriously; the many technical terms impeded her progress. Nevertheless, she saw at once that something had gone wrong at the First National. As she read on, her face turned ashen pale; her head bent forward; her long nose seemed to want to tear the piece out of the paper; her small eyes shot dangerous gleams.

"Get the cart ready!" she ordered, a metallic ring in her voice. "We had better hurry!"

VII

In an incredibly short time they were rattling down the road, in the old rickety cart which they had bought with the farm, Louis clucking impatiently and using the lines to make the horse trot faster.

Both sat silent, each absorbed in dark thoughts. But

not for long; Louis had the sensation of being strangled slowly, either he must say something or he would choke . . . perhaps Lizzie—she was so much smarter—might understand what was wrong?

But she would not talk. "Drive on, can't you?" she snapped, with the same metallic ring in her voice, and fell silent again; her face was closed and set.

. . . It's no use to talk to her the way she feels now, thought Louis, though she can't blame me! and so he tried to figure out the mystery by himself. He was like a man groping about in a strange, dark room. . . . What could have happened to the bank? . . . Must be something terrible, since the papers wrote about it? . . . Far away Louis saw a faint light, dimly at first, but gradually growing brighter: the money must be safe . . . their money, anyway . . . the bank hadn't burnt . . . it hadn't been robbed—the paper mentioned neither fire nor theft. . . . These fellows at the bank must be honest? If people entrusted with the job of taking care of other people's money weren't to be relied on, then who in the world could be trusted? Before this clear process of reasoning his dark mood lifted and gave way. . . . If the bank had closed, all they needed to do was to go there and ask for their money. . . . They would probably get no interest for this year . . . well, they'd have to stand that . . . just so they got the principal. . . . The bank must have closed because it didn't pay to run it. He would have liked to discuss the matter with Lizzie, but her face looked so set and foreboding that he decided to leave her alone.

Having reached town they hitched the horse to the rusty iron bar in front of Jenkins' Grocery and went straight to the First National.

The bank was closed all right, no doubt about that; but the brick building stood just as solidly as ever. No sign of violence anywhere. The front door was locked; though Louis bore down upon it with all his might, it refused to budge. To his repeated pounding, it gave a dull, dead sound. From the door Louis ran to the window, trying to peer in; but the shade was drawn clear down. . . . This began to look funny . . . uncomfortable . . . where could the fellows running the bank have gone?

Remembering that there was a side entrance to the building and that sometimes he had seen people go into the bank by that way, he grabbed Lizzie by the arm and hurried around the corner. They found the entrance, but that door was locked as securely as the other.

Louis looked bewildered and excited. What the hell was this, anyhow? The bank closed, deserted, and empty, not a soul there to look after the money, and he had nearly $900 in this place! Lizzie stood mute; not a sound came across her lips.

Louis, not knowing what to try next or where to turn for help, sat down on the cement steps. A groan escaped Lizzie as she sank down beside him. Oblivious to everything else save their own problem, there the two sat, with the scorching hot sun mercilessly beating down upon them. People coming by on the sidewalk stopped a moment, looked at them and grinned; then went on; a few curious ones came past the second time —some more suckers that had been caught . . . poor fools! The passers-by spread the news of the two sitting on the back steps of the bank, and so more people came, eyed them, whispered and grinned.

Suddenly, Louis, hands clasped below his knees, began to curse, in a dejected, hopeless monotone. Once started, he seemed unable to check himself; in an uninterrupted flow of broken English, all the curses he had heard during his years of threshing now welled up in his consciousness; to relieve his pent-up emotion he said them—maledictions, oaths, obscenities, anything and everything vile that he could lay hold of.

"Can't you shut up!" groaned Lizzie, breaking into hysterical sobs.

Louis stopped short, holding his breath. What was the matter? . . . Gosh almighty! Lizzie crying? During all the years they had lived together he had never seen her act up in this way. Now she was choking with tears . . . a strange fear gripped his heart.

There they sat in the hot sun. On the other side of the street people went forth and back in the shade, eyeing them. Lizzie wept and Louis tried to hush her up; not knowing what else to do, he patted her awkwardly on the back. He felt so badly that he could not find his voice; if he had, he would have burst into tears himself.

Of the two she was the first to regain composure.

"We must see a lawyer!" she said, resolutely, drying her eyes with the fold of her skirt.

At that proposal he too was on solid ground. . . . Of course they must see a lawyer! How foolish of him not to have thought of it!

But, walking down the street, he plucked timidly at her sleeve. "I'm afraid it might cost us a lot?"

"Never mind! Can't you see that we must try to get our money back?"

The lawyer, a good-natured Irishman, was fat and jolly; just now in the middle of the summer, business was slack; he seemed glad of the chance to have some one to talk to. And when he found out what they wanted of him—which wasn't an easy task, because they talked so fast and excitedly, and both at the same time—he grew really friendly with them; he even found chairs and insisted that they sit down and rest themselves.

Both declined the offer . . . they weren't going to stay long . . . they couldn't take up his time . . . no, they must hurry!

With a quiet but uncontrollable glee the lawyer explained to them that the First National had gone the way of all flesh; absolutely no doubt about it; the sooner they accepted that fact the better they'd feel. All the books and papers were now in the hands of the government; no one could tell yet just how bad the situation was—no danger, however, that it wasn't bad enough. Perhaps they'd get a few cents back and perhaps not; he had grave doubts. The slipshod business going on in that bank had to stop sometime . . . people ought to be thankful that the end had come, that the game was up. . . . Oh no, it was hardly possible that they'd ever see a cent of that money; they might as well kiss it good-bye at once and be done with it . . . How much had they been fleeced of? So—nine hundred? Now they ought to go right home and have a private Thanksgiving because the amount wasn't larger . . . they had surely been let off easy! Thereupon the Irishman, himself a member of the board of directors of the other bank in town, The Merchant and Farmer's State Bank, advised them earnestly to patronize that institution in the future, for then they need not be awake nights and worry, no matter how many thousands they put in! That was a real bank, he'd tell them, as safe and sound as old Uncle Sam himself—he'd say even safer and didn't care who heard it!

But that was not the kind of advice Lizzie had come for, and so she asked straight out what the First National had done with their money.

—What they had done with it? chuckled the man, joyously. Why didn't she rather ask what they had *not* done? She might just as well inquire of the north wind where it put the dust it swept up along the road! All he could say was that the money was not where it ought to be, and that she probably knew herself. . . . Done with it? Ha-ha-ha!

—What had they used the money for? demanded Lizzie, angrily. Had they stolen it outright? Wasn't there a law against such things?

The lawyer seemed much amused by her innocence. If she entrusted her money to fools and crooks, it was hard to tell what they might do with it; people of that sort had strange notions of right and wrong! Again the man laughed heartily. . . . She might go and ask them—why not? Two of the First National's gang were spending a few days in the county jail . . . it might prove a good stunt to ask them! Yes, why not?

"They haven't skipped, then?" she asked, breathlessly.

"Skipped, my good woman! What are you talking about? How could they skip, I'd like to know? When the bank closed there wasn't enough money left to take them to the next town!"

The only satisfaction they got from the lawyer was that he charged them nothing. Oh no, not this time would he take anything, they had had enough outlay for a while! The man was so polite that he escorted them to the door, on the way giving them the fatherly advice to do their banking with The Merchant and State, for then they would know where they had their money.

Again they were in the street. The sun was roasting hot, the air blazing with heat. The dogs sought the shady places, panting hard, their red tongues hanging out, quivering.

But the two on the sidewalk did not notice the heat. Louis, thinking that any further effort to recover the lost money was useless, walked stooped, like a man that is being led to the gallows. At the first corner he turned down the street where the horse was hitched. Lizzie realized what he had in mind and stopped indignantly. What was he thinking about? Had he lost his senses? Didn't he understand that they were being robbed of nearly one thousand dollars? Suddenly a new thought had struck her, something about the government and those in authority, executives ordained by God for the protection of the innocent—the Bible mentioned them too.

Not at once grasping what she wanted, Louis' dejected face looked silly with its puzzled expression.

His helplessness exasperated her. "Don't you know that much—you a man?" She stamped her foot impatiently. . . . "How about those we pay for seeing to it that everything is done right and according to law, who jail people when they steal and rob? . . . Oh, don't stand there like a . . . What's the matter with you?"

"Aw, hell!" Louis understood what she meant and regained his wits. "Why, that's the sheriff, you certainly know that much, Lizzie!" His voice was mildly reproving.

"Why don't you say so, then? The sheriff? Where does he keep himself?"

The next moment they were heading for the sheriff's office, Louis leading the way.

The sheriff was a Norwegian, and a Sogning [1] at that. Louis knew him well; years ago they had worked together in the same threshing crew. To him they could speak Norwegian. Both Louis and Lizzie brightened—

[1] A person from Sogn, Norway. The Sognings are noted for their quick wit and clever repartee; their speech is lively, and musical in its cadences.

finding this man was like coming home . . . here they'd be sure to get help!

The sheriff lapsed into his native dialect the moment he saw them, speaking fast: Yes, yes, he knew all about it, they need not explain . . . he was just this minute thinking of driving out to them to ask their advice . . . he was in need of comfort himself! How much did they have in the bank? Nine hundred? Holy God! only nine hundred! . . . If his case hadn't been any worse than that, he wouldn't have cared to mention it —no, really. But in that circus over at the First National he had been skinned out of twenty-five hundred dollars . . . what did they think of that? And he had a peevish woman at home and eight hungry kids. Damned funny they didn't want her and them into the bargain! . . . His twenty-five hundred they had put roller skates under, and that was every penny he had to his name, his total savings in twenty years. . . . How would they like to trade with him?

After hearing about the misfortune that had befallen the sheriff, somehow their own trouble seemed to give way; they felt easier, they could reason more clearly about what ought to be done. Since the highest representative of the law himself had so much money in the bank, with such conditions at home, he'd surely try all he could to get his money out . . . just so he didn't beat them to it and get his before anyone else could get theirs!

Lizzie, seeing the danger plainly, asked, guardedly, why he, who had the authority, didn't go over to the bank and break open the door? Why not go right now? They would go with him and lend a hand. . . . They'd go right away!

The sheriff gave her an odd look, then broke into a sardonic laugh. "My dear woman, you go home and go to bed. You don't know enough about business to last you overnight!" Thereupon he swung his swivel chair around to the desk; there was a big pile of letters and documents before him; apparently he had dismissed the two from his mind.

Lizzie was not a bit satisfied with the advice given her. Stepping boldly up to the desk, she asked in a harsh voice: "Aren't they in jail? Well, then, why don't you make them tell you where they are keeping the money? You're the law, aren't you, and can do everything?"

The sheriff, full of important business, turned to Louis—to Lizzie he paid no attention:

"Take your woman and go home, Louis! Don't let her run around town, making a fool of herself. A man came in here awhile ago asking me to lock up the two of you. I tell you I have no more time for your dog-gone foolishness—I've a wife and eight kids to worry about; the ninth is on the way. . . . Now get out!"

Presently Louis and Lizzie sat in their old rickety cart, jogging across the flat prairie homeward. A breeze from the north had sprung up; with evening coming on, the sun had changed from bright yellow to a deep red; the heat was less intense now than earlier in the afternoon.

For a long time neither of them uttered a word; but at last Louis began thinking aloud:

"Can you understand it, Lizzie?"

She only shook her head and remained silent. But about a mile farther up the road she spoke:

"I certainly can't. . . . I don't think anybody can."

Again the silence lasted for a long time, each sitting bent over his and her own thought.

Suddenly Lizzie's face brightened, like a bleak landscape over which the sun breaks out:

"Suppose we drive over and see the minister?"

Louis ahemmed once, twice . . . the minister would hardly know what to do in a case like this. But before he was ready to object, she spoke again:

"Because if anybody can make them cough up the money, then he's the one . . . that man can get money out of a stone wall; we might.promise him ten dollars for the missions?" she added, questioningly.

Remembering how difficult it was to refuse Reverend Christensen money when he was out begging, Louis agreed thoughtfully that it wouldn't hurt to see him. He was a learned man. . . . They would probably have to promise him more than ten dollars, though! Louis fell silent again. . . . They might even offer to take one of the kids from the Orphans' Home—they wouldn't need to keep him longer than necessary . . . she had been too sharp that time . . . doggone it if she hadn't! Louis whipped up the horse and drove fast, keeping his thoughts to himself.

On reaching the next crossroad, they drove westward

instead of going home; from there to the parsonage was only two miles; it wouldn't take them long to make the extra trip, and it wouldn't hurt to try.

Coming into the yard of the parsonage, they saw two rigs standing there, and their spirits fell. Nevertheless, they tied up the horse and went in the back way. Mrs. Christensen herself met them, pleasant and smiling, telling them that just now her husband was in the study, marrying a couple, but if they'd please sit down, he'd be ready in a short while.

Lizzie said, in a crestfallen voice, that their errand was such that it couldn't be postponed, they just had to see him . . . since it was only a marriage he was performing, it would perhaps not take him so very long. Just then they heard the couple leave by the front door, and Mrs. Christensen showed the Houglums into the study.

No sooner had Lizzie entered the room than she was overcome by a sense of timidity, almost of awe. . . . It felt so queer in here; so quiet and so strangely silent. With the stench of stale tobacco smoke, which filled the air, was mingled a peculiar odour, unknown to her, yet pleasant to the smell. The room was filled with things invisible. Along the walls, books from floor to ceiling, four solid walls of books! Her eyes stole furtively up and down the shelves. Mysterious life, intangible yet vitally alive, emanated from these walls, was afloat in the air and everywhere present. Involuntarily she folded her hands. . . . Could one man have use for all these books? They must have cost a lot! . . . Now she understood why this man could get people to do what he wanted, whether they were willing or not.

The minister, having seen the bridal party off, came in again. He wore full canonicals, both ruff and gown. Coming close to them, he shook their hands warmly in greeting. Lizzie could not find her voice. But eyeing the minister closely, she suddenly noticed something so comical that she almost broke into a giggle . . . really, it was too funny for anything: wrapped around his left forefinger was a banknote, a worn ten-dollar bill. . . . Now did you ever see the beat! The mystery of the room was gone.

"Well, well," said the minister in a friendly voice, stepping over to the table and filling his pipe, "what important matter can have taken you from your work?" Lighting his pipe, he took a few deep puffs. Louis could see how thoroughly he enjoyed it and grinned . . . the minister was a real man, no doubt about it!

Louis waited for his wife to speak first, as she had done all day, but seeing her sitting there silent, folding and unfolding a pleat in her skirt, he began, hesitatingly:

—Well, it was like this . . . a great misfortune had come upon them . . . a calamity too awful to mention . . . they didn't know what to do about it.

"What can that be, Houglum? There is nothing wrong at your father-in-law's?" The minister was all sympathy.

Lizzie spoke up quickly: "It's us, and we don't know what to do, so we've come to you."

Pure Gold

"But, my dear children, you both seem well; it can't be so terrible?" the minister inquired concernedly.

"It certainly is," replied Lizzie, sadly; "I don't see how it could be worse; we've lost all we had!"

"Yes," added Louis, "we're just about ruined!"

"No, no, no!—what are you saying? Your home hasn't burnt?" The minister was sincerely sympathetic.

Their loss became so terrible now they sat here telling about it, that tears flooded their eyes. Burnt? Oh, no, it was worse than that . . . if it had been a fire, they might have managed it somehow! exclaimed Lizzie.

"You see, we've been robbed!" added Louis, in desperation.

"That's just what we have, and that's the truth!" repeated Lizzie. "They've stolen from us what little we had!"

"Robbed, d'you say? I can't believe it—right here in the midst of a Christian congregation?" There was a note of paternal reproof in the minister's question.

Lizzie had begun to weep and could not speak. And so Louis had to tell the story as best he could, though his voice, too, was not at all steady:

"It didn't happen at home . . . those fellows in town, you see . . . yes, that gang at the First National . . . they've cleaned us out—of nine hundred dollars in spot cash!"

The minister was greatly relieved; he even smiled cheerfully. "My dear friends, you mustn't take that to heart. No doubt that will be straightened out in time, and, furthermore, it is only a matter of money!"

To Lizzie his words were blasphemous; they outraged her sense of propriety. That a minister of the gospel could have such silly talk in his mouth! . . . And still beg so hard when he was after money! . . . Here he himself had a ten-dollar bill wrapped around his finger . . . she could see plainly how he fondled it . . . easy enough to admonish other people!

"Well, now, my dear children," said the pastor, consolingly, "such tribulations we must not take to heart. Let us rather give thanks to the Lord for having removed this stumbling-block from your path. No, no, friends, let us not grieve over a few dollars!"

But, sobbed Lizzie, angrily, he didn't know how hard they had toiled for them . . . besides, should they give thanks for being robbed by thieves?

"No, no, no, I don't mean it that way—you mustn't misunderstand me! But money is, after all, only of the earth, and will finally be destroyed by moth and rust as all corruptible things. We must never put our trust in money!"

Sick at heart and thoroughly disgusted with the minister, Lizzie dried her eyes, got up hurriedly, and started for the door, there waiting for Louis to get ready. No use wasting time in listening to an old man's silly chatter . . . he couldn't have got much wisdom from all these books! . . . Or maybe he was making money too easily? Again she glanced at his left hand, and sure enough—he was still fondling that bill!

Rather impatient with his wife, Louis arose: Why was she running away mad like that? They hadn't said a word to the minister about what they'd really come for! Couldn't she stand a doggone thing today? The minister was dressed for church, in his holy clothes, but just the same he'd better risk speaking to him. Assuming the greatest possible innocence, Louis stuck his tanned, square face close to the minister's, saying, artlessly, "It's like this, you see: Lizzie and I were thinking, that you being a learned man, could maybe help us; you're so smart at collecting money. . . . If you could get it back, there might be a little something for the church . . . Lizzie and I have been talking about the missions!" There was naïve earnestness in the man's pleading voice.

The minister chuckled kindly as he shook hands with Louis. "That's fine of you, Mr. Houglum. Think of the Lord always lest He forget you! We'll remember that promise. The affairs of the bank are now in the hands of the law; the law will tell us what to do. No doubt you'll get some of the money back. I'll keep it in mind and make inquiry from time to time." The minister spoke encouragingly, puffing comfortably at his pipe.

"How much d'you think we might get back?" Louis asked, hopefully.

But that question the minister would not undertake to answer. It would hardly be less than fifty cents on the dollar. Probably more. He had read of bank failures where the depositors had got every penny back. They ought not to set their minds on any figure. No doubt, this was a visitation from the Lord, just a reminder to them. Money was of value only to those who used it rightly, and the proper use of money was to do good with it!

Lizzie had been holding the door knob, waiting for her husband. Now she tossed her head back defiantly, an indignant gleam in her eyes; suddenly she faced the minister, in her voice a scornful note, the words snapping out of her mouth: "Those who slave for the money and come by it honestly, have, I suppose, the first right to say what it ought to be used for—talk is cheap!" Flinging the door open, she stepped out on the porch.

"Don't mind her; she means no harm!" apologized Louis, humbly, again grasping the minister's hand. "You see it's this way: we've struggled so long for the money; she just can't get over those fellows stealing it from us . . . Lizzie is a hard-working woman!" He did not let go of the hand; a soft, kind hand it was. The grasp of it had a singular effect upon Louis; here as he was standing face to face with the minister, dressed just as in church before the altar, he had a sense of blessings being poured out upon him. "Now you will try to help us, won't you?" begged Louis, guilelessly. "For if you can't get the money out of those fellows, then no one else needs try—I know what you can do!"

"Now, now, my good friend, never put your trust in man!" admonished the minister, kindly, as he went with Louis to the door.

III. On the Mount of Temptation

I

NEITHER husband nor wife recovered from the shock of the bank failure. The crash marked a turning-point in their lives, for with it began the great change which gradually crept over them.

But when the bank, shortly after Christmas that same year, paid each depositor fifty cents on the dollar (Louis succeeded in getting forty dollars of this money exchanged in gold at the State Bank), they enjoyed a few days of comparative happiness. Four hundred and fifty dollars, absolutely lost and suddenly recovered, was not a matter to be taken lightly. Short-lived and empty, however, as the morning dew, that happiness! Their feeling of loss grew only the more acutely unbearable at the thought of the other four hundred and fifty dollars which they would never see again.

For Lizzie, who had mothered all these nine hundred dollars, the loss proved the harder to bear; the longer her mind lingered on the misfortune, the keener she felt the bitterness; the denser the gloom gathering about her. It was not the amount of the loss which distracted her; but rather it was this, that never in all eternity would she see those fives and tens and twenties again. And she had tended them so well, making them comfortable, had watched over each one with such anxious care; they were hers—part of her own self . . . now they were gone irrevocably, never to return. She had been lured into ambush and wantonly stripped! . . . And such things were allowed to happen in the broadest daylight in a Christian country . . . nobody sweating in the penitentiary . . . nobody punished . . . nobody hanged. Oh no! the government stood by, letting such outrageous deviltry go on . . . did nothing . . . apparently, did not care one rap . . . yet the taxes mounted higher and higher every year! Had all justice gone from the face of the earth?

The attitude of the Houglums to the rest of the world underwent a gradual change; what previously had been indifference and aloofness became lurking suspicion looking for underhandedness in every man's word and act. Both had been fond of dickering for a bargain. Whenever they had tried to screw up the price on things they offered for sale, and the buyer, just as determinedly, sought to bring them down, it had been to Lizzie a capital sport, the most glorious she could think of. And she had never cheated anybody. How could she? Didn't the buyer see what he was bidding on? If he didn't like her price he could say no—the same as she. . . . If he lacked wits or failed to use them, that certainly wasn't her fault!

But now she had learned that no one could feel safe, even the most careful—there was no such thing as safety. When the bank, an institution existing for the sole purpose of keeping people's money safe and making it grow, no longer was to be trusted, then what in the world could be counted safe? The fact that one stayed quietly at home, never doing harm to anybody, did not make the least bit of difference. There actually were people who lived and thrived by devouring others, just like the worm in the apple!

There was one puzzle in the whole affair, which neither of them could figure out: Who had their money? Where was it now? None of those fellows in the bank, they were told. Well—where had it gone? If some one had borrowed it, why wasn't he dunned, his mortgage foreclosed, and the money recovered? It hadn't been stolen? It hadn't been burnt? Nor was it in the bank? . . . There must be some master thief running loose, but the Law sat idly by!

They had been saving before, their manner of living always simple and frugal; now a fervoured purpose had come over them; in every possible way they stinted and pinched; saving became a sacred religious practice that must not at any cost be broken; they seldom bought clothes; shoes still more rarely: Lizzie mended and patched; Louis cobbled.

By and by Lizzie learned to be more careful in preparing her meals. Though they were farming two hundred acres of the most fertile land in Greenfield County, and though they had both granary and corncrib so full the greater part of the year that the bins were bulging, still she saw clearly that she must be more careful in her cooking. In spite of the fact that they milked ten cows morning and evening, she now served skimmed milk with their morning porridge. Sweet cream, these days, brought good money, and milk was just as nourishing.

The prick that goaded her constantly, the thorn in her flesh, was the waste of money in tobacco. Every once in a while she chided and nagged him mercilessly. It was so foolish a habit, so downright stupid, so brutally selfish of him. . . . Didn't he see that they could not afford to be throwing money away that way? The idea of his chewing up and spitting away money every day in the year—what was he thinking of? What was the use of her turning each penny twice, so long as he persisted in squandering dollars? Had he minded her and stopped when they were first married, by now they'd have had enough saved to cover the whole loss; she was sure of it . . . either he must quit or take the consequences, now she was telling him. . . . What? wasn't he listening? Then what was he gawking at?

Louis weathered the storms bravely; gradually he learned to predict their coming on . . . he had certain signs; some did not fail; about once a month there'd be hell to pay. Usually he dodged, or hunching his back, he'd let the tempest rage. And he had a certain philosophy which stood him in good stead: no use to talk to anyone about things he couldn't understand!

In order to pacify her and get a day's rest, he promised to stop. Doggone it! he'd try, even though the attempt would cost his life. . . . Didn't she see how hard he was trying? . . . Well, then . . .

As a matter of plain fact he did not try; not in real earnest; he smoked and chewed on the sly, got caught

at it, again and again. Shamefacedly admitting his guilt
and assuring her that all he had was a tiny, wee snippet
he had found in the pocket of an old overall hanging
in the granary, didn't improve his case any; trying to
wiggle out of it by insisting that now she was mistaken
—honestly, he hadn't tasted tobacco for weeks!—made
matters worse than ever. Was he standing there trying
to deceive his own wife? She flew at him: did he dare
to lie right up in her face? Couldn't she smell the nasty
stuff? He stunk worse than an old manure pile . . .
wasn't fit to come near a woman!

Twice he tried another tack with her. Flaring up in
a terrible fit of anger, he flung it right into her teeth
that he *had* laid in a new store, and what was more, he
intended going right on; he'd buy some more as soon
as he got to town. . . . If she wanted to leave him on
that account, well and good—the way was open . . .
Now he'd hear no more damned foolishness! Did she
understand what he meant?

And apparently she did, for she cried hysterically.
Both times he left the house. But when his temper was
gone he felt ashamed of himself for having been so
rough on her. . . . Lizzie was an unusually able
woman!

The times were good, prices on farm products kept
rising steadily, and the Houglums prospered. Frequently Louis brought home babies, and brats, and shillings in heaps. Often they sat counting and sorting and
recounting money long after other folks were sound

asleep. This mystic devotion could only be held during the dark, secret hours of the night; then they could give themselves up with undivided hearts.

But no longer could they get the same enjoyment out of the money as in the good old days before the smash-up of the bank. Somehow, a new element had come into their joy, a strange craving, a hot excitement, a peculiar thirst that would not be quenched: How could they get more? They must increase their treasures! Unless they could make money faster, life wasn't worth living. Love was slowly changing into unquenchable desire.

Their faces bore marks of the change. Their features grew sharper, thinner—somehow, longer; their eyes were uneasy and roving.

Thus the years passed.

Without realizing it themselves, Louis and Lizzie Houglum were getting to be wealthy people. Their farm with stock, machinery, and all other equipment might easily have been worth $20,000. At home they had a strong $6,000 stored away, some in the barn, but most of it in mysterious places in the house.

In a far-away corner in the barn, where light, even on the brightest day, did not penetrate, Louis had discovered a square hole in the floor. It must have been there since the barn floor was laid; the board had not been long enough to reach to the sill, and the builder had forgotten to put in the piece. There Louis kept $500 in silver. The housing was really ingenious and of Louis's own invention: To a short piece of stovepipe he had made a cover and a bottom, both tightly fitting, with a smart leather handle in the cover. A stranger would hardly find that hiding-place.

The hole was dear to Louis; not only had he discovered it, but the scheme of the stovepipe treasure-chest was his own invention. After the money had been placed there the barn became ever so much more interesting and cozy. Going into the barn after dusk to do chores or to look after his horses, he felt a sense of comradeship, of friendly spirits meeting him, who were glad at his coming. Puttering about, he communed with them by humming and crooning softly to them— they would understand perfectly! When he had finished the chores he would often sit down on the threshold and light his pipe, for after the last set-to it was no fun to smoke in the house. But here he had good company! Often he stayed here by the hour . . . until he thought she might be through with her work in the house; then he dared not risk it any longer. Had it not been for her violent objections, he would have liked to cradle a few more in that nursery under the barn floor, but she wouldn't hear of it. . . . She might be right, too—in case of fire it might be a risky place, though those fellows would hardly suffer much.

The other piles they kept in the house, ingeniously hid. Under the clock on the kitchen shelf lay five one-hundred-dollar bills . . . a pretty smart place that was! One could stand right in front of the clock and stare for all he was worth, and no sign or sound would he detect. In the event of fire, one need only tilt the clock back, grab the money, and run. . . . It was fun to have people sitting in the kitchen looking at the clock.

In the northeast corner of the cupboard lay no less than $600 in an old molasses can, which was totally disfigured by rusty blotches; at the bottom of the can slept $300 in bills, mostly tens; on top of them another $300 in silver, arranged in neat little piles like troops of soldiers on parade; the space above was filled with old jelly-glass covers. Anyone who looked at the can would never suspect it of holding a fortune. But the can was so heavy that Lizzie had to step up onto a chair whenever it needed looking after. . . . Risky, of course, in the case of fire.

And in the upper drawer of the commode in the bedroom, she had laid away $500 in bank notes of various denominations. To be exact, the fifth hundred was not entirely complete yet, but would be as soon as she received settlement for the last month's cream. These bills were stuffed into two undarned stockings, which were rolled neatly together. As soon as one opened the drawer, the stockings lay in plain view— Lizzie possessed a keen sense for the picturesquely dramatic . . . here people might snoop all they pleased and not find a thing!

But the mattress on which they slept every night was, after all, the fairy couch; in it were concealed two leather pouches, each containing exactly $2,000 in pure gold, four hundred round, plump pieces, languid and dull until you held them up to the light; then they woke up; they would gleam and sparkle, winking at you until they blurred the vision of the eye. Lizzie would come away dazed by the strange sheen. Was the light living in them the same that came from the sun? Was the sun in them also? It might be—who could tell? . . . Of this she was sure: these fellows belonged outside, in the warm, sparkling, bright day, for only then did they fully wake.

On nights when they were not too tired, they would bring the pouches out and indulge themselves awhile with their mysterious contents. They alternated in counting the gold back into the pouches. Lizzie kept track of whose turn it was because Louis got angry unless he was given his chance.

II

Shortly past noon one day in mid-autumn—Louis had just left for town—a Ford runabout drove into the yard at Houglum's and stopped in front of the house. In the car sat a tall, well-dressed man, in a broad-brimmed black hat.

The engine died with a loud roar. The man stepped out and walked slowly around the car, examining it with a critical eye, tapping the back tires with his toe. Having completed the inspection, he deliberately pulled off a pair of gauntlets which he threw onto the seat. The condition of his long, shapely hands was apparently a matter of concern because he turned them slowly, scrutinizingly; but discovering nothing seriously wrong with them he came up on the kitchen porch. He had on a long duster, under it a black suit, spotlessly clean linen, and a black tie in the centre of which stuck a gold pin in the shape of an eagle. From the long clerical face, rather angular and gaunt, it would be impossible to predict age with any degree of certitude; one might guess fifty, while another would be just as likely to stop at thirty-five. The face, though meticulously cared for, showed considerable wear.

From the moment she heard the car drive up, Lizzie, through a corner of the kitchen window, had had her eye on the occupant. She did not care to go out to meet him . . . easier to dispose of him through the screen door. . . . Most likely an agent? Many of that kind loafing around the prairies this time of the year.

Whether he had detected signs of life in the kitchen or had just surmised that at this hour of day he would be most likely to find the lady of the house there, it is difficult to say; but now he was standing on the porch, giving respectful raps at the door.

The screen door was hooked inside, the other slightly ajar and opening into the room. By the time he had rapped the third time she pushed the inner door open and looked at him through the screen.

Tipping his hat politely, the stranger greeted her deferentially, rather bashfully, it struck her, in a curious mixture of English and Norwegian:

—Might he buy a bite to eat at her hospitable board? he asked, pompously. Seeing her hesitate, he hastened to add, "It doesn't much matter what you have, Mother, just so it is plain food and home-cooked. I think I can pay for it!" Giving a short laugh, he took hold of the door knob.

Lizzie had gone to the door to dispose of the fellow in a hurry; she had developed a certain knack for getting rid of agents. Now she stopped, uncertain. She couldn't quite make him out . . . the coffee was still warm, and the man looked fully competent to pay. Undecided what to do, she nevertheless unhooked the door, opening it slightly; which gesture the man interpreted as an invitation to enter, and straightway came in.

Lizzie was not at all pleased over what she had done. This afternoon she was alone, without much to do . . . many interesting things around the house to look at, and now she was spoiling the chance! She told the stranger, curtly, that if he would be satisfied with what little she could offer, he'd better sit down. She added, warningly, that these were busy times for the farmers . . . she had no time to fool away on getting up meals for high-toned city folks.

—High-toned? he exclaimed, facing her honestly. No, not he! How could she speak such evil words? He detested high-toned people; they always got on his nerves. No, indeed not, he was no aristocrat! For him the thing that mattered was to get a bite to eat. . . . Didn't she have cream? and a couple of eggs? Plenty good enough; he was a democrat, born and raised in democratic ways; his own mother—God bless her!— was a simple farm woman down in Iowa . . . the best food he ever had was what she prepared with her own hands. "Believe me," he concluded in an unctuous voice, "there're no pies like the ones Mother makes!"

At that he fell silent, not uttering a syllable till the food was ready and Lizzie had asked him to sit up to the table. During her preparations he had been deeply absorbed in a sheet of paper, seemingly oblivious to what was going on around him. She had to call him twice before he heard her.

Before beginning to eat, the man folded his well-shaped hands, letting them rest on the table, and said grace, aloud·and solemnly, in the Norwegian language.

Lizzie, watching him narrowly, concluded that the man must be a minister. She felt chagrined and disgusted with herself for having been so foolish as to let him into the house. She ought to be ashamed of herself for not having learned better by this time. Here she was wasting all this valuable afternoon, and of course, she could not very well take any pay from a man like that! With him blabbering around the neighbourhood and telling how she had demanded money for a cup of coffee, it would cause a scandal.

During the meal her forebodings changed to depressing certainty—no doubt he was a minister, she could tell it by his silly talk! . . . Did they have a large congregation here? Were the people faithful in their church attendance? The man ate slowly, as one enjoying his food thoroughly; his many questions, Is that so's, and You don't say's impeded his progress. How did they get along with their minister? Was he an able man, and did they pay him a decent salary? . . . Is that so?—Had they a large Ladies Aid? She attended regularly, didn't she? No time? You don't say! Having received the information asked for and in monosyllables, the man launched into sermonizing on what a blessing it was for any community to have a church in which they might unite their effort for the good of mankind. The world was full of wickedness and evil. Just look at the young people! No restraint anywhere. The god of this world smote among them with blindness. . . . Did they contribute liberally to foreign missions, and could she spare him one more cup of coffee?

In sheer exasperation Lizzie chewed her tongue; the man was a minister, not the least doubt about it. And of course he was out begging! . . . For Foreign Missions again, or perhaps for one of the schools. . . . She was thankful that Louis was not at home. . . . He was too soft-hearted. Any fool could talk him into giving a dollar—even two. Now she'd tell this fellow where to get off! . . . Lizzie keyed herself up for the coming attack.

To her great surprise, no assault came. The man having finished eating, again said grace (this time also in the Norwegian language), got up and came over to where she was standing. Grasping her hand, which she reluctantly gave him, he thanked her warmly for the excellent dinner she had prepared for him, and thrusting his thumb and forefinger into his vest pocket, he fished out a silver dollar and handed it to her. Bewildered, dumb-founded, Lizzie stood looking from the coin to his face and back again, not knowing whether to accept it or not.

"Take it, Mother," he said, warmly. "That dinner is worth a dollar any day; a man who wouldn't pay that would be a fool!"

There Lizzie stood, the dollar in her hand, puzzled and ill at ease, but finally letting the coin slip down into the pocket of her apron. It was too much pay; in fact, much too much, even from a total stranger. . . . But now she had money in case he should start any begging foolishness! There was a glint in her eye.

Apparently the man had no underhanded intentions whatever. Having settled for the dinner, he lit a cigar and sat down by the wall, not paying the slightest attention to her. While she washed the dishes she eyed him with increasing curiosity. What kind of fellow was he, anyway? His behaviour mystified her. He offered nothing for sale; nor did he seem to be out begging. Judging by his clothes, he was no ordinary agent . . . such fellows didn't dress in black. He looked for all the world like a minister, though from his manners she'd hardly think so . . . young ministers nowadays didn't make an effort to talk Norwegian to people who understood English readily!

Her curiosity could stand the strain no longer; coughing ever so little, she asked, cautiously, what kind of man he might be?

The stranger glanced up quickly, then was busy over his paper again:

—Oh, just a plain man.

—What was his business?

—Business? he repeated, abstractedly.

—Yes?

—Nothing at all . . . no, really.

—Nothing at all! she ejaculated, incredulously.

"Yes, Mother, that's it, nothing at all. Just travelling and looking around." From out of the papers he volunteered a little more information: he had always been interested in the farm . . . he knew from his own experience how hard the farmers had to work . . . he honoured them for it . . . nevertheless it was the only occupation worth while . . . he might be called a farmer himself.

—He a farmer! Lizzie had to laugh. Remembering his soft, white hands, she laughed again, but more easily and naturally.

—Indeed he might be, he insisted. . . . But not all farmed alike. . . . Perhaps his methods were a bit different, that was all. Beyond that he would say nothing. He did not seem to be at all anxious to talk.

Lizzie had lost her curt reserve. The man looked honest enough, though he was hardly a farmer. . . . Well, she concluded, as she put the last dish away, he might be anything he pleased for all she cared, as long as he behaved himself and didn't start begging for money. If he wasn't a minister, one of the slyest kind that ever walked the earth, she'd let him alone. . . . Perhaps one of those fellows just out for his health; he looked skinny . . . seemed to have plenty of money?

After a while he had finished his cigar. Now he put the papers away, got up, and made ready to leave. Lizzie sat by the table, mending a threadbare overall.

The stranger went to the door and stopped, his face wearing a puzzled expression. He seemed to be debating a question and unable to decide what to do. Suddenly turning toward her, he asked whether she could tell him of a place in the neighbourhood where a forlorn stranger might put up for a few days; it would have to be a quiet home, preferably one without children; he felt tired, very much worn out, and had to have absolute rest at night—the doctor had expressly ordered rest and quiet; the price was no object—no, really; just so the people were not of the stuck-up kind, for that would drive him to distraction. Standing there by the door, he looked so depressed and haggard that she almost felt sorry for him.

—She hardly knew where to send him, she said. It wasn't easy to find a place like that. He might try at Gilbert Olson's.

—Gilbert Olson? he noted the name. So? Any kids there?

—Yes, the Olsons had children, but they owned a fine house.

—No, he said, decisively, then he needn't go there; he'd rather curl up and sleep in the Ford. With innocent, suppliant eyes on her he added, homeless birds sleep in strange places! Then suddenly, as if struck by a new thought: What about her? Didn't she have a spare bed, a cot or something? Her house seemed so quiet and peaceful, and he took her to be a plain woman, with no fandangos of any kind (Lizzie had not heard the word before and wondered what it might mean). What if she took pity on him for a few days? He would need only breakfast and supper, because he would be spending most of his time in the Ford. The man begged entreatingly, in an insistent monotone.

Lizzie eyed him searchingly. What was he, anyway? she asked. A minister?

—Minister? The question seemed to amuse him. No, indeed! . . . What an idea! No, unfortunately, he could not lay claim to so high a calling, though in his youth he had thought much of entering the ministry . . . a higher power had willed it otherwise. . . . Well, what did she say?

—If he'd be satisfied with what she had to offer, he might come and try. If he didn't like it, he could go elsewhere. But the house was quiet—he might sleep till noon if he wished . . . she would, of course, have to ask him reasonable pay, for they were only poor people.

The stranger seemed touched by her kindness, so much so that he came over and took her hand. That was fine, real hospitality, he'd call it! He'd be back this evening sometime; she must not feel put out if he should come a bit late. He'd try to arrange his business so that it would not happen another time. . . . No, he'd not be here for supper, not tonight.

III

Not until ten o'clock in the evening did the stranger return, and by that time the Houglums had given up looking for him. When he arrived Lizzie and Louis, long since through with their work, were sitting in the kitchen, resting and getting drowsy, preparatory to going to bed.

The man appeared taller now, and much darker—the lamp gave only a dim light. In his hand he carried a small, worn satchel, which he deposited in the corner. After a polite "Good evening, folks!" he came over to the table and shook hands with Louis, giving his name as Robert Nelson. . . . No, thank you, he said to Lizzie, he had had supper, and a most sumptuous feast that was! Tonight he had intruded himself upon their pastor . . . fine, Christian gentleman of great erudition! They had talked theology; he had forgotten himself, place, time . . . queer about one's first love! As if now suddenly remembering time, he pulled a gold watch out of his pocket and looked at it, his face assuming a troubled expression. What? So late already? It couldn't be possible! The man was standing in the middle of the floor, tall, black, an odd fidgetiveness in his manner. Would they mind, he addressed himself to

Lizzie, if he stayed up awhile? And might he use the kitchen table? He had some work that must be done tonight.

Having obtained her permission, Mr. Nelson looked about the room, fastening his attention on the front window. Might he pull down the shades? They didn't mind, did they? His voice was low; there was a nervous tremour in it.

After pulling down the shades, he took from his satchel a bunch of papers and a pair of dividers which he placed on the table; then he drew up a chair and sat down to work. He was soon lost in his problem.

Louis, sitting at the opposite end of the table, had brought out his pipe and begun to smoke . . . with the stranger present, there couldn't be any danger! Pretty soon he was watching the man intently. Lizzie, with her arms crossed, stood leaning her back against the range. No one spoke a word.

Spread out on the table lay a map on which the stranger was concentrating his attention. From time to time he stuck pins into the surface, grouping them about a mark in the centre. Then he measured the distance from one to the other, writing down the figures on a sheet of paper at his right hand. Having all the measurements down, he took some more sheets and began to figure, talking to himself in brief, cryptic ejaculations; his features were drawn taut; from his eyes shot gleams.

"Let's have one good, square look at her! Now

we'll see . . . the total perimeter of that county is 280 miles, exactly . . . hm!"

With astounding rapidity the man was writing down figures on the sheet; sums and products came to him in flashes of inspiration; for him to multiply numbers in millions was apparently no more of an effort than to wink an eye; and the adding up still easier.

Of the two onlookers Louis was the first to break under the strain. Hawing cautiously by way of introduction, he asked Mr. Nelson guardedly what kind of problem he was trying to figure out. Was he—er—a land-buyer?

"Land-buyer's right!" For an instant the man glanced up; the next he was buried in his calculations.

"You both sell and buy?" inquired Lizzie.

No answer. It was so quiet in the room that the silence spoke, repeating her question. The man was trying to verify some figures which evidently refused to come out right. After some time he said, absentmindedly, in a far-away voice:

"Unfortunately, I've nothing to sell. We're buying . . . nothing to sell . . . no . . . really." His voice trailed off, then changed into a soft, low whistle; his glance was fixed on the paper, his head tilted to one side.

Louis had more questions to ask. He would like to know, before he went to bed, what this fellow had up his sleeve; but somehow, he couldn't bring himself to the point of asking. Something in the man's whole make-up forbade familiarity.

Lizzie was less timid. She had talked with him a long time this afternoon and felt she knew him. Coming over to the table, she asked straightforward whether he had bought any land today.

The silence which followed lasted so long that he could not have heard her. Not daring to speak, Louis looked at her, telling her plainly to ask once more. . . . Good God—if this fellow was buying land, they ought to know it!

"Well, anywhere between two and three hundred millions—that much is certain!" the man muttered as he ran his pencil across a whole row of calculations. "Lord, but that's some dirt—I don't mind telling you! . . . Beg your pardon, Mrs. Houglum, did you say something?"

Lizzie repeated the question she had asked a minute ago.

—No, he answered, shortly. Not interested in Minnesota land; no, no!

—Not in Minnesota land? both spoke up at once. "No better land can be found outdoors than right here in Greenfield County!" Lizzie didn't like his smartness and wouldn't mind telling him so.

"No, ma'am, I'm not. There's greater game elsewhere."

Forthwith he had forgotten them. So deeply absorbed was he in his calculations that he seemed totally unaware of the two who stood watching him. His brow lay in deep furrows; all his energy was concentrated on the solution of the problem before him. Thus he sat for a long time.

But by and by his features relaxed. He looked up musingly, his eyes blinking fast as if suddenly exposed to a too strong light; in his voice trembled an infectious excitement:

"Bet your life, she may easily go over two hundred and fifty millions, yes, easily!" His eyes rested in space; he seemed to be speaking to some one far away.

Then suddenly aware of their staring faces, he beckoned to Lizzie:

"Pull up your chair, Mother! You have befriended a stranger; in return for your kindness I'll show you something out of the ordinary. Say, lock that door first, will you!"

He waited till she had sat down and was leaning forward on the table.

"Here," he said, pointing to the small area on the map, enclosed by the pins, "you see that, don't you? Well, that little strip of land is a county in Arizona; the name doesn't matter, you wouldn't remember it anyway. Right here, in this spot—you see?—is where I was last summer, I and my friend, Jim Hansen from Nebraska. Listen! Now I am going to tell you a fairy tale: Here"—he pointed with his pencil—"here is where we roamed with our herd of sheep—right *here*. Did you ever herd sheep? Well, that doesn't matter, pray God that you never may, pray morning, noon, and night! . . . In this very spot one night Jim and I pitched our camp. The soil in this place is almost clear sand, it's so light. That night a rain storm came up; talk about a storm—oh, it was awful, terrible; why, it was a regular cloudburst, it rained pitchforks and nigger babies, and old women fried in butter—you have never seen the like! We were dead sure, Jim and I were, that we'd never again see a single sheep out of that entire herd, nor did we expect to see the light of day ourselves. Well, it did stop, all right, and the storm blew over. There we went splashing through pools of water all night long; but when morning broke, the ground was dry again—water, you see, disappears fast in that kind of soil."

Here Mr. Nelson made a short pause. "You are sure you locked that door?"

When he resumed his story his voice was full of secret excitement:

"What do you suppose I saw after the sun came up? I'll give you just one guess each, might as well give you a whole million, for you could never guess it, no —not in a thousand years! Well, sir, would you believe it, my eye was blinded by some peculiar-looking grains of sand which I had not noticed the evening before, too big to be just ordinary sand kernels, and they gleamed so oddly in the sunlight; I tell you, it was like sun blinking against sun, only these on the ground were of a deeper colour. Without saying one word to Jim, who had begun to hunt for the sheep, I went over and picked up a few of the biggest kernels, and, by gosh! if it wasn't gold . . . pure, *genuine gold!"* The man's voice had sunk down to a low, awed whisper.

All the while Louis had been listening in mute wonder, not wanting to believe, but not able to resist the spell of the story. Into his brown cheeks had crept a redness. Lizzie was bending over the table; in her half-closed eyes burnt a strange light; her lips were shut so tightly that the wrinkles around her mouth deepened.

"Well," she panted, speaking with an effort, "how much did you pick up?"

Nelson gave a pleased laugh:

"I called Jim, yes, sir, so I did. 'Just let the damned sheep go Gallagher, Jim boy!' I shouted. 'You come here!' But do you know, at first he wouldn't believe me —thought I was just fooling; you see, he couldn't understand that luck should have found us in the middle of the blackest night we ever lived through, and I don't blame him. Not until he had his hand half full and could feel the weight did he believe it, but then he had to—that man Jim is no fool, let me tell you!"

Through Robert Nelson's story ran a suppressed rapture that came from deep within his being. He leaned back in his chair and chuckled joyously.

"Well," he continued, "there wasn't any longer a doubt about what we had found; so we marked the place and drove the sheep back to the ranch—that is, you understand, all we could corral, which weren't very many. But we didn't care much, for now Jim and I were through herding! The owner of the ranch, when we told him we were going to leave him, flew into seven fits; he threatened to kill us, and what was worse, now that we needed money, the rascal refused to pay us any wages; we never got a red cent. But we didn't argue the point! How could we? For us the question was how to get away quick. A time we had, all right. Not until the next night just after midnight did we clear out. You can just bet your last dollar that that night we did some travelling!—By sunup we must have been about twenty-five miles away from the ranch, the only human habitation in the whole region. But we had no difficulty in locating our gold mine, no—not the least. By sundown we had all we could carry, and were off for civilization. Would you believe it"—Robert Nelson made a dramatic gesture—"we never spoke to a soul until we were walking on Michigan Avenue in Chicago? Didn't trust ourselves, you see; our heads were just a bit wobbly from having lost so much sleep—might have said too much. From now on the rolling was easy: We hunted up the most reliable firm in the whole city of Chicago. And those fellows understood a thing or two; they pronounced it the genuine article quicker than you could say Jack Robinson—always deal with people who know, that's my principle! After that, Jim and I made nine trips out to our sand piles, always just us two. Then we quit. 'Better leave her alone now for a while,' I said to Jim; 'this is too dangerous a business!' When we finally had settled up, Jim and I, we had a full one hundred thousand in spot cash. That's the first time in all my born days I've seen a grown-up man weep for joy; but that day Jim Hansen started bawling, just

like a kid. It was a sight, I tell you. I was afraid he'd
go crazy before my very eyes. I just didn't know what
to do with him. Not strange at all that it did knock
him over, for, don't you see, only a few weeks before
we had been just two ordinary sheep-herders, worth
about forty a month when we had a job; now we owned
a fortune, and as many more as we cared to pick up!"

Robert Nelson's eyes had grown small and drowsy;
his voice, though still elated, filled the room like the
droning of a bee; he had made many pauses; were it
not for the bright flush in his cheeks, one might have
thought that the man felt sleepy; now he leaned back
in his chair, letting his eyes rest on man and wife—
first on Louis, then on Lizzie, where they sat. Apparently, the woman puzzled him. For anyone sitting
quiet, her breathing was too irregular, there was a
catch in it; and the lines around her mouth he had not
seen there earlier. Not a word did she utter, nor could
he catch her eye.

"D'you mean to tell me you haven't been there
since?" Louis asked as soon as he could get enough
voice.

"There? Man alive, what do you take me for?"
Immediately Robert Nelson calmed himself. "No, not
there exactly. But Jim and I have been many other
places." In a low, excited voice he told them some of
the practical difficulties in the way; there were many
complicated ones, it appeared:

"You see—that whole county is owned by a big gold-
mining company. Once upon a time, several years ago,

rumours of a rich strike sprang up out there; nothing of any consequence was found; but the boom was big enough to cause one of the mightiest syndicates in the country to buy up the whole county—they just grabbed the whole darned pie. Prospecting was started in several places, but they did not find anything, which doesn't surprise me; fact of it is, that a lot of prospectors have no more sense than the sheep Jim and I herded, no, sir! For some time Jim and I have been negotiating with the syndicate (they are now operating on a big scale somewhere out in Nevada) for a block of about one thousand acres. But the rascals won't sell in small parcels. Did you ever hear the beat? they won't sell that worthless sand for good money! Their answer is: 'Take all or nothing!' Either Jim and I will have to buy the whole county, or else we can't get a spadeful, and so we're stuck in the mud right there."

Robert Nelson paused; through his half-closed eyes he was observing the man opposite him. Louis had removed his elbows from the table and sat with them planted on his knees. His mouth had opened in amazement:

"How much are they asking?"

"Only three hundred thousand. That's all!"

"Hm!" came from Lizzie, her eyes blinking rapidly, "if you two could pick up that much in a short while ——"

Robert Nelson checked her by a deep whistle:

"Now, Mother, you're getting us in on the right track. I've figured out on this here sheet of paper, that if the sand on just three quarters should be as rich as the half acre Jim and I have picked over, then the three quarters are worth upward of three hundred million dollars; most likely twice that much because Jim and I didn't get all there was—we just walked around picking with our bare hands!"

"Three millions! Gosh almighty!" shouted Louis, and tilted his chair back against the wall.

Tapping the table impatiently with his pencil, Robert Nelson broke in:

"Brother, I didn't say three millions! I said *three hundred millions*—likely as not twice that amount! Now do you get me?"

"O Lord!" groaned Lizzie, a hushed awe in her low voice. "And all that is pure gold?"

"You bet, Mother, as pure as any in the United States Treasury!"

"Have you bought yet?" cried Louis.

"No." Robert Nelson spoke deliberately. "We haven't. Not yet."

"Hm—you must be crazy!"

"You think so, do you?" In Robert Nelson's voice was a note of reproach. "Could you and your wife have handed over three hundred thousand dollars in cold cash?"

Louis shot back on his chair. "We?"

"Yes? That's what I said? You couldn't have done it for the simple reason that you haven't got the money. Well, nor can we; for the present we happen to be a couple hundred thousand short—that's all."

"But isn't it risky," stammered Louis, excitedly, "to let all the gold lie there, and nobody watching it?"

"That's where you're quite right. In a way it is risky," the man admitted. "But the danger is less than you think. For one thing: in that particular spot of the globe human beings are scarcer than hens' teeth, especially since the professional prospector left it as no good. The only real danger is from stray sheep-herders, and, luckily, they are few and far between because there's nothing but sand in that whole blessed region; sand everywhere, and here and there a lonely cactus. Another good thing for us is that it hardly ever rains during the time of the year when people are likely to pass by; and then the wind blows day and night everlastingly—oh, it's an infernal wind!—and it covers every inch of ground with a fine, yellowish clay dust. Take it all in all, the Lord is protecting Jim and me pretty well; right now we're in the hollow of His hand."

Robert Nelson took a cigar out of his pocket, lit it, leaned back in his chair, and smoked in silence. He was studying his two listeners. Especially Lizzie. In that woman lay a hidden secret force that he could not fathom.

No sound came across her compressed lips. And never could he get hold of her eye; the minute he looked away, he felt her eyes on him, but turning to her, he failed to find them. Her cold, expressionless face showed no further interest in his story. Louis, on the contrary, he could read like an open book, for he was the man who has come upon an unbelievably rich treasure and does not dare to touch it. He had refilled his pipe and lit it, entirely unmindful of consequences. . . . The silence in the room became a bit strained. The map, the pins marking the county, and the other papers were still spread out on the table.

Unexpectedly, Lizzie broke the silence, asking in an innocent, careless voice:

"Is that the land you are selling around here?"

Both men gave a start and looked her way. Robert Nelson replied musingly:

"Well, Mother, whatever else you may be I cannot say, but you are not a foolish woman."

He gave the fine compliment time to sink in before continuing: Not exactly selling, no; just scouting around and calling on people. After a moment he went on to explain what he meant: It would, of course, be an easy matter for him and Jim to go to one of the big companies, show them what they had found, and sell them stock for all the money they needed; easy enough, no trick at all; most people would do that very thing—only to let themselves be done out of a fortune! For in a big syndicate he and Jim, even though they had put in $100,000, would eventually and inevitably be frozen out. That was the way it went, always; sooner or later all large stock companies were bound to fall into the hands of Big Business. And if they went to one of the big financiers of the country, the identical, selfsame thing would happen to them— exactly! Thereupon he launched into the history of big corporations, which he seemed to have at the tips of his fingers—names, dates, figures, everything to the least dot, never slipping on a name or stumbling on a year or a figure: lumbering, coal, railroads, shipping on the Great Lakes, and mining of all descriptions; he knew their history as though he were reading it out of an open book. Into his narrative flowed an epic earnestness that gripped his listeners, each instance ending like the stanzas in an old ballad with the same refrain: The small investor has no chance; he is kicked out and pushed aside, and that's that!

But now he and Jim were going to try out a new plan—quite modestly he revealed later that it was he who was the originator of the idea—one that would give equal rights to all. He and Jim were themselves only small investors; they didn't care to become anything else, even though they had the chance; they were just part of the common herd and perfectly satisfied to roam with it. Well—now they were going about in a quiet way, organizing a stock company of their own, consisting of small investors exclusively, just like themselves. And they were picking their people, yes, sir! They weren't taking anybody and everybody, but only people they could *trust*. To avoid the danger of Big Business they did not want too many stockholders —oh no, they weren't going to run the boat ashore on that rocky coast! In short, he might as well state the whole plan plainly: they were picking out two hundred and fifty persons, preferably farmers, who would go in with them with one thousand a piece. He and Jim stood ready to put in $100,000 in *spot cash,* which was all they had; that would give them a capital of $350,000, out of which they first of all would pay up the land and get clear deed, and then have a working capital left of $50,000. More than they'd need, of course! Yet, it didn't hurt to have plenty; considerable machinery would be needed—they must not forget that; and they'd have to have a strong force of picked men to patrol the tract as soon as they got going. . . . "Why, after a good rain she fairly blinds your eye!"

In a heated, entranced state of mind Louis and Lizzie had been listening to the unfolding of the plans. No sooner had the man stopped than Louis asked:

"Have you sold any shares yet?"

Lizzie paid no attention to her husband:

"S'pose you took a thousand, how much could you expect to make?" Her voice, cold and business-like, showed no trace of emotion, but on her face was a strange pallor.

Robert Nelson shook his head soberly:

—No, that he would not undertake to say; for that could only be a gambler's guess. . . . But anywhere between 150,000 and 200,000 would be a conservative estimate. The man mentioned these sums as nonchalantly as though he were speaking of transactions involving a few pennies.

"Two hundred thousand!" puffed Louis, clasping his hands back of his neck. "Gosh almighty! are you crazy?"

For a while Lizzie sat mute, her hands working nervously under her apron. In a voice that sounded far away she asked, without looking up:

"Do you happen to have any of that sand with you?"

For a moment the man seemed to hesitate. Again he was conscious of her strange power; never before in a human being had he experienced anything like it; an uncanny feeling came over him. . . . He arose slowly and went over to the door to see if it were locked securely. That done, he crossed the floor to the window and tried the shade; then to the door leading into the living-room, closing it tightly. Between the table and the door he stopped, asking in a forced whisper if it was absolutely certain that they were alone in the house. The lamp cast a dim, blurred light; darkness lurked in the corners of the room.

The two of them nodded affirmingly.

Advancing a step toward them, he spoke in the same mysterious voice as before:

"I take it for granted that you two are honest people who won't do harm to a lonely stranger?"

Both speechless because of the choking in their throats, they could only nod; the tenseness in the room was fast growing unbearable.

With the assurance that no harm would be done him, the man began to take off his clothes: first his coat, which he hung across the back of a chair; next his vest; and, turning away from them, he unbuttoned his shirt; then he unbuckled a belt which he wore around his loins next to his bare body, and with some difficulty pulled it out. After buttoning up his clothes, he laid the belt on the table without letting go of it.

None of them uttered a sound.

The belt was made of leather, extraordinarily wide, somewhat worn, with several pockets stitched on the outside, the pockets, too, furnished with buckles. After opening one of them, he drew out a small pouch, made from soft skin; the contents, golden-brown grains, the size of coarse sand, he let run into the hollow of his hand.

Then he spoke:

"Here we are, gentlemen! Now take a look at her!" He addressed himself to Lizzie, who stood bent over the table like a hawk over its prey.

"No, no, no," he warned Louis, who was about to run his fingers down among the kernels, "don't you touch her!" Having allowed a brief inspection of his treasure, he carefully let the sand run back and tied the pouch securely. Handing it to Lizzie, he said, joyously:

"Feel the weight of her, Mother!"

Lizzie did not wait for a second invitation; grabbing the pouch she weighed it in her right hand, deliberately, with the air of a connoisseur. To make absolutely sure she shifted it over to her left hand; then handed it over to Louis, who proceeded to weigh the pouch in very much the same manner. "About eighty dollars . . . no, wait a minute—hardly eighty; what do you think, Lizzie?"

"About seventy-five," she nodded, paying no more heed to him. Her attention was concentrated on another pouch which the man was taking out of his belt.

And he seemed to divine what she wanted. Opening the pouch, he exhibited the contents in the hollow of his hand. But this was not sand; the kernels were larger than in the other pouch—about the size of small peas; some larger; some smaller; of various shapes; and these had a brighter colour; the same dull, lazy hue which both Lizzie and Louis knew so well.

With bent heads they stood looking intently into the man's hand. Louis' mouth drivelled; Lizzie's was closed tightly; but her head craned, like a hen's who is about to peck at a kernel. In order to let them view it still better, the man stirred among the golden grains with the point of his pencil. Shaping his hand into a funnel he let the kernels run back into the pouch.

"Me first this time!" exclaimed Louis, eagerly, holding out his hand.

But Lizzie anticipated him. Unceremoniously she stretched out her hand and snatched the pouch before Louis could get it. This time it took her longer to make certain of the amount.

"How much?" cried Louis.

"Not so very much. Perhaps two hundred and fifty dollars." She spoke curtly, perfunctorily.

In an astonishment so great that he almost forgot himself, Robert Nelson, stock promoter of *The Arizona Pure Gold Company*, stood staring at Lizzie.

How could this common farm woman, with her coarse, toil-worn, bare hand, judge the weight of gold down to the ounce? Did she possess a sixth sense? Or was he suffering a nightmare?

"Yes, sir!" cried Louis in childish enthusiasm as soon as he got the pouch, "I believe you're right—about two hundred and fifty."

Lizzie paid no attention to him. "Have you more in the belt?" she demanded. "Any more?" There was a harsh, brittle note in her speech.

Instinctively Robert Nelson took a step away from her, quickly, as if he had come too near a flame. But unbuckling one more pocket, he stuck two fingers down in and fetched out a large, heavy, very heavy gold coin, much bigger and thicker than any either Louis or Lizzie had ever seen, which he let fall before them on the table. It was a hundred-dollar piece.

Like a child that unexpectedly gets his wish, Louis threw himself forward and grabbed the coin.

"Holy God! See that, Lizzie?" He held it in his hand, awed, shaking. "Feel of it, Lizzie!" Generously, he handed the heavy coin to her.

But Lizzie showed no ecstasy. Turning it over and weighing it, she handed it back to the owner, asking in the same curt manner as before:

"Is this made from the same sand?"

Robert Nelson had regained his balance. In a deep, thrilled voice he answered:

"Yes, Mother—that and many more like it!" He returned the coin to its place in the belt, put on his vest and coat, rolled the belt together and stuck it into his pocket. Whereupon he lit a fresh cigar and blew out big clouds of smoke.

The stock promoter of The Arizona Pure Gold Company had, apparently, nothing more to say. His half-closed eyes shot searchingly from one to the other of the two, as some general trying to find the weak point in the enemy's line. Well, he said, presently, perhaps they felt tired after their long day's work? Sorry he had kept them up, inexcusable of him; it would not happen again! He, too, felt sore and quite bunged up from driving the Ford all day over these wretched roads. . . . He walked over to the stove, lifted a cover, and threw in the half-smoked cigar. Coming back to where Lizzie stood, he pulled a five-dollar bill out of his pocket and threw it on the table:

"You take that for the time being. I don't know how long I'll be staying; but I always rest better when I go to bed with the feeling that I am not owing anything."

Lizzie would not take the money; she insisted that she wouldn't. She seemed put out with him for offering it . . . they weren't that kind of people—they didn't need to be!

Robert Nelson yawned, stretching his limbs, as a man would who is so sleepy that he can't get himself off to bed.

"You take it, Mother. Tomorrow I might not feel like offering you a penny. Hard to tell where I'll be then, and now I want to hit the hay! Oh, I'm tired!

May I sleep as long as I want to without upsetting the house?"

—Of course he might!

—Just so it didn't cause her too much trouble to prepare two breakfasts. . . . Ouch, but he was done up!

—No, that would be entirely all right. She couldn't prepare anything elaborate, anyway. For that matter, he might sleep till noon if he wished! . . . Lizzie spoke naturally, and showed real concern for his well-being.

IV

For the two Houglums, the quiet, serene autumn night, with a glorious full moon, proved anything but peaceful. Yet there was nothing in particular to worry them; all their possessions were as safe as ever; stretching out his arm, Louis had made certain of the cradle in the mattress on his side of the bed.

The lights blown out, an uneasy darkness moved throughout the whole house. Not a sound could they hear from the room above them where the stranger slept. But in their own bedroom no peace. By now Louis had tried every known device, but in vain; he just could not go to sleep. He had tried both sides, had for a long while lain flat on his back, had even turned around on his stomach. All to no purpose; he was as wide awake as ever.

If he only could have talked to her for just a mo-

ment! Then he'd have found out what she thought of
this fellow and he could have gone to sleep right away
. . . he felt sure about it . . . but he couldn't possibly
even say a word . . . no house like this for sound!
The walls themselves were made of sound . . . and
of big ears . . . and then, that doggone register up
in the ceiling! Louis gave a deep sigh and yanked himself over on his left side.

His thoughts roved restlessly:

Bet you, *that* fellow had done well in America! He
must be lined with money. . . . Wonder if he slept
with that belt on, or if he took it off at night? . . .
Funny how some folks walked blindfolded into luck
. . . didn't see it before they stepped into it! Gosh,
what piles they'd heap up, once they got properly going
in that sand! . . . Provided he wasn't a faker? . . .
Yet he had the goods right there to back up his claims
with . . . still—what business did he have up here in
Minnesota? Seemed strange, all right . . . why did he
not operate among the corn-huskers down in Iowa? Or
out in Nebraska, the home of the other guy? . . . No,
he better try it on his back again—might at least get
some rest that way. . . . Suppose, for example, that
he had brought back that sand . . . to this neighbourhood? . . . Had come with one load after another?
He'd first of all have gone to Tom Öien . . . next to
Jens Haugen . . . perhaps to Tostein Hegg . . . no,
not to Tostein, that old skinflint he'd leave alone. . . .
No, this is what he *would* do: he'd go right to Reverend
Christensen and get his advice . . . that man was no-

body's fool. . . . Pretty soon Louis was counting on his fingers the people he would invite to go in with him; before he knew it, he was up in the fifties and had to stop because he couldn't keep track of whom he had counted already. . . . If he struck any doubting Thomas, he'd simply take him out to the sand piles and say, "Now you see for yourself!"

—Gosh, how that rascal was pulling the wool over people's eyes! Turning to Lizzie he gave a light cough and waited a moment before whispering right into her ear:

"Are you asleep, Lizzie?"

"Keep quiet!" she breathed. "We'll get up early in the morning . . . I'll call you."

The suggestion was so simple and yet so practical that peace descended upon him, and in a little while, he was sound asleep.

Lizzie kept her promise. At the first streak of day she called him; it was yet so dark in the room that they could barely see to get into their clothes. They dressed hurriedly and went out across the yard in the direction of the barns. On the ground lay a light hoar-frost. At this early hour, the autumn air had a sharp tang in it which went right to one's bones. Louis shivered; he had to bite his teeth to keep them from chattering. He was miserable and downright out-of-sorts.

Though outwardly calm, Lizzie was in a towering state of excitement. Throughout the night she had beheld bewitchingly fair visions of a steady, ever-increas-

ing golden stream flowing into her yard, visions so
glorious that her nerves were kept constantly on edge.
. . . The question which she could not decide alone
was, whether they should take one thousand each, or
only one thousand together. When she got up she had
practically made up her mind to take two, for supposing
this was the chance of their lives? Today it was here,
right in their house, tomorrow it might be gone for-
ever. Such things did happen.

"Let's go into the corncrib," she suggested to Louis;
"from there we can keep an eye on what's going on."

Louis yawned heavily, not fully awake yet, and
followed her. He shivered like a dog, and got crosser
and crosser the fuller he awoke. He didn't even take
the trouble to ask what she meant to do in the corncrib. . . . What the hell was the big idea of getting
out at this unearthly hour?

Leaning up against one of the studdings and keeping an eye on the house, she wanted to know what he
thought about it : should they take one or two thousand?

—Take what? Louis was sour as vinegar. Once more
he yawned.

His torpidity irritated her wrought-up nerves like
the sting of a thousand mosquitoes. In that instant she
could have laid hands on him . . . now look at that
ape of a man! The way he had snored all night, he
ought to be waking up pretty soon! Lizzie did not
mince words in telling him what she thought.

—He was awake, doggone it! Couldn't she see?
What should he use the night for? Were they to have

breakfast in the corncrib, or did she have a corn-shelling job on? Louis spoke cutting, mean words and didn't give a hang who heard them.

In desperation she began to plead with him:

"Don't be so mean, Louis! I'll make breakfast; the coffee and oatmeal are on the stove. You know we can't talk about this in the house. . . . Shall we risk a couple thousand in his company? I really think we ought to try with one thousand each."

Louis was suddenly wide awake . . . so—that was what she wanted of him . . . his consent to gamble? The experience of last night stood vividly before his eyes, the glib stranger and all his bunk talk. But today there was no trace of romance about it. Louis was back in Minnesota, with both feet firmly on solid ground, in a cold, stark reality; he had not even had a bite to eat yet, and not a sip of coffee. Never had the state of Arizona seemed more unreal and farther away than now. . . . And she really wanted to risk money on a deal of that kind? That was the reason she had dragged him out of bed and down to the corncrib! Not foolish of her, he must say . . . here they could discuss matters privately without fear of being spied upon. Louis felt considerably mollified.

"No, Lizzie," he said, soberly, "we ain't going to throw away good money on a circus like that . . . we've lost enough as it is. . . . How can you think of such a thing? Do you mean that you are going to trust this stranger with a whole thousand dollars?"

"I think we'd better make it two—one for each of

us. We see what we're buying. I've figured out that this way we'll make more money than you and I could save up in four hundred years."

"Are you crazy, Lizzie?" A note of fear had come into his voice. "Suppose it's only a fake? How can you tell—you've never been in Arizona!"

"While you slept last night I was lying awake thinking of that; that's why I can't make up my mind whether we ought not to take only one thousand." Conscious of how attentively he was listening, she continued more slowly, expressing herself with that peculiar deliberation which he both respected and feared in her:

"Even with only one thousand, we'll be making a nice sum of money . . . we will have more to stow away than any farmer in this county ever could make. And if it should go wrong, I suppose we could stand that, too. We're going to sell for considerable over two thousand dollars this fall . . . not counting cattle or hogs." She was silent for a moment. "We might take five hundred dollars of what we have in the kitchen, and the five hundred dollars you're keeping in the barn. . . . If you can scoop up two hundred thousand dollars with one scoop, you'll be on easy street for the rest of your life, and have nothing to do but to smoke your pipe and count your money—that's worth risking something for, I am thinking!"

"*I*, you say?" Louis sprang up as if stung. "No, I tell you, I'm not going to throw any of my money away on this doggone wildcat scheme!" He spoke with so much vehemence that she was startled. "If he has found so much gold, why the devil doesn't he go peddling his stock down in Iowa where he is acquainted? What's he up here for? And there's that fellow out in Nebraska. Why don't they go there? Not a red cent are we going to throw away on this humbug. . . . Shut your mouth, woman," he snarled at her as she tried to interrupt his flow of angry words. "Can't you see he's only a fake? Suppose I had found all that gold and had wanted to sell stock? D'you suppose I'd be running around down in Iowa—among strangers? Don't you suppose I could have found buyers enough right here? . . . Gosh—what nonsense!"

For a while things went from bad to worse in the corncrib at the Houglums' that morning. A terrible storm broke loose, the equal of which neither of them had experienced before. His violent objections fell like explosives into her overstrained mood. At first she just sat looking at him, coldly, disdainfully. . . . How oldish he looked with the greyish stubble of unshaven beard on his chin! How shrunken and good-for-nothing . . . just a haysack! . . . What she so often had vaguely sensed before now blazed forth with awful clarity: a man with so little guts in him as he had would never dare seize an opportunity coming his way . . . as once it must come to every man. . . . Her own feeling of superiority, of strength, rose in proportion . . . how she'd like to give him a sound beating, the good-for-nothing imp of a man! . . . Without sparing the words, Lizzie spoke her mind. Tall, towering, an enraged woman, defamed in the eyes of the world—married to this clod of impotence. She confronted him, emptying the vials of her wrath over him.

Finally Louis kept still altogether, letting her rave on unhindered. It was perfectly useless for him to try to reason with her or chastise her by words, for whenever he tried to object she brushed him aside, told him to keep still, and began all over again; which was the worst part of it, because the starting-point was always the same, to wit: he was only a no-good, he couldn't do anything, he had no sense . . . if it hadn't been for her, they'd have landed on the Poor Farm long ago. "Now see if you can get your eyes open and get some work done!" So saying, she slammed the door and left him.

For a long time Louis remained sitting on the sack of shelled corn, dazed, in a half stupor. He felt unwell; he must be getting sick, for he shivered with cold; and right through his heart was an ache which would not leave him; but the worst was an odd sensation that he was crying inside himself—he could both hear it and feel it, and he felt ashamed and told himself to stop —doggone it! couldn't he shut up? . . . He heard a question repeating itself; right in his ear: how could she be so crazy? Now how could she, for she was so much smarter than he? She was a good manager . . . nobody could figure quicker than she. . . . It beat all how she was carrying on lately, he thought . . . if it only had been on account of the tobacco, he might have understood it . . . because there she was right, in a

way, though she didn't know how a man felt about it.
. . . But this time she was wrong, plain crazy—huh,
clawing his eyes out because he refused to let her throw
away a fortune on this mare's nest! . . . Whether it
got straightened out between them or not, she'd never
take those fellows he was keeping in the barn! he muttered as he grabbed the shovel lying beside him and
began to throw in corn to the hogs.

After feeding the hogs he went into the barn, closing the door behind him. There he took the stovepipe
out of the hiding-place under the floor and dug it down
into the further end of the haymow. . . . The temper
she was in now, it was hard to tell what she might want
to do . . . these here fellows were not going to be
squandered for nothing, no matter how terribly she
acted up! The nest securely hid, Louis felt so much
at ease that he could risk going in to look for a bite to
eat.

He didn't stay in the kitchen longer than necessary:
the atmosphere was too storm-laden for comfort.
Hitching the team to the wagon, he drove to the cornfield and began to husk corn . . . until noon at least
he'd have peace!

About nine o'clock Robert Nelson came downstairs,
smiling and in the very finest humour, as a well, healthy
man ought to be after nine hours of sound sleep. So
peacefully, he assured Lizzie, he had not rested in years.
Oh, but he had slept fine! And so quiet and nice! He
hadn't heard the roosters, even! Didn't she keep roost-

ers? Or had she perhaps trained them not to crow when she had tired people sleeping under her roof? What a blessing once in a while to get out into the country, such calm, such peace and perfect rest! In the supreme enjoyment of well-being Mr. Nelson stretched his shapely body.

Lizzie eyed him secretively, and the hovering shadows of doubt, which her husband's obstinacy in the early hours of the morning had cast upon her, began to disappear. . . . The way the man talked, his straightforward trustfulness and all—it didn't seem possible that he could be a cheat and a crook? And such a nice, upstanding man, too!

Seated at the breakfast table, he told her of how last night he had lain awake for a long time thinking of his own dear mother, and of how he planned to make it easy and pleasant for her. Soon there would be no more difficulties for her to contend with . . . her days of worry and hardship were over.

—Was she, too, buying stock? Lizzie asked, trying hard not to show undue interest.

—Indeed she was! He himself was taking two thousand in her name. In case anything should happen to him, he wanted to feel sure that she was protected. . . . Here she might see for herself! Pulling out of his inner coat pocket the stock list, he unfolded it and pointed to his mother's name: "Mrs. Carrie Nelson, New Prague, Iowa." . . . Jim Hansen had done the same for his mother—here was her name: "Mrs. Lena Hansen, Church Hill, Nebraska."

Lizzie was touched by the sheep-herders' thought-fulness for their mothers. She took his cup and went to the stove to fill it. So far she had said very little, but having brought the coffee she began to talk, hesi-tatingly, guardedly . . . there was something she would like to ask; he must excuse her if it sounded foolish : . . she was only an ignorant country woman.

"Bless you, Mother, that's just the people I love to talk to, for they are so straightforward, one doesn't need to be on his guard. In what they say is the wisdom of experience. You ask all you want!"

—Why did he not peddle his stock down in Iowa. where he was acquainted? Word for word she repeated the objection Louis had raised.

"Now that's what I call a proper question," ex-claimed Robert Nelson, heartily, "one that I should have thought of myself, really—that's foolish of me!" Laying down his knife and fork and placing a hand on each thigh, he looked her straight in the face, openly, speaking with the utmost candour: "There are only a few Norwegians down our way; about four or five families in all, counting ourselves; one is an old, crabby bachelor, who hasn't got much; the other two I have on the list. The rest of the country is Catholic, every last one of them, and they are a hard lot to deal with. If I, who am a good Lutheran, always have been, and am known as such, should try to go from house to house among those Catholics, they'd simply slam the door in my face and sick the dog on me—that's what kind of neighbours they are. They would like nothing better,

I tell you, than to drive the few there are of us out of the country. You, who are living in the midst of friends, brethren in the same good old faith, can hardly appreciate such a condition. And to be perfectly frank and admit my own shortcomings, I don't care to shower riches upon people of that kind. No, sir. I'd much rather cast my lot with strangers, for I tell you, Mother, those people don't deserve to have anything done for them!"

He attacked his food vigorously; but all of a sudden he stopped eating and began telling about the social conditions over in Nebraska where Jim Hansen lived: "You see, out by Church Hill, so Jim tells me, there is just a small pioneer settlement. Some years ago, a few Danes, mostly destitute immigrants, were fooled to move out onto those sand prairies; too poor to get away, they have had to stay ever since. In that country it would be as impossible to find a man with a thousand dollars as to change an old rooster into a canary bird—it just can't be done! Now, does that explain your question, Mother?"

"Why, yes, thank you!" Lizzie was moved; she felt tears coming to her eyes . . . anybody could understand that no stock could be sold in such neighbourhoods—anyone with an ounce of brain in his head!

Presently she had more questions to ask:

—Where was he bound for today?

—That he could not very well say before he got into the Ford. First of all, he was going to call on the minister.

—The minister? He wasn't buying, was he? Lizzie became greatly interested.

—He wanted to bad enough, just so he could raise the money. "Do you know," he confided, innocently, "I like to help our poor Lutheran ministers; they are so interested, and so deserving!"

—Did he have many preachers on the list?

—Indeed yes. They were the easiest to get. At first Jim and he had been considering selling only to ministers, but had given up the idea because most of them were bankrupt, it would take them too long to find enough.

—Had Reverend Christensen said he would buy?

—Yes, that he had. It was only a question of raising the money. Both he and the missis were terribly enthusiastic and wanted to buy. Well, all did who had sense enough to see a real opportunity. But he didn't know how much more he might have to sell, because yesterday just before coming out here he had had a wire from Jim telling him to go slow. Would she care to see the telegram? Taking for granted that she was anxious for the information, Robert Nelson poked among his papers and produced a yellow slip on which was written the following message:

Stock going very fast. Be careful not to oversell.

JIM.

—Before evening, he continued, he'd have to run to town to see if there were another message from Jim, for he certainly wouldn't like to run around the country fooling innocent people—no, sir, he wouldn't do that.

Not until he was ready to leave did Lizzie ask another question, and then she quite surprised him:

—What guaranty for their money did people get who bought stock?

Without answering right away he drew a cigar from his vest pocket, bit off the end, and lit the cigar slowly, turning it around so as to get an even fire. . . . Guaranty? They got their stock certificate. Just look here! Opening his satchel, he took out a small portfolio of papers and documents. In the portfolio he found a certificate which looked much fancier than a hundred-dollar bill, with beautiful pictures on it; in the left-hand corner was a bright gold star, a good deal larger than the hundred-dollar piece he had showed them last night; in the star was stamped deeply: "$1000." . . . This particular certificate was for Dr. Hansen in Akron.

Lizzie seemed much interested in the paper:

"Well, I declare, has Doctor Hansen bought? We know him well. Father and Mother always go to him."

"Yes, ma'am, the minute he saw what it was, he took a thousand."

"Do you have other high-toned folks?"

—He wouldn't call doctors and ministers high-toned. But they were good customers—easier to sell to than any other class of people, if they only had money. "Pretty nice, isn't it?" He held up the paper in order that she might see better. "Believe me," he said, enthusiastically, "a year from now that man won't be cutting out appendixes for his living!"

"How do you know that it is safe to invest money in

your company?" she asked, in a tone of motherly solicitude.

Mr. Nelson noticed that her attitude toward him was changing perceptibly. "Well, Mother, when you ask me that question, I am stuck and I don't mind owning up to it."

Taking a chair, he sat down again and began to talk, calmly, in a business-like way, yet very simply, as he would to a child: Safe? It all depended on what she meant by safe. Was bank stock, for example, a safe investment? Most certainly it was not, and could not be considered so. What about bank deposits? No, of course not—she need only go into Greenfield and ask some of the people there how safe bank deposits were, for they could tell her. Would she call first mortgages safe? Well, he would not; many people had been bankrupted on buying mortgages. On the whole, was there any business that might be called absolutely safe? No, Mother, there was not, at least none that he could name. For example, was it safe to invest in land? Or take the business of farming? The farmer who ploughed and seeded his field in the spring, was he sure of harvesting a crop in the fall? All sensible people would answer, if they were honest, that he was not. There was no absolute safety, and that was why ninety per cent, at least, of all business was done on mutual confidence. Even U. S. Government bonds were not safe in the absolute sense of the term; for the government might go bankrupt, not at all an unlikely event the way they were running the country now. "No, Mother," he concluded, gravely serious, and arose to go, "nothing in the world is safe. Let us assume that you are keeping money in your house; some day your house burns down and your money is gone. But Arizona Pure Gold is as safe an investment as I know of. I haven't the heart to fool innocent hard-working people. Simply couldn't do it!" Thereupon he went.

Lizzie stared at the door through which he had disappeared, confused, bewildered. Should she run after him and call him back? . . . There he went and had not offered her stock—now, wasn't that the limit! Perhaps he was as rattle-headed as other men? . . . He might not intend to offer her any, either? Perhaps he thought she had no money and that he better dicker with Louis? . . . Well, she'd show him who was running this place!

Throughout the day Louis stayed in the field, husking corn, only taking time out for dinner; but his dinner hour lasted longer than usual.

As soon as Robert Nelson was gone Lizzie got her noon meal on the stove, put on some ragged clothes, and went out to help Louis husk.

Husking side by side, they finished two rows, turned and husked two more; not a word had been exchanged between them by the time they reached the other end of the field. But whenever Louis spoke to the horses he used no Sunday-school language. His face was dark and foreboding. After the quarrel they had had in the morning he did not feel disposed to do any talking— yet he was pleased to see her, because she was a fast husker. Besides, since she came to help him, the storm must have blown over? Well, doggone it, it was about time she found her senses!

Though she left him to himself, she was in excellent spirits; the corn snapped easily; it was great fun to work; she could outdistance him any time she wanted to; but today she didn't care to try it. The good talk she had had with Robert Nelson had soothed her like a warm bath after a hard day's work. Her mind was functioning clearly; she saw what must be done: Even though Louis failed to grasp the opportunity, she could not stand idle and let it slip by. A plan was revolving in her mind, a unique scheme it was—the longer she looked at it, the better she liked it, and the greater the possibilities she saw in it. . . . Just as well that she acted independently . . . it would give her more freedom of action in the future . . . she would show him a woman that *could* manage! . . . She was wondering whether to put the proposition before him now or wait until after dinner. She chose the latter course; from past experiences she knew that, having had a good dinner, he would be more tractable; then he would mellow, no matter how crusty his temper . . . she hoped he wasn't out of tobacco!

Today she had a real wedding dinner for him, cooking on the stove. The night before, thinking that she might have to prepare something extra for her lodger, she had gone to work and beheaded a rooster. But likely as not, Mr. Nelson would shift for himself tonight, too, and so, this forenoon, thinking of the plan she was going to propose to Louis, she had put the fowl on the stove to cook before going out. Now all she needed to do was to go home a few minutes early to boil the potatoes. . . . Louis would need softening before she could discuss anything with him—anyone could see that. . . . Perhaps she had been a bit hard on him this morning? Too bad that he never could understand that it was only for his own good!

A short while before the load was full she left him and went home to get the meal ready. Not a word had they spoken to each other.

They ate in silence; Lizzie very little. Louis wondered at the company dinner she was dishing up for him. He was still in a grim mood, but as he ate he thawed out gradually. . . . Just like her, this is, he thought. Never saw such a woman! She behaved like that old horsepower he and Jens Haugen used to operate years ago—the old thing had to be run just so, or else she would not work at all . . . either they couldn't budge her, or she would send all the grain into the straw, or she might get a fit and run days on end without the slightest hitch . . . why, you could shove more grain through her than through any new machine in the country! . . . By now, Lizzie must have seen her madness and was trying to make up again? The breakfast wasn't much to brag about—he'd do justice to her dinner!

And she saw to it that he helped himself. She passed him food and waited on him as though he had been the returned Prodigal Son himself.

Louis, always so slow of thought, at last began to fear that there must be some hidden meaning under this unusual generosity; it was too much, too unlike her; he chewed more slowly. . . . Doggone it—if she went to work scattering their hard-earned savings, then he'd eat his fill! . . . Most likely she had bought already . . . this was the funeral feast over a whole thousand dollars! Tears came to his eyes as he speared the second leg of the rooster.

The minute the meal was over he picked up his duck coat and made ready to leave the house. No talk, except a few monosyllables, which could not be avoided, had passed between them.

—Did he have to go so soon? Better let the horses rest a while longer, she advised. She appeared to be in an amiable mood.

—Louis guessed he might as well start right away. Nevertheless, he lingered by the door, studying the condition of his coat . . . there was a nasty tear on the right elbow.

—Why not sit down and smoke his pipe? Was he out of tobacco perhaps?

—Tobacco? No; he had plenty, he replied, glumly. Still hesitating, the coat over his left arm, he sat down on the corner of a chair.

In the meantime she walked to and fro between the table and the stove, clearing off the dishes. . . . Easier thus to get said what was on her mind, and now was the time for it. . . . She had thought of a good scheme, she began boldly; did he have time to listen?

—He supposed he could take time . . . she better spit it out.

His sulkiness made it harder for her to go on, but once started she would not stop. Suddenly she sprang it on him:

"Now we're going to divide our money, Louis."

If a hundred-dollar gold piece had dropped out of the sky and right down into his hand, Louis could not have been more dumbfounded.

"You mean for—for—for each of us to take our part and keep it separate?" he asked, incredulously.

"That's just what I say. You take your share, I take mine; we each manage our own as we think best. Whenever you receive settlement you give me one half and keep the other yourself . . . then you can buy tobacco as often as you please. But I want to take care of mine in my own way . . . that's fair enough, certainly?"

With his coat over his arm Louis sat twirling his cap. Never before had he felt so down and out. Even her tantrum in the corncrib this morning was nothing compared with this. . . . She wanted her share separate? So it had come to this between them: she insisted on managing for herself? . . . She no longer trusted him, the no-good that he was! . . . Finding nothing to say, he just sat there on the edge of the chair. He would have liked to get up and leave, but dared not, for then there would be another storm . . . he could sense it in the air already.

His sluggish dumbness irritated her. Now look at

him! Here she had fussed and fixed up a banquet for him . . . she had thought out the best scheme, so smart and so interesting . . . a plan that any man with a grain of ambition in him would have welcomed, for it would give both of them something to strive for and have fun with, and there he sat, a fat frog on a log, not understanding a thing! The dishes rattled ominously.

By and by Louis found words which he spoke in a dejected, hopeless tone:

"Are you really going to buy stock with all of yours?"

"No," she said, partly appeased, "I should say not. But I am going to have a thousand, provided there's any left by the time he comes back."

Again Louis was silent; his square face with his mouth drooping at the corners was blank dejection. "Ya-ya-ya," he groaned, pulling himself up with an effort, "if you, Lizzie, are bound to throw away a fortune, you better have your way"—there was a catch in his voice—"but we've lived together all these years . . . we better try it awhile longer . . . that's my way of thinking!" He reached the door where he stopped to blow his nose. "You'd better take the molasses can and the rest from the bureau drawer." His voice had reached the breaking point: "I certainly wish you good luck!"

The next morning Lizzie Houglum bought one thousand dollars' worth of Arizona Pure Gold stock.

The deal was consummated behind locked doors.

Robert Nelson had finished his breakfast of cold chicken, boiled eggs, oatmeal, and toast, and was about to light his morning cigar; all the time he had been chatting intimately with his landlady. He told her confidentially that yesterday he had found time to run into town for his mail and that he had received both telegrams and letters. The telegram told him to quit selling and come right back; the few shares which were left they could dispose of later. . . . Here she might see with her own eyes what Jim had sent:

Stock going like hot cakes. For the love of Mike, don't oversell, otherwise we shall get ourselves into trouble!

Then Lizzie had acted. But, the transaction finally completed, Robert Nelson swore long and softly under his breath. Though he was well seasoned, having peddled stocks of almost every description all the way from the Rio Grande clear into Canada, this was the strangest case he had ever run up against. Once, some years back, he had had an experience of which this particular case reminded him. It had happened up in Minneapolis; there he had attended a prayer-meeting and had been forced to take part in order to dispose of some Texas oil stock which simply refused to move. That time he had done a fine business, but had felt miserable for quite a while afterward.

Now, too, he felt sick. To begin with, this farmer woman paid him the whole thousand in cash, picking up every cent right here in the house. No less than $500 was in silver; he had all he could do to lug the load out to the car. The rest was all bills, in denominations of fives and tens.

But that wasn't the worst of it: As she stood there counting out the money to him, in piles of one hundreds, he got the feeling that she was slicing up her own body and handing piece after piece to him. In her grave seriousness was an eerie, uncanny element which gave him the creeps. The impression would not leave him for the rest of that day. "What queer fools these mortals be!" he reflected as he got into the car. "Yes, sir—queer is right!" He started up the motor and was gone.

v

During the year after Robert Nelson had practised his tricks of black art on Lizzie, Louis led a wretched existence. An evil spirit that would not let itself be cast out was loose at his place.

Haunted by a secret fear, particularly during the first weeks after Nelson's visit—Louis went about watching his wife. Talk to her about it he dared not for his very life. Gradually, inevitably, he was being driven to the conclusion that Lizzie had lost her mind.

His mood was such these days that every misgiving, of whatever nature, immediately assumed alarming proportions. . . . It had happened before in Greenfield County that folks had gone crazy and had had to be taken to the asylum at Saint Peter; he had heard of them . . . there was this man Henrik Tharaldson, over on the prairie west of town, and Petrina Gunderson who had such a terrible time with the devil that her husband could not keep her at home. Both of them were still living. Just how they had acted before they had to be taken away Louis did not know, nor did he want to ask about it, but he doubted whether they could have been any worse than Lizzie. . . . Worse? How could it be possible? Imagine a sane, sensible person throwing away a round thousand dollars on that hot-air artist, every penny of which she had slaved so hard to save up! Not many in Saint Peter could be acting nuttier than that. If this wasn't insanity, then what could it be?

At night he would lie awake, worrying for fear the neighbours might find out about it, and come and take her away, which would make matters still worse, for how could he get along without her? Gosh almighty! get along without Lizzie, how could he? Over and over again he would repeat to himself: If they came and took her, they'd have to cart him off at the same time —there was no other way! . . . It was this fear which kept him from mentioning the name of Robert Nelson to a single soul.

He could not help observing her secretly. She was a changed woman. In reality, another. During the first weeks after making the plunge she lived in a hot flurry of excitement; her energy was inexhaustible; she did the work of two ordinary hired men; her body seemed made up of tempered steel springs, for she never got tired; there was a strange buoyancy in her, a constant exaltation, in her face a flushed radiance; often she would sing—in a deep, big voice throbbing with happiness. And she was so playful; frequently she would make Louis cross because she could not leave him alone. But worst of all, she would talk so much nonsense. Just wait, she would say to him, teasingly, until she had her $200,000! . . . It might be more, even! . . . For a while she was sure that the returns would run considerably higher.

Mostly she lived in another world, far away from the one in which her husband moved. Had he known all her thoughts, he would have had greater cause for worry.

For several weeks she was happily busy trying to decide what she should do with her fortune, once she had gotten it. The working out of a solution she found more exciting than any game she had ever played. . . . She would keep the money at home—to that she soon made up her mind . . . right here on the farm, and she would take care of it herself!

By and by she worked out an elaborate plan, which she didn't care to reveal to Louis—not yet, anyway, because he was so terribly slow and stupid. A short distance east of the house, just a few steps, was a steep hill, at the foot of which ran a small creek. In the slope she would dig a deep, wide cellar which she would have cemented up. There would be an inside room with extra-heavy walls of cement around it, but spacious so

that several people could be in there at one time. . . .
In this inner room she would have a safe, like those
the banks used. . . . She would hide the key to the
safe well . . . no, not hide it, perhaps, but carry it
under her clothes on a chain . . . the key to the inner
room she would also carry. . . . Just for fun she
would invite some of her old schoolmates down to the
room and show them her treasures . . . not many, and
only people she could trust . . . they would clap their
hands in wonder and envy her. . . . On counting days
she would take Louis with her . . . he was smart and
reliable when it came to handling money—and so fond
of it! . . . Quite a job to count so much money;
one day, she figured out that it would require two whole
days for her to check all her possessions. . . . She
would, of course, store her other money there, too—
she might even consent to housing what little Louis
had . . . but then he'd have to be a good boy!

. . . Whatever she got above 200,000 she would
give away—that is, if it wasn't too much . . . she had
to be careful or people would say that she was trying to
make a splurge. But to Reverend Christensen, who
hadn't been able to buy any stock for himself—Robert
Nelson had told her that he could not raise the money
—she would give a big sum for Foreign Missions . . .
perhaps $500? The idea pleased her; she laughed at it
. . . wouldn't he look surprised, though! No—she
would do better than that, even. After she had given
him the $500 and before he got through blessing her
for the gift, she would hand him another $100 for the

Orphans' Home. . . . Then he would go around telling people what a good woman Mrs. Houglum was! . . . The story might get into the papers . . . suppose they came and asked for her picture? Lizzie laughed joyously; in her eyes shone a bright light.

. . . Another thing: they must buy themselves an auto, they would just have to have an auto! The cart was getting entirely too old-fashioned . . . even after Louis had had new wheels put on and a new seat made . . . especially these days when everybody was buying cars. . . . They might get the car before she made the big donation to Foreign Missions—you didn't need to be a spendthrift just because you had plenty!

There was another idea around which her fancies loved to play: First of all, she would go to the old folks and count out on the table to them $500, provided there was that much above 200,000 . . . yes, she would take care of that item first. The $500 was to be used for a trip to Norway next summer . . . the folks, especially Mother, had been talking about making a trip to Norway as long as Lizzie could remember. . . . Father, too, was anxious, though he never said much. Now neither of them would talk about anything else. . . . Only pure foolishness to squander money on such a venture, but that was the way with old folks near their second childhood. The last time she went over to see them Father had actually proposed to her, in all seriousness, that she and Louis rent out the farm for a year and go with them. The idea was so ludicrous that Lizzie, even now, laughed out loud. . . . But in the end she'd lose nothing by giving the folks this money—she'd get whatever was left after them . . . something more to take down to the cellar!

. . . And another thing: they'd soon have to fix up the house a bit . . . perhaps get a piano—a piano looked smart in the parlour . . . it was so handy to set things on, pictures and such like. . . . She might buy the piano first of all? Well—she'd see about that, though!

One day she gave Louis a terrible scare: He came in at noon from a long half-day's husking, tired, quite worn out; she noticed it and spoke up encouragingly:

"This will be the last fall you'll have to slave with the corn; you can be glad for that, anyway."

"Are we going to farm with only small grain from now on?" he asked, disgustedly.

—Not that, exactly . . . no. But soon they could leave all the hard work to good help. . . . As soon as her ship came in, it would be the end of drudgery for them . . . all he'd have to do would be to smoke his pipe and go around bossing jobs, perhaps now and then helping with the chores. . . . For her part, she was not going to slave the way she had been doing.

—There she goes again, thought Louis in despair; she's crazy as a loon already, and getting worse every day! He felt so badly that he could have sat down and cried.

Whenever she was not in a gay mood an evil spirit of nagging possessed her; she fussed and blustered, scolded and domineered until Louis didn't know on what foot to stand to please her or where to run for shelter. He became more silent and morose than ever, shunning the company of others for fear that they might find out what had happened to her, and perhaps come and take her away. If she should start that kind of talk, well —— Between spells she would have days when she was no loonier than other women in the neighbourhood . . . all were cracked, more or less— that much he understood now.

With the nearing of winter a sweet expectancy came over her; she wanted to be good to Louis; only he could not return her tendernesses.

But by the first balmy days of spring, which that year fell early in March, her mood changed perceptibly again. A queer restlessness possessed her. She figured that those boys out in Arizona must have been working several months by this time, and that she soon would have good news. Every day she went down to the mail-box herself to look for letters. Not long after Robert Nelson's departure a letter had come, announcing that they were almost ready to begin operations; they were being held up for the present because certain pieces of machinery had not arrived yet, but soon they would be going full blast. She heard nothing more until Christmas, when she received a short letter, stating that they were just beginning work, and that she might look for good news almost any time.

After reading that letter she was so elated that she could not keep the news to herself; in the evening, as

Louis sat by the table with the *Courier* spread out before him, she thrust the letter under his nose and told him to read it. *There!* Now he could see for himself . . . there it was in black on white. . . . What did he say now? Had it not been for his silly stubbornness, they might now have been worth $400,000 . . . perhaps half a million . . . did he see what his obstinacy had cost them?

Slowly Louis spelled his way though the letter, grasping little of what it was all about, and making no effort to understand it. Only one thing was plain to him, as clear as a bright day: they had been swindled out of a round thousand dollars, which was all her doing—just a damned whim she had to satisfy! Saying nothing, he shoved the letter aside.

Not before the second week in April came the third letter. During the many long weeks of waiting Lizzie had been counting the days, anxiously, fretfully, as one whose time of birthing is drawing near. Every evening on going to bed, she consoled herself with the old, worn-out thought: I will surely hear tomorrow . . . they don't care to bother with sending money in small lots . . . the other way is cheaper . . . I'll be getting 20,000 at a time . . . that will save a lot of stamps, too. . . . Those fellows are doing business on a big scale! But day followed day; weeks passed; still no letter; all of March went by without a word of any kind. There were nights when she didn't taste sleep, but had to get up and walk the floor. Finally, the idea came to her that they would not be sending anything until the work was finished, and that all would come at once like a mighty flood. . . . I wouldn't wonder a bit if that's just what they will do, she thought, and enjoyed a day or two of comparative peace of mind.

That spring proved hard on Louis, for she hovered over him like a storm-cloud, ready to burst at any moment.

But the second week in April, the letter for which she had lost so much sleep, arrived. Lizzie had been on the lookout for the mailman and was down at the box when he came, and got the letter herself.

Back in the kitchen again, her hand shook so that she couldn't open the envelope; her heart was pounding madly; the sight of the letter frightened her . . . it was so thin, and it looked just like an ordinary letter that anyone might have sent.

But she hadn't much time; in a short while Louis would be coming home for dinner—she must open it right away.

—No, it contained no money, that she saw first of all, but it did contain a long jeremiad of misfortunes. In cold, cheerless words it told of a series of unforeseen mishaps: Some of the machinery had turned out to be useless; a new set had to be bought and installed; the late spring had hampered the progress of the work; and on account of the long distance to the railroad, operating expenses were running higher than had been anticipated; but worst of all: the company from which they had bought the land was bringing suit against them (for what reason the letter did not state). It closed with an urgent request for more money: unless each stockholder came across with $500 more, they would lose every cent they had put in. Would she please forward said amount by return mail!

That April day Lizzie Houglum wept until her heart broke and until she feared that she would lose her senses. All her beautiful castles lay smashed, by one cruel blow ground into dust.

Mechanically she got up from the table and looked through the window. The outhouses were floating in the air. Through a mist she saw Louis' stooped figure coming behind the horses. Down by the water-tank she saw him stop . . . tie up the lines . . . take the bridles off . . . water the horses. . . . Pretty soon he would be coming in for dinner.

At the sight of the dusty figure down by the water-tank an unseen hand came, giving her support. She got the fire started, the coffee-pot ready, and some eggs on to boil. She cut bread and set the table, then washed her face . . . never would she give him the satisfaction of telling him, *never!* It was his fault; he claimed to have seen through it from the first . . . then why hadn't he stopped her? Why . . . and he had stood by the altar in church and promised before God to protect her! . . . And he a man!

Having set the table and prepared the meal she went into the bedroom and lay down.

For a whole week Lizzie kept to her bed, only getting up at mealtime to prepare the most necessary things. At noon she went out to do a few chores. At Louis' repeated question—what was the matter?—she always gave the same answer: it was her head; she was suffering with a terrible headache. . . . No-no-no, she didn't want help! . . . Doctor? Was he out of his mind? Who could afford to waste money on the doctor? It would cost at least ten dollars to have the doctor come out there!

Otherwise she was silent for hours at a time, just sat there listlessly; all of which Louis took for bad symptoms.

But one forenoon during her illness, while he was seeding, he saw their old cart rattling down the road with Lizzie in the seat and she was driving fast. This frightened him so that he did not know what to do, and so he kept on working . . . if she was gone, there was nothing to do about it—not that he could see.

Just as he was about to unhitch for dinner she returned. To his question of where she had been, the only answer he got was that she had gone to see the minister. After that he inquired no more, for now he knew what he needed to know: the blow must have struck at last!

VI

Though nothing at the time had come of Lizzie's proposal that they divide their savings, each one keeping and managing his and her share independently of the other, yet without their being conscious of what was taking place, from that day on they had drawn wider and wider apart; the process was still going on; slowly, themselves unwitting, the gulf between them widened.

Lizzie's cooking had become still more light-handed. In a manner, that was excusable; the way she worked these days she could find no time for the preparation of elaborate meals. Louis saw it, accepted it as something that could not be remedied, and did not blame her, yet he chafed under it. She ought not try to regain what she had squandered by starving them to death, for that was foolish—doggone it, he had to have food! How could a hard-working man get along without proper nourishment?

But it's an ill wind that blows no one any good; one blessing the catastrophe had brought him, one for which he could only be thankful: she never mentioned the word tobacco any more; he might chew and smoke to his heart's content without the slightest fear of being nagged—that much good sense she had left! In a way there was peace in the house now, and Louis enjoyed it.

Still, he wasn't getting enough to eat; the way he was working, trying hard all the time to save money on hired help, he needed better tending; his experience as an old thresher told him so plainly: you can't crowd a machine without proper power . . . the horse that was being worked hard all day long required a lot of good care!—He couldn't just figure out how she herself got along on so scant a fare . . . maybe she took a bite now and then between meals . . . perhaps all women did the same thing . . . that was how they could get along on nothing.

Determined to let sleeping dogs lie undisturbed as long as possible, Louis never mentioned her parsimony . . . considering all they had lost, they needed to be careful—by golly if they didn't! One morning he sat in the cowyard, milking; it was 6:30 already; he had been working since sunrise, and felt empty as a pair of old shrunk bellows; before his eyes sparkled black stars; they seemed to pop out of his very eyeballs; he was afraid of falling into a faint. Just as he had stripped the first cow and was ready to get up and move to the next, he lifted the pail to his lips and, blowing the foam away, he drank his fill. The fresh, lukewarm milk revived him; pretty soon the feeling of faintness had gone, only a slight dizziness remaining. From then on, every morning he drank fresh milk the minute he had finished the first cow. After a while he began taking a few deep sips in the evenings also, but always on the lookout lest Lizzie should catch him at it. By fall, his face had filled out again; on his cheeks lay a peculiarly fresh complexion, soft and delicate as that of a child. People wondered at how well Louis Houglum looked.

Thus little by little the two drifted farther apart, each building up his own world into which he withdrew. Seldom now that they sat down to discuss plans of any kind.

The summer after Robert Nelson had dealt them the

cruel blow, Louis invented a wonderful device, one so
clever in both conception and execution that he had to
marvel at his own ingeniousness:

One Sunday forenoon, while tinkering in the machine shed with the new binder which had to be got
ready for the cutting the next day, Louis' attention
fastened itself on the canvas of an old discarded
McCormick he had standing there. About finished with
his job, he walked over to the old rig. . . . That canvas
is still in pretty good shape, he thought . . . much too
good to be standing here rotting. He walked around the
platform, ripping the canvas off. Turning it and examining it on both sides, he studied it critically. . . .
That was a whole lot better linen than people were
weaving nowadays!—A light shone in his eyes . . .
one should be able to make something out of that, all
right . . . something smart and useful. . . . Tucking
the canvas under his arm, he went to the door and
looked across the yard. Not a sound came from the
house . . . most likely she was lying down at this time
of the day . . . too early yet for dinner. Certain that
he would be left in peace, he began to work. The zeal
of the inventor was upon him; he measured and cut,
fitted and did some more cutting, stitched and riveted;
with the excitement of invention burning in his blood,
his hands worked deftly.

That Sunday forenoon Louis made himself a wide
canvas belt, with six pockets stitched on the outside,
each pocket locked with a small buckle. When the job
at last was finished and he had unbuttoned his clothes

and tried it on, he could have shouted for pleasure. In these six pockets he'd keep all his paper money; here he could easily store several thousand dollars. He couldn't remember when last he had felt so thoroughly pleased with himself. Again life was worth the fight. What a fool he had been to go around all these years worrying about the safety of his money; his square face rounded, satisfaction beaming out of it. . . . He would exchange every piece of silver for bank notes . . . and the gold also . . . he would carry the money with him wherever he went, and he would have it on him at night—gosh darn it, if it wasn't the smartest invention ever made! . . . Not for anything in the world must Lizzie find out about this . . . she might take a notion not to like it . . . women are queer ducks, you offer them candy and they won't have it!

Louis' apprehension was quite groundless; since they no longer shared the same bedroom, there could be no great danger of Lizzie's finding out about his wonderful invention. In the spring, when she had been so very restless at night, tossing and twisting and turning around all the while, he had left her and taken an upstairs room, and had not moved back again. Lizzie had made no objection to the separation, only remarking that, if he could do without her, she was thankful to get a night's peace . . . how did he expect her to sleep with a log in the bed? He better not be saying anything, or she'd tell *him* a thing or two! Louis obediently took the hint. Since then nothing more had been said about their separate sleeping quarters. Occasionally he had gone into her bedroom to look after the babies in the mattress, had had them out and counted the money, but he had found little joy in them because every time his grief over all they had lost had come upon him. What was there left to count? They were nothing but poor farmers; they had nothing . . . they never could have anything, the way they conducted themselves!

On every trip to town that fall Louis brought back with him some silver and the same amount in bank notes. Whenever the wads of fives, tens, and twenties grew big enough he would step into a bank and ask for a hundred-dollar bill, going about the business in a shrewd way; rather than running the risk of returning to the same bank too often, he would go to one of the neighbouring towns, not minding the matter of a mile or two of farther hauling. By October he had a hundred-dollar bill tucked safely away in each pocket of his belt.

One day in late October, full of drowsy, yellow haze, he was sitting perched high on a load of hogs, jogging into Greenfield. He felt a bit lazy, but otherwise in fair spirits; the day was warm and balmy for so late in the year. The thought of Lizzie's misdeed had been in his mind all morning. Now all of a sudden an idea came and stood before his eyes; pretty soon there were others; the jolting of the wagon over the rough road made them come and go: How idiotic he had acted that day last fall in opposing her proposal of division! Of all the foolish acts he had ever done, that was certainly the damnedest . . . otherwise he could now have

sat here with five more—land o'living how foolish he
had been that time! . . . He might now have had his
share all to himself! . . . How could he get her to
divide now? . . . Supposing she got another crazy
streak? Many agents and salesmen came to the farm
in his absence!—The wagon jolted and shook him up,
but of that he was unconscious.

. . . Lizzie had misappropriated common funds, yes,
so she had . . . taken out of his money and thrown
it away when he had told her in plain words not to.
. . . How could he make her see that she had done
wrong? For it was wrong . . . criminal; good God,
take another man's money and just gamble it away!

. . . Perhaps? . . . Louis saw an idea which made
his tanned cheeks flush deeper and his heart beat faster.
. . . He could, of course, get his money back . . .
there was a way . . . without her knowing it, which
would make it easier for them both . . . for then
there'd be no fuss about it. . . . He took in most of
the money himself . . . he could hold back a small
sum each time—that's it: just a little each time . . .
occasionally a five or a ten . . . until the whole five
hundred was paid up. Why, doggone it! he'd only be
doing the right thing on her behalf without her knowing it. Wasn't that his plain duty as head of the house?
As long as she couldn't be trusted? . . . He'd keep
good track of what he paid himself back . . . not take
a cent more than he had coming—he certainly would
not go around nigging from his own wife! Louis'

honesty made him chuckle out loud at the preposterous-ness of the idea.

That very day Louis tried the scheme of paying him-self back a little of what he had coming from Lizzie; the hogs brought $68.45, exactly; when he came home he laid $63.45 on the table and told her to put the money away; the five-dollar bill he had already tucked into his belt.

From now on he put the plan into operation and found that it worked splendidly. An exciting game, this was. On the way home from town he would make up stories, plausible explanations to have in readiness in case she should question him why the amount was not larger. After a while he had a stock of stories, which he rehearsed but never found any use for, be-cause she never questioned him. Oh, it was a great game, even more exciting than threshing. When he received settlement for the wheat that fall a whole twenty-dollar bill stuck to his fingers, but then he felt he owed her an explanation and volunteered it . . . the wheat had not graded as high as he had hoped . . . that elevator in Greenfield was run by a pack of thieves . . . these days the farmer couldn't turn around with-out being robbed!—Lizzie received the news absently, making no comment of any kind.

All in all, conditions at home were improving. For one thing, Lizzie never mentioned the matter of the tobacco, which Louis appreciated more than he could tell . . . she really acted square, Lizzie did—he'd say that much for her! And somehow, she was less

domineering than formerly; by looking out and using
a bit of forethought you could easily get along with
her . . . really, she wasn't worse than other married
women—not a bit. . . . If he only had had sense
enough to agree to dividing up the money. . . . What
could have possessed him that time, anyway?

Suddenly an awful rumpus broke loose between them,
threatening to smash up things worse than ever. But,
fortunately, the storm proved of short duration, passing over as quickly as it had come; afterward they enjoyed calm weather and the brightest sunshine.

The trouble started in this manner:

One day in late fall Louis had gone to town with a
load of grain. A nasty day it was, with a lowering sky,
full of heavy, raw clouds out of which a cold, pene-
trating wind mourned. There was snow in the air; winter would soon be upon the prairies. While out doing
chores Lizzie had had a hard tussel with some young
cattle which had not been under a roof since early in
the spring, and which she had been trying to get into
a shed for wintering. When she came back to the
kitchen she stirred up the fire and sat down to rest.

But not for long. During the last two weeks she had
had no time to herself; they had worked early and late
to get the corn out of the fields before snowfall. "No,"
she said to herself, getting up, "I better be looking after
them!" She went into the bedroom and, taking out the
two pouches and emptying the contents on the spread,
she counted the money slowly. As she replaced the
treasures, tears came to her eyes, a frequent occurrence

lately; she was hardly aware of it herself and could not have helped it.

Coming back to the kitchen, she examined the five hundred under the clock; again tears came—there might have been a whole thousand more now in that pile! She went to the cupboard for the molasses can, brought it over to the table, and counted the contents. Not much to be proud of. It held $191 in silver and nothing more. Replacing the can, she sighed heavily.

In the middle of the kitchen she stopped suddenly, perturbed because of her forgetfulness . . . how muzzy she was getting . . . here she had been to the bedroom, and forgotten all about the bureau drawers! Going back to the bedroom, she took out the $600 in bank notes which lay hidden in different drawers and counted them caressingly . . . nice kids these were, mostly twenties . . . an odour of sweet perfume emanated from them. Her sadness got the better of her as she sat on the bed looking at the wads. . . . A whole thousand poorer than last year about this time . . . and all because she had married that dolt of a man who couldn't look after anything . . . was there ever a fate more cruel than hers?

Arousing herself and hiding the wads, she went to the summer shanty which she had stopped using for this year. From under a heap of old clothes in the farther corner she brought out a crock which to all appearances was filled with empty fruit jars. Placing the crock on a small table, she removed the jars, and next an old stove lid of about the same size as the crock.

She looked down into the crock and smiled—the kids were sleeping serenely!—then she began to count the money out onto the table, mostly bank notes with some silver. The crock contained $1,400 exactly, which sum represented the greater part of last year's savings. With much care she counted the money back into the crock. It made a fine heap, almost like that she had seen in the bank. . . . By right she ought to have six hundred more here . . . she would see what the corn brought . . . she might, of course, bring out the few dollars she had in the cupboard?

Having returned to the kitchen, she saw it was too early for dinner; besides, she would not need much, with Louis gone. Since she had nothing particular that must be done, she might just as well take time to look after the five hundred that Louis kept in the barn— poor, abandoned things . . . shameful of her to let him take them out of the house . . . and stick them in such a place! Whoever heard of people keeping their money in the barn . . . he was getting more slovenly every day . . . she'd just bet anything that he never remembered to look after the money!

A moment later Lizzie was on her knees over in the dark corner of the barn, feeling with her hand under the floor. Finding nothing, she grew frantic, a benumbing fear gripped her heart. Thrusting her arm down clear to the shoulder she groped about as far as she could reach, but she could feel only the wall and the dank, cold earth which was hideous to the touch. Realizing at last that nothing else was there, she pulled her arm back and broke into hysterical sobs. . . . Now he had gone and done it again! Squandered $500! What could she have done that Evil should single her out above all others? Was she condemned to be eaten up by robbers?

After a while her reason began to function normally: It couldn't be possible? No stranger would have discovered that hole, most certainly not thought of searching there for hidden treasures? . . . Oh no, there was a nigger in the woodpile—somewhere! Her face became hard and set.

She arose and walked slowly out of the barn, her head nodding to the thoughts that she saw floating in the air, determined as one who has made up his mind on a momentous question.

. . . He has hid the money in some other place, that's what! . . . A bitter laugh escaped her . . . he is afraid that another Robert Nelson might come and beguile me . . . there you have it! . . . She leaned up against a post, thinking hard.

. . . All right, since he wanted it that way, she'd see to it that he got it, now she would make him divide. No ifs and buts about that . . . she wasn't going to stand for his scattering her money all over the farm, no, sir! He could just take his share and do with it whatever he pleased—then they'd see how far he got! . . . She didn't fancy his snooping about in her bed, either, the old good-for-nothing, since he no longer cared to stay with her as a decent husband ought to do! Returning to the house, she walked with a firm step; involuntarily her right hand closed tightly.

That night Louis had no sooner seated himself at the supper table than she demanded to know what he had done with the money in the barn; her voice had the old metallic ring in it which he knew so well.

"In the barn?" he repeated disconcerted, looking for a way to escape.

"That's what I am asking you!" her eyes blazed with anger.

"I suppose it's ——" He was going to say "where it has always been," but caught himself in time. "I suppose it must be in some other place," he explained in a careless voice.

"You suppose so?" she cried, indignantly.

"Yes." Louis continued to eat.

In order to get better hold of him she came closer:

"Good and well!" There was an awful finality in her voice. "Since you go hiding from me what we own together, we're going to divide right now; this kind of foolishness I won't stand for. You aren't going to hide *my* money and now I am telling you!" She stamped her foot on the floor; the storm had broken and more would be coming.

For some time Louis ate in silence. Twice he cleared his throat to speak and twice he hesitated, fearing that his voice might betray him. But at last, without looking up, he asked, cautiously:

—Did she mean fifty-fifty? Dollar for dollar of everything?

—That was exactly what she proposed: dollar for dollar of all they had and of all they'd get . . . she wouldn't stand for this another day!

—Well, he conceded, amiably, since she insisted, she better have her way, only she needn't get so mad about it. Louis was trying hard to conceal his satisfaction, but didn't quite succeed in keeping his voice even enough.

Lizzie detected it and blenched, her anger blazing up anew. So! he was actually jumping at the chance, was he? There he sat feeling pleased because she no longer trusted him. She raked her brain for a caustic remark, one that might scorch his mean old hide.

But before she could find what she wanted he arose abruptly, snatched the milk-pails and left the house. To tell the truth, he wasn't half through eating yet; and it was a fine supper, with nice fried potatoes and fresh bread; but he was afraid to stay longer lest she might change her mind. On his way to the barn he made a détour to the machine shed to see if there was canvas enough for another belt . . . he might need it.

With shades drawn close, Louis and Lizzie sat by her bed, dividing the money they had saved up during their married life. All through the deal there was in Louis a generosity which Lizzie was at a loss to understand and which puzzled her more and more . . . it was so unlike him . . . it disgusted her. To begin with, he suggested carelessly that they might first of all count out five hundred in gold to her to balance what he kept in the—well—in the barn. Seeing her astonishment, his spirit of sacrifice soared still higher: "If you prefer to have all yours in gold," he said, blandly, "it will be all right with me . . . I am not particular . . . besides, it's not so easy for a woman to handle safely all this paper and silver . . . just give that to me!"

In speechless wonder Lizzie looked at her husband. What had come over him, anyway? Was he joking or had he lost the little sense he had? . . . He must have something up his sleeve, that's certain! But she had to watch the business at hand, his madness she would figure out later.

When Louis that night went upstairs to bed he carried with him a milk-pail full of money; at the bottom all silver; on top of the layers of silver, rolls of bills of different denominations; and on top of the rolls, several gold coins. He was chuckling to himself —now he'd have some real fun!—He placed the pail on a chair right by his pillow and left it there for the night, falling to sleep in an endless sea of contentment.

The next day he hitched up a team and took a load of corn to town, and so every day during the rest of the week, but to different towns. All his shelled corn had to be hauled out, anyway . . . he might as well take it now as later. . . . On Saturday night he went to bed with nearly $4,000 in his belt. Never before had life been so exceedingly interesting.

IV. The Day of the Great Beast

I

TIME passed; silent, calm-eyed, inexorable; unnoticed by most; unchallenged by all; but adding
seasons and periods to every living creature, and day
unto yesterday: to the young, strength and golden
aspirations; to manhood, maturity and the fullness of
life; casting its soft, thin mantle of hoar-frost upon
those who had begun to age; no one escaped the touch
of the unseen hand; but few took notice thereof. The
Houglums least of all, because they could not afford to
stop and look.

By and by came the fatal fall of 1914. Then the
farmer of the Mississippi Valley had something else to
think about than such unimportant questions as Time
and Existence, for prices on all farm products began
suddenly to soar, like the lark—up and up, ever higher,
to unbelievable peaks. Wherever one turned his eyes,
gold glittered in the sun. The fair promises of the
millennium were at last about to be fulfilled.

Ever since 1908 times had been good and money easy
to make, but nothing comparable to this. Now Aladdin
himself was visiting the prairies, and his wonder-lamp
he had with him. By 1915, in the deadening heat of
midsummer, eggs were selling at 40 cents a dozen cash
and butter at 55 cents a pound. All other farm products

brought prices in proportion. Louis and Lizzie rejoiced like the Children of Israel in the wilderness at the sight of the manna.

Louis had just entered upon his fifty-fifth year; his wife was not far behind him. He looked so well that his neighbours often remarked about it. How did he do it? That man must have found the Fountain of Youth. Though he slaved from sunrise until after dark, he had the fair complexion of a girl and was as spry as a lark. Lizzie, on the other hand, was growing scrawnier every year; only mere skin and bones. But she had lost nothing of her old energy. Woe unto any man who tried to get the better of her in a deal! To his dismay, he would soon learn that he had barked up the wrong tree.

After dividing up their money they got along remarkably well, though there was no longer any intimacy between them. Once in a while she would ride him rough-shod, but Louis had acquired a placid stolidity which no storm, however bad, could seriously ruffle.

Whenever Louis returned from town after selling produce from the farm, they would cut the proceeds squarely in two, that is to say—they would divide the money which he laid before her. But truth to tell, if he saw his chance he would filch outrageously.

Now they farmed only the home forty; the rest of the land they had rented out on shares. On the forty they produced all the fodder and corn possible, kept a good-sized herd of milk cows and a lot of hogs and poultry. Both of them were as busy now as they had ever been.

Not the slightest interest did either of them take in the struggle going on over in Europe. Save for the fact that the war created such uncommonly good times in this country, it did not affect them. They had nothing to do with it; in no way were they responsible for it, and it was so far away and so unreal. To them it was ridiculous beyond words that people could argue themselves into blows about Huns and Allies—how foolish of them! . . . Incredibly silly it was! Why not enjoy a good thing as long as it lasted? It was only a matter of wisdom to make hay while the weather was fair. For the life of them, they could not understand why the Norwegians out here should be so furious at this fellow, Kaiser Bill. Not a bit nice of them. Had he done them aught but good? If it were true what people said of him, that he had started the circus now going on in Europe, and thus caused prices over here to go sky high, then his picture, beautifully framed, ought to hang in every farm home in America! Lizzie made the statement often, and for once her husband agreed heartily. She would take his compliments complacently and add: The Norwegians around here had so many high Moguls adorning their walls, such as Roosevelt and King Haakon, Fritjof Nansen and this here LaFollette, fellows who had never done a tap to help this neighbourhood along, that they might just as well pay a little respect to Kaiser Bill!

The war was making the whole country flow with

milk and honey—that was clear to anyone who stopped to look. During the first year Louis and Lizzie each put aside a whole thousand dollars. If one could have checked Louis' account closely, he might have found a hundred or two more, but Louis had gone about his business so deftly that Lizzie, who never suspected perfidy from that quarter, had no cause for any misgivings.

Her interest nowadays lay elsewhere. After the money had been divided, her mind concentrated on her own share. This was hers, hers only; she alone had the sole right over it; she could do with it what she pleased without asking him. Frequently she would slip into the bedroom to count and add up. Some of her old joy had come back to her; on Sundays she might close herself up in the bedroom and pleasure herself with her possessions, staying there for hours at a time. At night she would take the two pouches with her to bed and go to sleep with her hand on them.

The question of where to hide her treasures puzzled her considerably. The old hiding-places that Louis knew about would no longer do. . . . For all the world, she would not allow Louis to poke his nose into her things, oh no, thank you—nothing doing!

One day in spring when she was cleaning the cellar an idea flashed on her mind: wouldn't this be a good place? Over here in the corner where it was almost dark? She was much pleased with the thought. Every day when Louis went to town, she worked like a mole, spading up a hole and carrying out dirt until her back ached. In the darkest corner of the cellar she dug a hole big enough to house a wash-boiler. Having got the hole ready, she first set the boiler in, and then she lugged down to the cellar the top of a discarded cook stove, so heavy that the strain nearly tore her. The top covered the hole nicely. Over it she spread two gunny sacks; on them she placed some crocks and fruit jars. When at last all was ready, the corner looked so innocent that one would have to be endowed both with a sixth and a seventh sense to smell rats here; the place was not only foolproof but fireproof as well; she needed only to re-move a crock and a couple of fruit jars, turn over one of the gunny sacks, lift a stove cover, and reach down with her hand into the boiler. All the silver and all her bills she brought down here; but the gold she con-tinued to keep upstairs . . . somehow that belonged where the bright light of day reigned and where the sun once in a while could rouse it, she saw it clearly.

Many a wakeful moment did she have trying to fig-ure out where Louis kept his money; she wasted hours in hunting for it. Upstairs there was not an inch of space that she had not searched, not a crack that she did not look into; again and again she examined both quilt and mattress, and the pillows, too. To every outhouse on the farm she went, even up into the haymow—not a penny did she discover. Like all mysteries one is trying to solve, this one became an obsession with her: she must find out where he was keeping his money. At times she was downright worried over it, for he was so slovenly and forgetful. One night a terrible idea occurred to her, causing her to lie awake for hours: supposing that foolish man had let himself be lured by the interest and had again put his money into some bank? 'Twould be just like him! It was he who had thought of the bank the other time, and who would not give up. Well, if he was as hare-brained as all that, he could lie in the bed he had made for himself . . . not a penny of her money would he get!

Louis, on the other hand, gave no thought to what she might be doing with her money; he had his safe—that was enough for him. The belt, once in a while, gave him considerable trouble, particularly when he was working hard and the sweat flowed heavily. Before he got used to wearing it, he developed collar-sores around his loins, which caused him much annoyance. In the barn he always kept a bottle of horse liniment; having no other remedy on hand, he daubed himself with handfuls from the bottle. Gradually the skin calloused and he suffered no further inconvenience.

By now the pockets were beginning to bulge rather seriously. Soon he would have to provide more room. One day while perched on top of a load of corn, he began to wonder if there might not be bills of higher denomination than one hundred dollars? He gave a chagrined laugh—what a fool he had been for not inquiring about this before.

As soon as he was through with his business he stepped into the State Bank and, approaching the teller's window, inquired diffidently whether he might ask a question:

—Of course he might, as many as he liked.

—Well—er—hm—he had often wondered if there might be such a thing as a thousand-dollar bill?

—You bet you . . . plenty of them. The clerk was a young man who spoke with a swagger.

—Did they have them here?

—Certainly, they had. Did he have money he wanted to change?

—Oh, no, no, no! No, he was just asking. . . . In case he should ever get that much money, it would be fun to have one . . . but that wasn't very likely to happen, he added, resignedly. Louis walked out of the bank with the waters of happiness welling up in him.

These were busy days for Louis; jobs of all kinds kept piling up on him. But finally a day came which began with a cold drizzle from the southeast, of the kind that is likely to settle down to an all-day rain. For a while Louis studied the sky, then hitched a horse to the old cart. There was a remarkable quality about that vehicle: it never wore out so badly that it couldn't be patched up again. To discard it as long as it held together Louis refused to do, for that would be wasteful. . . . Let the youngsters poke all the fun at him they pleased . . . if they wanted to spend their money on costly automobiles and burn it up in gasoline, that was their business . . . he'd rather keep his and get some fun out of it. Besides, there was nothing the matter with the cart yet!

In getting himself ready that morning Louis spent so long a time upstairs that Lizzie fell to wondering what he could be up to. He wasn't putting on his Sunday clothes to go to town on a day like this? She called up the stairway, asking in a sharp voice if he intended to have the poor horse standing out in the rain all day?

From his room came the sound of shuffling feet that all of a sudden were in a great hurry. No, he called back, warningly, he would be down in a minute. . . . What was she stewing about? The horse didn't melt because of a few drops of water! His tone was irritable. Yet it was some time before he was ready to come down.

Presently Louis sat in the cart, rattling over a muddy road toward Akron. His mood was pleasantly expectant . . . in Akron were no less than three big banks; he had never set foot inside any of them . . . today he was out to make a haul! . . . Now stretch yourself a bit! he exhorted the horse.

On reaching town he tied up his horse and walked down to the business centre. There were few people in the streets; he saw no one that he knew. The first bank he found he walked into.

—Would it be possible to obtain a couple of one-thousand-dollar bills? he asked, deferentially.

The clerk gave the dripping, unshaven figure in the ragged coat a close look, and guessed indifferently that they'd try to accommodate him. Did he have the money with him?

Without saying another word Louis unbuttoned his old raincoat and, going deeper into the duck coat underneath, he fished out from the inside pocket a small package, carefully wrapped and tied up; after removing the cord, he counted out and shoved through the window twenty wilted hundred-dollar bills, soft as the most delicate silk.

The clerk sniffed and coughed, got his handkerchief up to his nose and held it there; with the finger tips of his left hand he picked up the bills one by one and slung them into a till. "Gosh! what stink!" he muttered to himself. Coughing, he went into the fireproof vault and came back with two new notes.

A boyish curiosity in his face, Louis took them, handling them as if he were afraid to touch them, studying each one in silence. . . . Correct enough—here was the figure one with the three ciphers after it . . . and the sum printed in plain words! A deep sigh of relief escaped him. He folded the bills up and put them into his pocketbook; immediately he turned to the door; but on the way he stopped to make sure that he had put the pocketbook clear down at the bottom of his trousers pocket.

At the next bank he had a good deal more self-confidence. On coming in, he walked directly to the window, asking innocently if they could spare him a thousand-dollar bill or two?

—Certainly! The answer was prompt and businesslike.

This time Louis went deeper. From the inner pocket of his vest he fetched out a small package exactly like the first one, opened it, and counted out on the marble slab twenty much-mutilated bills.

The scene at the first bank was reënacted here also: the clerk put his handkerchief to his nose, drawing back a step or two, and then, with a do-or-die determination, he rushed up, counted the bills, and swept them down into the till. "Great Scott! Where did you get them, anyway? Did you dig them right out of the manure pile?"

Grinning good-naturedly, Louis with much deliberation folded together the two bills which he received in return and placed them beside the others.

On the way to the third bank he walked with a light, springy step. Coming up to the window, he spoke in a care-free, business-like manner:

—He was in need of two one-thousand-dollar bills. Did they have them? And would they please help a poor fellow out? But when he had counted out his twenty bills the teller swore and carried on worse than any rough-necked threshers Louis had ever known. "Hell and brimstone! Say, old fellow, how many thousand years have you slept on these, anyhow? . . . Of all the rotten stinks ——!" That was as far as the man got because he had to pull out his handkerchief; he coughed, making frightful sputterings; between spells he used the vilest cusswords Louis had ever heard.

On the way homeward Louis let the horse take its own gait. Out of a low, wet sky the rain dripped unceasingly. But he was oblivious to both roads and weather; to him the day could not have been fairer if he had made it himself. His thoughts lolled, satisfied, lazily, picking up ideas here and there. What a doggone smart invention this belt was! He could easily carry one hundred thousand dollars in it, and not a soul would be the wiser—he was a walking gold mine. . . . The way those white-collared gents had sniffed at his kids! Well, they had looked a little worn down at the heels and smelt a bit tough . . . but evidently the value was still there. Louis broke into a pleased chuckle: Gosh darn it—if this wasn't the best fun he'd ever had!

In his beatific state of mind Louis fell to thinking of Lizzie: kind, generous thoughts, of how helpless she was and how hard it must be for her—only a frail, foolish woman—to take proper care of her money. She got no real fun out of it, either . . . just sitting there counting and worrying. . . . Where was she keeping it now? Louis' face sobered; his thoughts took a definite course: suppose something should happen to her? and she suddenly fell away? Nobody would know where to look . . . perhaps her money never could be found? . . . That girl could think of queer hiding-places . . . the way she had fooled him that time with the mattress! . . . He, being the head of the family, was hardly doing the right thing by her in not telling her his secret. . . . He ought to show her . . . then he could move downstairs again? During the winter this bachelor's life wasn't what it was cracked up to be. . . . And her feet were nearly always cold, poor thing! . . . He'd sleep better himself, too . . . now if he woke up at nights, especially when the wind howled around the corners, he'd stay awake for hours, listening for sounds from her room. . . . One night he had heard her get up and go to the kitchen, and then he had sat up in bed, stretching his ears, waiting to hear her return . . . sometimes she walked so quietly that you couldn't detect a sound.

. . . Why not tell her? They might take her savings and go up to St. Paul or Minneapolis. . . . To exchange her money around here now, would be too risky . . . he could take his remaining two thousand at the same time—yes, he *would* tell her!

His clothes all dripping wet, Louis stepped into the kitchen, humming a merry tune. The supper was much too frugal after a long, wet day on muddy roads, but he didn't mind. Leaving the table and picking up the milk-pails, he started the same tune . . . he'd soon have something more to eat—just wait!

The chores done, the milk-pails washed and stacked up ready for the morning's milking, Louis did not go upstairs right away, but sat down by the table and lit his pipe. By and by Lizzie became conscious of his eyes. There was an air of mystery about him, some secret that he'd just as soon tell, and on his face sat a kind grin.

Lizzie guessed he had something important up his sleeve and asked curtly whether he intended to sit there all night? She was still puttering over by the stove.

In a drawling tone Louis presumed that he would go to bed . . . after a while, perhaps, and continued looking at her. Refilling his pipe, he stuck it between his teeth without lighting it. Suddenly he spoke:

"Tell me, Lizzie, what are you doing with your money?" In his voice was a paternal note.

His question must have displeased her:

—Huh! she said, was that any of his business?

Louis was so amused that he chuckled . . . now wasn't that just what he had expected . . . there she went off like a cocked pistol, and he was only wanting to help her!

—Well, he remarked, judiciously, it wasn't that he cared, for he had enough with managing his own affairs. But in case she'd listen to expert advice, then he had it. Louis was swelling up with importance.

Lizzie strove hard to quiet her curiosity. . . . Now that lump must be up to some kind of trick? It wouldn't hurt to find out just how crazy he was . . . not that she intended telling him!

"When did you get to be so smart?" she asked, not unkindly.

"Now I've found a way—it's all my own, too!" There was boyish delight in his words.

"So I hear! You haven't been to the saloon and filled yourself up? Is that why you're so smart? . . . Why don't you tell what you know?"

"If you'll listen!"

"Ain't I listening? What more do you want?"

"Well, now you are!"

But not yet was Louis quite ready to divulge his great secret. Lighting his pipe and taking a few deep puffs, he began in a low, confidential tone that held in it an odd joyousness—it didn't sound natural for an old man:

"Yes, sir, Lizzie, now I've found the way. You could never guess it . . . it's no use for you to try . . . I might as well tell you right out," here he stopped to give the information time to sink in: "I carry the money on me . . . no matter where I go or where I am . . . always!"

"At night, too?" she broke in, incredulously.

"That's what I'm saying—at night, too."

"Are you sleeping in your clothes, then?"

"I should say not!" Louis had to laugh at her silliness.

"You're crazy, that's what!"

"No, I ain't, Lizzie. Only I got a bit more sense than you!" And in order to convince her Louis did exactly what he had seen Robert Nelson do: he went over to the window and pulled the shade down; close; then he unbuttoned his clothes, unbuckled and pulled out the belt. *There!* he said, laying the belt on the table. "Now take a look at that! You have it around you night and day . . . after you get used to it, it doesn't hurt you the least bit. . . . In this here bank," he held the belt up to her, "you can easily keep one hundred thousand dollars if you only had them!"

"In gold?"

"Gold!" he pooh-poohed. "How silly you are! Gold, that's only for looks. . . . Besides, who would go lugging the heavy stuff around? . . . No, what you want is *value*," he added, instructively. Louis fetched out his pocketbook; opening it slowly and taking out the wad of bills, he unfolded one and showed her, fairly bursting with pride. "Now how's that for a baby? That fellow is worth just *one thousand dollars!*"

Open-mouthed, she examined the bill, absorbed, fascinated by the sight of it . . . one thousand dollars? It wasn't possible! Her eyes moistened; into her lean, angular features came a soft, tender expression, making her face handsome. She forgot herself: "I never saw the beat!" she exclaimed.

Louis laughed good-naturedly:

"No, I don't think you have, Lizzie—no, sir! It's doggone deviltry that a piece of paper not bigger than that can be worth a whole thousand dollars . . . and lighter than a feather!" To illustrate to her the ingeniousness of his invention he unbuckled one of the pockets, slipping the bill in. "Plenty of room in here . . . and you keep the kids around you all night. . . . If you want me to, I can make you one much nicer than this here one," he offered, generously.

For a long time Lizzie was silent. At last she remarked, meditatively:

"I'll never get enough to make it worth the trouble. . . . I'd have only a few."

Against her foolish talk Louis protested vigorously, but without meeting her eyes:

—What difference did it make whether few or many so long as the value was all there? He grew voluble in his effort to convince her: "You simply don't understand! Can't you see—you have them about you when you go to bed; they're there when you get up; you have them always . . . they never leave you because they can't get away. And can't you see the value?" Louis took another bill, waving it before her eyes. "Here I have a whole half-forty of good land . . . see me holding it right here in my hand?" His enthusiasm was running away with him: "I tell you, Lizzie, in a belt like that you could easily carry all of Greenfield Township and never feel it, yes, and then some." He paused for a moment and began from the beginning again: "You leave the place and go away—there's nothing to worry about. Let any thief come and ransack the farm . . . what will he find? He finds nothing. . . . If the house should burn down over your head, all you need to do is to get yourself out . . . the kids you have with you. . . . That belt there is the doggonest safest thing you ever saw!"

"Oh, I don't worry about any fire! I . . . well, never mind . . . I wouldn't lose anything."

"No, but you'd go around worrying just the same. You'd have to dig in the ashes, with the whole neighbourhood looking on . . . and you never can tell what a fire like that might do—I tell you: I wouldn't risk it!"

There was a pause, after which Lizzie asked, feeling her way: "Where do you get these fellows?"

—Aw, that was easy, Louis explained, with a swagger. No trick at all. He'd make a trip to Minneapolis. . . . The banks would be glad to get all the small change.

"We couldn't take all at one time ... it would fill a whole suitcase!" she objected.

"Course we can. Plenty of banks up in the Twin Cities. . . . I'll do that for you!"

Lizzie had gone over to the stove. She was fingering the handle of the water kettle. "I want to sleep on it before I say. . . . Could you be going one of the first days ——?

Already the next day Louis was on his way to Minneapolis to exchange the money for her. Thus it happened that Lizzie, too, began wearing a belt, and that man and wife moved together at night, sleeping peacefully, each with $8,000.

II

For some time now the Houglums prospered magnificently. Life was kind and good. The hens behaved well, showing fair diligence in their business of laying eggs. The cows gave an abundance of milk. Whatever they took to market sold at unheard-of prices; even an old scrub cow that they formerly could not have given away now brought whole farms. By the spring of 1917 Louis and Lizzie each had $1,500 more in their belts.

Louis had, however, gained a few hundreds on Lizzie. For several reasons, this money he did not keep with the rest. Whatever he paid himself back he stored up in a secret place, so ingenious in conception that no Pinkerton detective would have been able to ferret it out, no matter how many sixth senses he might have been endowed with.

They were still using the old hoghouse that had been on the farm when Louis bought it. Low and squatty, built of posts and straw, it had had to be patched up every fall; now the walls, and the roof, too, had grown to twice their original thickness. In the northeast corner (the door was in the south end) where the roof met the wall, some bird or animal had burrowed a round deep hole into the straw. One day while repairing the roof Louis had discovered the opening and had made an investigation. The hole seemed made to order. Unless one came clear into the corner the opening could not be seen. Even so, the hole would, more likely than not, not be discovered, because Louis had corked it up with a tuft of twisted straw.

In the bottom of the little cavern Louis was keeping an old shoe of Lizzie's, one that she had been forced to discard prematurely because it refused to fit, no matter how long she wore it. Louis had picked it up in the granary. In that shoe now lay $683, all in bills of small denomination. The money represented the total of what Louis had paid himself back, with interest and compound interest added. Though the sum more than covered her total indebtedness, Louis still continued paying back. He had several reasons: no one could foretell the future . . . she might get another spell . . . or she might go to work and spend her money foolishly—doggone it, she was only a woman! And, well, it didn't hurt to be on the safe side.

Louis found much pleasure in the wad of bills hidden in the shoe. It was his. Each bill was a good chum to him. As soon as he came into the yard they raised their ears, listening for him. He felt their presence clearly. . . . In a way they were dearer to him than the big fellows he had about him . . . these little fellows were bought with a price . . . for if she should find him out——!

At the declaration of war against Germany neither Louis nor Lizzie experienced the slightest ripple of excitement. Prices were good; the outlook was that they would go still higher, particularly now that the Government had guaranteed a minimum price on wheat. . . . Now there was an Administration for you! Louis swore loudly that from now on he'd always vote the Democratic ticket; doggone it! he'd be a fool if he didn't.

Not only was the wheat price guaranteed, but from out of Washington came an urgent request to the farmers of Greenfield County, that they plow up every strip of ground, sow all the wheat possible, and thus help win the war. And the necessity of raising much beef was just as urgent. The boys fighting for us in the trenches must have food, and so must our Allies. . . . Talk about an Administration that knew its business, and one that looked after the welfare of the farmer! Now just watch the prices soar! Aye, the millennium was dawning at last!

But then, like a bolt out of a clear sky, came the first Liberty Loan drive. The heavens were overclouding fast and threateningly.

Without Louis and Lizzie's being in the least forewarned, and hence not prepared to meet the attack, the committee in charge of Greenfield Township descended upon the two helpless elderly people. One beggar at the time is bad enough—no one will dispute the fact—but here came two who had been commissioned and sent out by the Government in Washington. In addition, these particular two were patriotic men who would leave no stone unturned in the great cause of winning the war; they were soldiers fighting the cause of Humanity.

The Houglums were thrown into a state of desperation; the earth itself was beginning to rock and sway under their very feet. Where could they flee for refuge? When the Government in Washington had to come out here to a small dirt farmer, begging for money at a rate of interest as low as *that,* then the whole outfit must be about ready to topple over!

And such begging one had never heard before. No sooner had one member of the committee talked himself dry than the other started in, keeping the argument going in a steady stream of strong words until the first was sufficiently rested to begin again. What one forgot, the other would be sure to remember. It was terrible to listen to them.

There were two pitched against two. None of the participants minced words in speaking his mind. To begin with, Louis told the committee courteously but firmly that it was useless for them to waste their time here, because neither he nor his wife had any money. Immediately Lizzie reinforced his position by declaring that, if they could find a penny on the farm, they were welcome to have it. If they didn't believe her, they could just look for themselves—the house stood open to them. Undaunted, the committee held its ground, maintaining the position that if the Houglums had no money at home, they must have it in the bank, which was still better; besides, they were not asking for cash, but for a subscription. . . . Here was the list . . . would Louis please sign up?

At the mention of the bank Lizzie laughed bitterly, maliciously.

—Bank account? They? Was that it? Would they please listen: They were welcome to go to any bank in the country and take what they found in Louis' name! Once they had had a few dollars saved up, and they had put the money in a bank; the committee could have all of *that* money now! Since that day they had had all they could do to make ends meet.

—All right, insisted the committee, then they'd have to do as thousands of others were doing: go to the bank and borrow the money . . . no two ways about it. Most people had to do that very thing. Would she sit here snug at home, with the boys fighting in Europe, and not do a bit to help them? Would she, now?

At that particular point in the argument Lizzie lost her temper; she pounded the table:

—Did the committee really mean that two old people, working a forty of land, should go to the bank and borrow money in order to loan it to the Government in Washington? So that was it? Who could best afford to borrow the money, Louis or the Government? Her eyes blazed with righteous indignation. No, sir, nothing doing! Those who had started this circus better pay for the fun of it!

All in all it was a spirited debate. Both sides used angry words, nasty invectives that were out of harmony with the holy cause of making the world safe for democracy. It ended in total defeat for the committee. Louis and Lizzie remained adamant. At last the two men had to leave empty-handed.

That day marked the beginning of an era of terrorism. From now on Louis and Lizzie lived in constant fear of dire visitations. A curse had fallen upon the earth, smiting the prairies with all that was evil.

And no escape—neither for saint nor for sinner! One team of beggars was hardly out of the yard before the next drove in. The Red Cross must have bandages with which to bind up the wounded; the Y. M. C. A. solicited money that it might provide wholesome entertainment for the boys in the army; the United War Workers was asking aid for its many branches of organized relief work abroad, particularly in the Near East; the Lutheran Soldiers' Welfare must have money in order to save the souls of American Lutheran boys in the service; while the Liberty Loans represented the war itself The different organizations had to have their drives for the raising of funds with which to carry on the noble work. Elaborate plans were made by a central board, usually with headquarters in Washington; these plans were sent out to the chairmen of the different states; the state board appointed the county organizations, which in turn organized the townships, and the township boards the communities—all as in a great army. In the lull between battles came the usual solicitations to the local church and to the synodical budget, for schools and charities, for home and foreign missions, with only this difference that these solicitations now were organized as drives—the war taught the people many useful things. The Great Flood itself was again deluging the earth, but now there was no Ark in which a poor sucker might seek refuge. And no more did beggars come singly; now they appeared in pairs. It was as in the day of the apostles: they were called and sent out two by two.

Louis and Lizzie lived in a state of constant dread, Louis more so than she. At any time some evil might befall them. The moment he opened his eyes in the morning, Worry would be standing there waiting for him. What was going to happen during the course of the day? Coming out on the porch, he would look down the road, keeping an eye on it all the while he was out-of-doors. To hide when he saw a rig coming he could not very well do, either, because it might be a cattle-man or a grain-buyer . . . the country swarmed with them these days . . . he might cheat himself out of a fine deal.

In the drive for the second Liberty Loan Louis and Lizzie suffered their first defeat; they were beaten— there had been no escape. . . . Louis signed his name for fifty dollars. That huge sum he let the Government have in order that it might go on killing people who had never crossed his path . . . taking twenty-five of his own money and making Lizzie pony up the same amount. But the committee was not satisfied; they held out for two hundred, insisting that they must have it. Finally Lizzie rose and spoke her mind, her voice choking with anger: If the committee wanted to do them harm, they better cast them into prison! . . . It would be worse for the cattle . . . the poor, innocent beasts would starve to death . . . Louis couldn't afford a hired man . . . but since there was no other way, well —they better go to it and have it done with! She waved her arms dramatically. The men seeing that no mere words would help, took the fifty, which Louis paid in cash, and left. There were loud curses as they drove down the road.

That night man and wife held a council of war. Both saw clearly that they must take greater precaution. To keep loose money at home now was simply out of the question—it would never be safe. But if they could say truthfully that they had nothing, it would be easier to stand their ground . . . then they could invite the robbers to search.

The next day Louis made a trip to St. Paul. In the morning he was up early and fed the hogs, staying in the hoghouse for some time.

When he returned from St. Paul late in the evening Lizzie's belt was made richer by a whole five-hundred-dollar bill, and his own by a bill of one thousand; but that she could not know because he had put his away before he came home. . . . Lizzie waited until she undressed. Buckling the flap of the pocket, she confessed that the belt was a true godsend. What would she have done without it? In these days of howling wolves and manslaughter, with thieves prowling about in the night, she'd have worried herself to death with all the money lying loose about the house. There was no hint of praise in her voice, only a cold statement of fact.

Louis was already in bed:

"It would have killed me for sure!" he agreed, heartily.

"I could never have stood it!" she stated, soberly, and blew out the light.

Then came the massed drive for the third Liberty Loan, more urgent, more insistent than any of the others that had gone before; in comparison they had been only skirmishes. Now there was no hesitation, no giving quarter, no mercy—the money had to be raised; the Allies said so, and old Uncle Sam blew his nose grimly.

After much time and planning the committee of Greenfield Township went at their job with a firm hand. No slacker would slip through, on that they had made up their minds.

They opened the drive by addressing a questionnaire to every person of age within the township, requesting a complete statement of what each possessed. The formal document contained words and phrases which carried little meaning to uneducated farmer folk. But it spoke in a sober tone.

After giving a whole night of study to it Louis and Lizzie agreed that this business was too serious to fool with; they must go down to Greenfield to seek the advice of a lawyer. "We'd better be sure of the Law!" said Lizzie. The hour was after midnight and she was much wrought up. "Doggone it—if you ain't right, Lizzie!" Louis agreed. "We must find out what the Law says . . . this looks bad . . . I can see that . . . they might take our farm!" He, too, was in a state of high excitement.

By nine o'clock the next morning they walked up and down the streets of Greenfield, trying to find a lawyer whose name they did not know. To go to one who was acquainted up their way might be dangerous.

The lawyer they picked out was an elderly man of few words but with a kind face. After asking them several questions, he stated frankly that this Liberty Loan was a serious matter and that it had to be raised, explaining to them that America could not go abroad to borrow the money; hence it must be raised at home. The committee having charge of the drive had the right to assess them a fair amount; if they refused, it had the moral backing of the whole nation to force them to show cause.

—But when they had no money, neither at home nor in the bank? objected Lizzie.

—Then they must borrow.

—Could the committee force them to borrow money with which to kill people they had never seen, even? Lizzie's eyes were watering; underneath lay a white sheen, giving her face a singularly odd expression.

—No question it could. In times of a national crisis the Government automatically received absolute power and democracy ceased to function. . . . The man spoke kindly, didactically. He tried to show them that, for a man owning two hundred acres of land in Greenfield County, unencumbered, it was no hardship to raise a small loan with which to aid the Government, because a man so favorably situated must be worth at least $20,000.

At hearing this unfavorable counsel Louis' face hardened. Lizzie was chewing her tongue—there was an intermittent smacking sound.

—How much did he think they'd be condemned to raise? asked Louis, darkly.

—That he would not venture to say, but he would guess between five hundred and a thousand dollars.

"That's impossible!" exclaimed Louis, his eyes widening in terror.

"They won't get it!" declared Lizzie, hoarsely.

"Where'd we take them from, Lizzie?" Forgetting where they were, Louis turned to her for advice. . . . As he stood there staring at her he suddenly remembered that in the shoe was left only $186 . . . where in hell would he take the rest of his share?

A week later came a letter from the committee, stat-

ing briefly that Louis had been assessed $600. Would
he please appear at the Town Hall of Greenfield next
Wednesday and subscribe said amount. Nothing beyond
these cold words! Louis was so down-hearted that he
put his hat on and left the house.

During the few days intervening, little was said between the Houglums. Louis couldn't get a word out
of Lizzie. Make talk alone he could not. Whatever she
was thinking, she kept her own counsel. Her continued
silence distressed Louis so that he did not know whither
to turn. . . . What would he do? . . . In the shoe
was only $186 . . . in case the committee insisted,
where would he take the remainder from? And he
worried on Lizzie's account, also . . . the poor woman
was caught in a trap . . . she'd never take a whole
five-hundred! How could she? . . . What on earth
would they do? . . . If they only could get some one
to take care of the place, he'd take her and go away!

The visit to the Town Hall threw Louis into a
despondency in which there was no ray of light. To him
it was a terrible experience. The moment he stepped
into the Hall he was all confusion. He had expected
to meet two people, and here he was face to face with
a whole roomful. In the centre of the floor had been
placed a long table; on one side of it sat nine people,
among them three women. . . . Worse luck—how
could he chew the rag with strange womenfolks! And
they were dressed up in their Sunday fineries and sat
quiet as in church, their chairs slightly tilted back, with
their hands folded across their stomachs. . . . It was

simply awful to look at. . . . How could he and Lizzie hope to stand up against a gang like that?

Along the wall by the door stood a group of men, waiting for their names to be called and talking in low whispers. Louis and Lizzie went over to them and stood there for some time, she listening intently to what the men were saying.

Before Louis' name was called, Lizzie began to weep. Louis' efforts to hush her up only made matters worse; her sobs grew more tempestuous, finally becoming so hysterical that the chairman rose and came over to them, walking on tiptoe, with short, quiet step. An awful silence settled upon the room—it seemed that he never would get across that floor, and all the while Lizzie was getting worse.

"What is the matter here?" he asked in a whisper that could be heard clearly all through the room.

"I fear she's going to die on me!" whimpered Louis.

"Take her out of here." The man cleared his throat and repeated the command sternly.

"Get me out of here. . . . Can't you take me home?" Lizzie groaned between sobs.

Louis hurried her out and pushed her into the cart; two men untied the horse for him. Soon he drove off.

By and by she calmed down again till at last she seemed normal, except that she would not talk. Louis insisted that she go to bed—he'd do the chores alone— but that she would not hear of.

During the days following the visit to the Town Hall there was greater intimacy between man and wife than there had been since the first sweet days of their honeymoon, though a stranger listening to their talk would hardly have thought so because it sounded as if they had tangled themselves in a quarrel that never would end:

"There's no other way—we'll have to take it!" Louis would say, repeatedly.

"Not if I know it!" she would snap back at him.

"What are you going to do, then?"

"Going to do!"

"That's what I said!"

"Never mind!"

"Doggone it! can't you tell me?"

"No, I can't."

"They'll lock us up in jail. See if they don't."

"Let them do it!" Lizzie put an awful emphasis into each of the four words.

"What will you do about the cattle?"

"Never mind!"

"The beasts will starve to death!"

"Can't you shut up for once and let me have peace?"

"What will you do? . . . You hain't got six hundred dollars!"

"Leave that to me, only remember this: when they come you let me do the talking."

"Can't I say a word?"

"No, you can't. . . . Now go out and tend the hogs!"

One fine day the subcommittee, drafted for the unpleasant business of rounding up the slackers, came to the Houglum farm. The men assigned to this part of the township were Joe Veum and old Tostein Hegg. There was a broad grin on Tostein's face as he came in and sat down.

Lizzie challenged him instantly:

"When you two are out calling together it isn't hard to guess what the errand is."

"That's fine," laughed Tostein, genially; "then we don't need to waste time in bringing it up!" Taking the subscription list from his pocket and unfolding it, Tostein looked at it.

Lizzie came over to the table where the two men had seated themselves and stood before Tostein, her head bent slightly forward, her eyes blinking fast; in her words, after she began to speak, lay the calm distress of long suffering; her attitude of a moment ago had changed completely, now she seemed tired and deathly worn:

—She and Louis were more than willing to do their bit . . . whatever was reasonable . . . she hoped Tostein didn't think otherwise! They had made a special trip to town the other day in order to save him the trouble of coming here, but she had got so sick that Louis had had to leave before his turn came . . . she didn't know what had come over her lately. . . . Tostein must bear in mind that they were farming only a forty . . . both of them were getting old and worn out; neither was good for much. . . . She should have seen a doctor long ago, yet she had never thought that she could afford the money . . . she didn't like the idea of Louis' having to go to the Poor Farm after she left him. . . . Some years ago they had been caught in a bank failure and had lost every cent they had, and more too . . . they had been swindled—well, no use to mention such things . . . that wouldn't kill many Huns, would it? . . . Here she gave a bitter, tired laugh. . . . But they had agreed to borrow three hundred dollars to let the Government have . . . she hoped Tostein for once would leave their house satisfied!

Lizzie had been a long time getting this speech together, piecing phrase to phrase. It must have cost her considerable effort to deliver it, for now she reached for a chair and sank down upon it, her thin bosom heaving dangerously.

Tostein moved uneasily, trying to man himself. He had several accounts to square with Lizzie. Today he had come here with his mind made up to settle them. But this was not the Lizzie Houglum he knew; this was an old woman broken in both body and spirit, quite helpless, an object of pity rather than a formidable opponent against whom to measure one's wits. He felt displeased with the whole business and addressed himself to Louis:

—It was fine of them, he agreed . . . only not *quite* fine enough. He had figured that Louis must be worth at least $30,000, perhaps a good deal more. And inasmuch as it was a question of winning the war, he'd have to have six hundred, or any other sum between six hundred and one thousand. "Isn't that right, Joe?" he asked his partner.

Louis was standing in the middle of the floor, dry-smoking, one hand holding the bowl of his pipe, the other under the bib of his overall, looking helplessly at his wife.

The silence in the room grew heavy . . . stretched its ears, waiting for some one to speak. Tostein's fingers beat a meditative tattoo on the table. "Yes, sir," he repeated, slowly, "today we must get what we're asking for!"

"You better go and take 'em, then!" Lizzie spoke up. The ominous calm in her voice startled Tostein.

"I wouldn't use that kind of argument, no, sir. This time it's Uncle Sam who's out begging; that fellow won't take No the way he's feeling now!"

For the first time since they entered Louis spoke up:

"We hain't said No . . . this ain't fair of you, Tostein."

"It'll be six hundred, then?" Tostein asked.

As if stung, Lizzie sprang to her feet:

"No, it won't!" she shouted, her eyes ablaze. "You take what we say or get!"

"Now listen here, Mrs. Houglum!" Tostein was a bit impatient. "Joe and I have been your neighbours for thirty years. For your own good we ask you to come across. Six hundred is no hardship. There are people in this township whom the committee has treated a great deal worse."

"Some folks know a lot!" The scorn in her words lost its force because she seemed to be choking.

"So they do. And now I'll tell you something that you may not have thought of," Tostein's voice was firm: "This whole neighbourhood knows what you two are worth, every one of us—we don't need to guess. . . . There isn't a family around here having grown boys, that hasn't been forced to send some of them to the war; I myself have three there now. In every darned drive we've had we've been obliged to take part —all except you. What do you suppose people will say when it gets out that you have refused this time, too? I tell you frankly you just can't afford to let it happen!"

From now on things went from bad to worse.

"So?" Lizzie flew at Tostein. "You're going to sick the whole settlement on us? That's what you're after?" She was short of breath and had to pause. "And just because we can't give what you're demanding!"

"Go easy now, Mrs. Houglum! That sin I won't have on my conscience when I die. But we'll have to hand the list to the authorities; it won't be our fault that your name is left out. You remember, I suppose, what happened this spring to that German, living over west here on the prairie? You, Louis, must have better sense. Here's the list; now put your name down!"

"We hain't got six hundred!" protested Louis.

"All right, then I'll go to the bank and borrow what you're short!"

Lizzie pounded the table. "Put down three hundred, Louis!"

"No, you don't!" Tostein snatched the list. "It will be six or nothing."

Then Lizzie had a fit. She stormed, she wept hysterically, she stamped her foot on the floor, whirling vile names at Tostein, in between taunting him for his godliness . . . such a Christian . . . a trustee of the congregation . . . an annual delegate to all church conventions . . . always hanging on to the minister's coat tail and wiping his nose . . . what an example . . . what a man of God!

Without another word Tostein got up and left the house. That Lizzie was an impossible old hag he had known all along, but that Louis had no more sense!— Driving down the road, he remarked to Joe Veum: "I suppose the old proverb is true: 'A crazy woman makes a crazy man!'" He was still too riled up for much talk.

III

In justice to Tostein Hegg let it be said that he did his utmost that the Government might borrow $600 from Louis and Lizzie Houglum. No sooner had he swung the car into the main road than he suggested to Joe Veum that they drive over to Tom Öien. . . . Lizzie was his daughter; perhaps he could talk a little sense into her? For Tom—that Tostein knew—was a man who always wanted to do the right thing.

They met Tom in the yard. Though an old man now and compelled to use a cane because his feet were wobbly, Tom was hale and vigorous, carrying his eighty-three years easily.

After Tostein had explained his errand, Tom was silent, gazing off into vacancy, as old people often do when weighing a difficult problem. He stood thus for a long time.

At last, addressing no one in particular, Tom spoke, making many pauses: "You see . . . there is this about Lizzie . . . that she . . . she . . . ah, well . . . never mind—let me see your list, Tostein."

Tom took the paper, tottered up to the porch, where he sat down and wrote in large, unsteady hand: "Mrs. Lars Houglum $600." Then he returned the paper to Tostein. Again his gaze was on vacancy:

"I suppose . . . that this needn't . . . get any farther . . . that it may be between us, Tostein. . . . I'll see to it . . . that the money is paid . . . when the time comes." There was a great weariness in the old man's voice.

"Well——" Tostein was going to protest, but Tom interrupted him:

"Ya . . . it will be all right, Tostein! . . . I'll tend to this matter myself . . . the money will be paid when the time comes . . . you needn't worry. . . . You see, Lizzie . . . well, never mind. . . . Come in and have supper before you go. . . . It'll be paid on time."

There Tostein stood in the presence of the aged man, feeling so ashamed of himself that he didn't know whether to sneak away or to weep. This was certainly not what he had intended!

But old Tom never stirred. His dim eyes rested on blue space. He seemed utterly oblivious of Tostein's presence.

Had it not been for the young lady who was chairman of the Red Cross Auxiliary of Greenfield Township, Louis and Lizzie Houglum might have come through the World War without serious injury. But, alas! there was that chairman!

Everything about her spoke of American efficiency. Take her name, for example—Hazel Knapp, so short and with such a snap to it, with no trace of foreign origin, neither in sound nor in spelling. The old folks still persisted in using the old form Knapperud, which was a source of constant annoyance to Hazel; but she just couldn't make them drop it. Old folks are so stupid! The other young Knapperuds—there were thirteen, all told—agreed with her perfectly; it was an ugly duckling of a name, and more: absolutely impossible in this country! Good Heavens! what chance would a young American have going around with a pump-handle of a name like that? No chance at all. Real Americans would think they had come over from Norway only yesterday, and would call them greenhorns and dirty foreigners; the young Knapperuds wouldn't stand for it, and Hazel least of all. Rather than have to suffer such unbearable humiliation Hazel resolutely went to work and performed an amputation; and so the old family name that had been used for centuries was shortened to Knapp, with the K silent. After the operation Hazel felt much better. Now she dared lift her head and look people in the eye!

Hazel was now well along in the twenties, had taught country school for four years, and was engaged to Clarence Hendrickson, second lieutenant in the Rainbow Division, serving in France since last spring. A great girl Hazel was, short, a bit inclined to plumpness (which she was aware of and was trying to fight by occasionally denying herself starchy food), auburn-haired, bright-eyed, fair-complexioned, active, full of energy, with her mind always bent on reform and social uplift—the very embodiment of American efficiency.

No sooner was the suggestion voiced that Greenfield Township get its own Red Cross Auxiliary than she took the lead; she called the women together and got the work started, assuming all responsibility until an organization had been perfected. That she did so was to her only a matter of plain duty, for wasn't Clarence in the war, her Clarence, and wouldn't Clarence be needing both mits and socks? The poor boy simply must be kept warm!

At the organization meeting she got up and made a touching patriotic speech in which she wept just enough not to lose control of herself, but which left few eyes dry in the church basement that afternoon. With an overwhelming vote she was elected to the responsible position of president.

But Mrs. Helgeson resented that election; she felt herself insulted, outraged, knowing within her own bosom that she was the only logical candidate for the office of president. This spring the spirit of sacrifice had visited her, inspiring her with a new idea: since that time she had taken a basket with her every morning when she went out to open the door to the chicken-coop; all the eggs she picked in the coop at that hour she sold and sent the money to the Red Cross. This unique scheme she told to all of her acquaintances. . . . How silly people were! Couldn't they see? Had they no judgment? What could this flippersnip of a school-ma'am do in a great war? She'd bet her old shoe that Hazel had never darned her own stockings. Yes, sir, so now the boys in the trenches needn't worry about their hands and feet! Mrs. Helgeson forgot herself and spat contemptuously.

Fortunately for the boys, Mrs. Helgeson's prophecy went wide of the mark: a more zealous and energetic chairman than Hazel the Auxiliary could not have found if it had gone to work and hand-picked the whole county. Her enthusiasm never gave out; her energy was inexhaustible; the many varied duties of the presidency gave her genius a chance to unfold. Soon the organization became a model for the whole state, receiving lengthy write-ups in many papers, even outside of the state.

The secret of its success lay in Hazel herself. There was hardly a soul in America to whom the World War gave greater moments of exaltation; it inspired her so. Her enraptured enthusiasm changed into religious worship to which she surrendered herself completely. How could she help it? The war was so mighty, so beautiful, so noble. Hazel saw clearly that an era of sweet brotherhood was dawning upon a sick world. Hereafter, nations were to dwell together peacefully, with all discords gone, in everlasting harmony. This war was the war against all wars, the last superhuman struggle against Wickedness. America had been chosen by God to lead the way, her country and its noble Allies! And her own Clarence had been consecrated to the mighty conflict! On the dresser in her bedroom stood three photographs, two of Clarence in officer's uniform, and between the two, one of herself in full Red Cross garb. Every night she thanked God fervently for permitting Clarence to take part in the greatest event since the creation of the world; in her consciousness the thought glowed warmly, giving her sweet comfort. In the last crucial trial of the cataclysmic upheaval on the West Front—she saw it clearly—her Clarence, somehow, in some mysterious way, would determine the final outcome: it was he who would cut the Gordian knot. How could it be otherwise? He so pure and noble, and braver than a god! And when the victory had been won and the roaring sea had stilled, her Clarence would return to her arms and receive his reward. He'd be so distinguished-looking in his uniform; wherever he went people would salute him and bow their heads to him. And then—they would marry, Clarence and she would, and live together intimately, just they two, day and night alone! Hazel blushed deeply; the thought sent hot thrills surging through her trembling body.

All she could find about the war she read. No other

reading could she endure because it nauseated her by
its emptiness and want of reality.

No one in that community was so well posted on
the subject of German atrocities as Hazel Knapp. She
absorbed it unconsciously and always retained it. In a
spirit of religious enthusiasm she passed on her knowledge to others. . . . On such and such a date—Hazel
rarely failed to mention the date—a Belgian child had
lost his hands; on another an unfortunate French-
woman, after being raped, had had both her breasts
hacked off. Just this last Friday a whole shipload of
maimed children had been landed in New York. At
Red Cross meetings and patriotic gatherings she edified
the people with the measureless barbarism of the enemy.
To her intimate knowledge she added colour out of
her own fertile imagination and out of the fulness of
her kind heart, thus giving to the pictures greater vivid-
ness and a glow of warm sympathy. But when she told
of how the Germans utilized the carcasses of boys by
boiling them up into cannon grease, she broke down and
cried because she thought of Clarence and just couldn't
help herself.

The picture of the maimed children shipped over to
America she could not get out of her mind. One night
after she had gone to bed, she conceived a brilliant idea.
Immediately she got out of bed and wrote an urgent
letter to Headquarters, requesting that they lend her a
child; at the end of the war she'd return it! That night
she could not sleep because she was so thrilled; the plan
had intoxicated her. With an object lesson like that

she'd stand Greenfield County on end. Wherever she went she'd take the child with her. Like a new Joan of Arc she'd go up and down the state and call people to arms against the last Wickedness.

It was after being promoted to the presidency of the county organization that she requisitioned her father's Ford. From now on she was on the go constantly. With paternal pride both in the car and in his daughter, Knapperud would often remark, jovially: "Hazel she sleeps in the Ford; but the old car finds his way home just the same. Now that's some outfit I'm telling you!"

These days Hazel met many people, mostly women, and with them she had influence. She could mould them, remake them according to her own ideal. With the men, especially the older ones, it was harder; they were such clods, so coarse, so lacking in lofty ideals; she so delicate—how could she prevail against their stolid brutishness? Many she suspected of foul play. . . . To her there were only two classes of people: the real Americans who in her terminology included those who saw the war through her eyes, and on the other hand these —these—well—these infamous foreigners who invariably had pro-German leanings. The Huns at home were, in reality, more dangerous than those brutes the boys were fighting overseas, because they lived right here; sometimes you could not tell them from decent people. They would go about, oh, so slyly, infesting ignorant hearts with their heinous propaganda! Always she kept her eyes and her ears open, and woe unto the slothful citizen who failed to measure up to her devotion to the holy cause of doing everything to win the war. Immediately he was marked, branded, his mind had been poisoned. If she had only been a man! Being only a woman, she could only watch and pray . . . the men came so seldom to her meetings.

Twice in her crusade for righteousness she had encountered Mrs. Lizzie Houglum, and twice she had suffered ignominious defeat; on neither occasion did she get a cent. And what was worse still, that old woman refused to take Hazel seriously. To all of Hazel's importunings, Lizzie grinned coldly, by her teasing silence inviting her to continue. It humoured Lizzie to have this snip of a girl, whom she had seen grow up like any other youngster, and who had never done an honest day's work in all her life, come and lecture her about what she must do. . . . Too ridiculous for any use!

"All right," Lizzie had told her at their last encounter, "you'd better go on knitting socks. I s'pose that's needed. As for me and Louis, we've decided to stick by this here fellow Wilson and go on raising wheat and a few more cattle. The boys will be needing something to eat . . . they can't be living just on woolen socks and sweaters!"

—Well, would she give an acre of wheat to the Red Cross? Hazel asked, quite taken aback by the woman's coarse jest.

—She'd have to see first what the acre yielded.

—What about giving a dozen fowl, or a calf, or a heifer?

—Yes, what about it?

—Could she give a heifer?

—Course she *could*. She could give two if she wanted to. "And now I'll tell you something, Hazel— I'm glad I came to think of it: if you were half as smart with your two hands as you are with your tongue, you'd some day amount to something . . . it's the plain truth I'm telling you." At that Lizzie turned around and walked away.

Hazel fumed as she drove down the road, her forehead wrinkling darkly. Here were two old pro-Germans right in her own neighbourhood, fattening themselves on the riches of the land, yet refusing to cross a finger for its safety. And her Clarence risking his life in France for the protection of such traitors—oh, it was shameful!

In Greenfield County, as in other places, a good many boys were still at home, waiting their turn to be called. As she left the Houglums' that day, Hazel met Roy Henderson, who was on his way to town. Roy, to use Hazel's own words, was a splendid fellow and a dandy worker, and had often helped her arrange Red Cross sales and rallies of different kinds. He was the only college boy in the neighbourhood whom the draft had not yet taken. Despite the fact that there never was much substance to what he said, he was a popular speaker and always full of fun.

The moment Hazel recognized him, she stopped her Ford. . . . Now she must speak to Roy!

Still profoundly stirred, she told him of her experiences with the Houglums, repeating Lizzie's words, her indignation giving them a new substance. . . . Was it right, cried Hazel, not to teach such people a lesson? Perfectly awful to have such people right here in Greenfield County, "and you know it, Roy!"

Roy was much amused over her patriotic zeal. As he leaned carelessly on the door of his Buick his eyes caught her flushed face, playfully, greatly pleased over the meeting. . . . Hell! but that girl was good-looking when you got her excited . . . her eyes sparkled pure fire! All summer Roy had been cussing himself because he had let Clarence Hendrickson snatch that girl right from under his nose. He could just as well have had her himself.

"What do you want done to Mrs. Houglum?" Roy laughed teasingly, and held Hazel's eyes.

"Oh, how can I tell?" she cried, in dismay. "If I were a man and not just a helpless woman, I wouldn't be asking you." Hazel leaned over, pounding the door of the Ford. "I'd teach her and that old skinflint of a husband of hers a lesson in patriotism that they'd never forget—they are a disgrace to the whole state!"

"Do you mean for me to go and hang them, Hazel?"

"I don't care, Roy. Just so you teach them what it means to be an American these days!"

"Perhaps I better stand Lizzie against the barn wall and shoot her at sunrise? But I'd much prefer to do it during the noon hour . . . I'm disgustingly lazy in the morning!"

"Oh, Roy, don't be mean! How can you take such things so lightly?"

Roy was in sparkling humour:

"All right, then, let's say shooting at sunrise for her. But what about the old man? You're doing the court-martialling and must name the penalty. What about sending him to France with a good sweater for Clarence?"

"Oh, Roy, you're such a tease!" Giving him a warm look, she started the Ford and drove off.

Roy let his Buick idle the few miles into town. Hazel's account of her set-to with Lizzie Houglum had come back to him. It was disgusting. She was right. Here these people did only what they wanted to, while everybody else. . . . In a few days he'd be off himself, though he'd have liked nothing better just now than to start in on his law course. . . . A shame that such people could do exactly as they pleased!

In town he ran into a crowd of neighbour boys; there were Olaf Holm, Arthur Nelson, Henry John-son, the two Wagner boys, and Andrew Steen—all of them adrift—lost, and leading an unnatural existence, because in a few days they would be off, to where and for what adventures they did not know; but it was romantic, yet so unreal. . . . They sensed a terrible grimness which they tried to ward off by affecting a care-free swagger. Roy told them jokingly about the encounter Hazel Knapp had with Mrs. Houglum, more in fun than with any purpose.

The boys knew the Houglums and enjoyed the story,

getting a good laugh. Arthur Nelson, a tall, rawboned youth given to coarse jokes, suggested enthusiastically that they get up a gang and drive over some evening —"just to scare the liver out of the old bitch . . . make her wet her pants or kiss the flag or something. Come on, let's have some good fun, boys! Aren't we the fellows to shoot hell out of the Kaiser?"

Other boys came by, joining the crowd. The story was repeated, and so was Nelson's motion. Plans were laid to notify a few more reliable fellows, and for all to meet at the Green Prairie Schoolhouse next Saturday night at ten o'clock. Then they would decide what more ought to be done. "Leave it to me," said Arthur Nelson; "I'll think of something . . . we'll have some fun all right!"

IV

It was half past eleven before the crowd was ready to leave the schoolhouse Saturday night. Some of the boys were slow in coming, and after they were all assembled it took a long time to find a plan of operation on which they all could agree. There were other things, too, causing delay: one of the Wagner boys, before coming out, had made a visit to Tom Olson's saloon, where he had so loaded down his Ford with pony kegs that he had been riding on the axle all the way out here. The other boys also didn't appear empty-handed, but had brought a drop or two with them. By the time the meeting began several of the boys were half-seas over already, and so jolly and full of bright ideas of what must be done, that you couldn't get a word in edgewise; all wanted to talk at the same time and no one would listen. Be it said to Roy's credit that with this part of the program he was much displeased.

A plan was perfected at last: eight men in two Fords were to be sent ahead and were to place themselves as guards about the house, lest the fox get away before the hunters should arrive, for then they would all be in a hell of a hole. The program proper was worked out in great detail. In the yard they would have a big bonfire; near it they'd put a pole with a flag tied to the top; at the foot the two culprits were to stand; around the pole the men were to form a circle, hold hands and sing "America" and "Star-spangled Banner"; after the singing Roy was to make a speech, whereupon Louis and Lizzie were to kneel before the flag; then the flag was to be taken down and the two malefactors would have to kiss it. But the oath of allegiance had to be abandoned because disagreement arose on several points: Should they take the oath kneeling or standing? Was it to be administered in English or in Norwegian? Was it to be the same for both Lizzie and Louis; and finally—should the oath be made up of common cussings, just for fun, or should it be a serious performance and hence dignified? An agreement being impossible, the oath was given up. The flag ceremony disposed of, Sam Barstad, the auctioneer for the local

Red Cross Auxiliary, was to step out of the heart of the night, dressed up as Uncle Sam, and solemnly command Lizzie and Louis to give $50 to the Red Cross and in addition demand a promise that they, hereafter, contribute liberally to every drive. To give his demand greater force, all who had revolvers and guns with them were to fire one volley. The final item, which had nothing to do with the program, was an agreement by the participants that all should smear their faces with mud in order that there might be no nonsense afterward.

When the program had been decided upon Steve Berg got to his feet, demanding to be heard in a matter that weighed heavily on his stomach. He had a special favour to ask: Would they hear him out of the generosity of their hearts? The man spoke pleadingly and seemed near to tears: would they entrust to him the responsibility of going into the house to awaken Lizzie? Because he had an old account to settle with the lady: Exactly four years ago when he, in all innocence, had paid a visit to her melon patch just to sample what kind she was growing, she had sneaked up on him from behind and had whacked him a hell of a crack right across his stern—she must have used a blacksnake. May God eternally forgive him if he didn't carry the scars yet! They might bar him from getting into the war unless the army doctors could fit him with a new pair of bottoms! It would be a disgrace if he should have to stay home and just suck his thumb while the other boys went overseas to hobnob with the Kaiser. "Believe me, boys," he concluded, dramatically, "that was some whack!" Steve spoke a strange mixture of Norwegian and English, a language all his own. The boys howled with laughter, agreeing unanimously that he was the man for the job. Iver Brun and John Pederson were appointed assistants:

At last the procession was off for the Houglum farm, the two Fords with the guards in the lead. In order to cause as little disturbance as possible, the Fords drove into a cornfield near the yard and the men hurried off toward the house. An intense excitement began to take hold of them. They were new at this business of making war, the night pitch dark, and so deadly quiet; a queer sensation gripped their hearts as they sneaked up to the house and took their positions.

Soon the others arrived, a long row of automobiles —Fords, Buicks and Overlands, but mostly Fords, breaking file as they entered the yard, driving over to the barn and to the corncrib to park. Not a word. Not a sound!

Some of the boys went to the woodshed for armfuls of wood; others brought kindling from an old strawpile down by the barn. When the bonfire had been lit and the flag pole placed near by, Roy Henderson drove his Buick close up, rose to his full height, and commanded in a loud, clear voice:

"All right, boys, bring 'em out!"

As Steve Berg and his two companions stepped out of the darkness and ran up to the house a joyous roar went up from the crowd. The fun they had come for was on; the bonfire crackled and blazed; yells and shouts rent the night; shot upon shot was fired.

"Now let's give 'em hell!" shouted Arthur Nelson, encouragingly.

In the meantime the three boys were prowling about in the house, Iver and John carrying flashlights. As soon as they entered the kitchen—the door was unlocked—Steve suggested that they halt and have a brief council of war; he pulled out a bottle which he passed around. "Pure rye, fellows! Let's have a drop before thrusting our heads into the lion's den!"

The three boys drank deep draughts, smacking their lips and declaring themselves fit to tackle Mrs. Goliath herself. And now they called in unison to their host and hostess to hurry into their breeches. The picnic was about to begin, they had come with the invitation!

Not a peep, not a sound of any kind in reply. The house was as dead and deserted as an empty grave. The light from the bonfire danced in through the window and cast a spooky glimmer on the walls of the room, forming fantastic, weird figures.

Steve proposed that they sit down and give Lizzie time to get her skirt on. They couldn't take her to the picnic undressed; the poor girl might catch cold and develop appendicitis—you could never tell what queer things the womenfolks might think up; he had taken a girl out once and she had suddenly got nosebleed. He had been scared stiff 'cause he was afraid she'd leak dry right there! . . . Steve was in a joyous mood and proposed that they sing a song to cheer up their hostess.

But the other two, wanting to get out, the quicker the better, called louder and more persistently than before.

Not a sound, save the echo of their own voices, answered them; the house might have been an empty church in the dead of night.

"Damn it all," observed Steve, rising resolutely, "then we shall have to dress her ourselves. It'll be a tough job, but I guess we can manage her all right. Well, come on boys!"

They went into the bedroom, threw the flashlight on to the bed and found it empty; the bed was all made, but not a soul to be seen.

"Now, if that doesn't beat the Devil!" Steve was so disappointed that he could have sat right down and howled.

"Cheer up, old boy!" said Iver. "This is only a spare bed; we'll find the folks upstairs!"

But when they got up into the loft, they found the rooms empty. Not even bedclothes on the beds.

—So! The foxes had hidden? Well, then they'd have to dig them out, no two ways about that! The three began to search, upstairs and down, every possible nook and corner in the whole house; but no sign of life. Only living shadows that whirled themselves on wall and window, bursting with uncanny, dark mystery.

Iver and John went out to the others with the distressing tidings that the nest was empty and the birds flown. There was not a cockroach left in the old den!

A council of war was held. . . . This was Saturday night. Perhaps the folks were out gadding? They must return sometime before morning? Most likely they were over at Tom Öien's? The boys decided to wait for further developments; the night was young yet; in the Wagner Ford lay three more kegs ready to be tapped. Why hurry?

By reasons of his scars, Steve was unwilling to give up. He had not come out with the other two boys. For the second time he had begun to search the house, cellar to roof. It was pitch dark now, but, fortunately, he had matches!—Going upstairs again and prowling around, striking off one match after another, he discovered in one of the bedrooms a trapdoor in the ceiling. "Aha!" he exclaimed, joyously. "There's the roost, and they've pulled the ladder up after them! . . . Well, old girl, you've bottled yourself up tighter than a teetotaler, but we'll try to get you uncorked—never you fear!"

Steve could not get his feet to mind him, because both insisted on being in the air at the same time, yet he got the table shoved into place and managed to climb up on it. Even so he could barely touch the sky with his fingers and the heavens refused to open at his knock. "Well, God bless her if she ain't sitting on it!" Steve listened and was sure he heard whisperings, whether prayers or something worse he could not tell because his mood was too exalted.

Getting down from the table, he placed a chair upon it and with much wavering and hesitance and many gruntings he managed to balance on the chair. Bracing his shoulders against the door, he forced it open with a bang, then held his breath and listened: Surer than hell, there she was!—He stuck his head up through the door, calling coaxingly: "Now you quit fooling with her, you old squaw-humper, and let the girl come to me!"

Disgusted because he got no answer, he caught a firm hold of two two-by-fours and raised himself until he sat on one of them. A musty smell took his breath away. What an awful hole for people to be in! In order to revive himself he drew the bottle from his pocket and emptied it in one draught. Then he crept into the dark loft, lighting his way with matches, of which he fortunately happened to have a good supply; otherwise he would never have got out of this hole alive.

When he finally came outside the festivities were in full swing and the boys so jolly that they couldn't decide which foot to stand on, trying now one and now another; sometimes both at the same time.

To Steve's solemn announcement that neither host nor hostess could be found, a grand scheme sprang up in Arthur Nelson's mind: They must leave some visible evidence of people having been here, or the expedition would have been in vain! Accordingly they fetched from the bedroom several garments, some belonging to Louis, others to Lizzie. The clothes were stuffed with hay and straw, and amid lusty cheers two figures holding hands were nailed to the barn wall. Both wore hats. Lizzie, being only a frail woman, was given stockings. The sight of the dummies partly restored Steve's good humour. "Well, siree, old girl," he said, patting her front, "I'd give a dollar if I could stand behind this wall and hear what you say when you see this picture of yourself! Oh, boys, won't she spit black, though!"

Suddenly some one saw sparks popping out of the roof of the house. The boys turned silent, looking helplessly into the black night. . . . What? Was Lizzie cooking coffee for them? Up so early in the morning?

With a loud roar the flames burst through the roof, sending an ocean of stars flying skyward, black smoke rolling after as if vomited out of the throat of a monster. In a moment the whole house was a huge bonfire. Amid the crackling and roaring the roof fell crashing into the sea of flames. The next minute the walls followed. Luckily the wind stood off the outhouses or they would have been in danger.

Instantly the boys sobered—that is, most of them did. With feverish haste Roy Henderson was trying to gather them. "Now, boys, this is dangerous business and don't fool yourselves. Get into your cars at once and take a roundabout way home. It must be clearly understood that not a single one of you has been here tonight, no matter how often and how much you're questioned. You simply know nothing about it. Otherwise we'll all go to the pen instead of to war. . . . Let's get away at once!"

In a heavy sea Steve went navigating about the yard, swearing and carrying on. . . . No, he would not leave yet—not *he!* He'd first see if Lizzie —— Two boys took him by force, threw him into a car, and drove off.

Tallakson and Bratlien were the first of the neighbours to arrive at the fire, and they came too late to be of any use. Stalking about in the yard, they saw some empty kegs and found a few bottles.

"These," said Tallakson, "we might as well take and throw into the car and save Louis the work."

"Guess we might as well," agreed Bratlien. "You're right there!"

Both were absolutely sure that they had passed their own boys down at the corner of the Green Prairie Schoolhouse, in Tallakson's old Ford, though the car drove at such a reckless speed that they could hardly see either the car or the occupants. But the auto had only one light . . . and it was a Ford. Bratlien had caught a glimpse of a light cap. . . . Both fathers had ambitions for their boys and thought it safest to remove all signs. For a long while they prowled about in the yard, looking for others.

—Ah, well, observed Tallakson, feeling the need of talk as they drove homeward, it would, after all, be a fine thing for Louis and Lizzie to get themselves a new house for the winter . . . the boys had, of course, seen to it that nothing worse had happened . . . Louis certainly carried insurance on the buildings . . . and he had plenty of money . . . no trick at all for him to build himself a new house!

—Certainly . . . of course! nodded Bratlien, who had been too deep in his own thought to hear what the other man had said. What he was thinking was so interesting that he must discuss it with some one.

—Did he say build? Well . . . it was about time for

Louis and Lizzie to give up farming. What? . . .
They should sell out now and move to town . . . could
well afford it. What did he say? . . . The man who
bought might not be satisfied with the buildings Louis
put up? What? "Don't you—don't you think he ought
to sell now?" he yelled into Tallakson's ear; they were
driving fast and the motor of the Studebaker hummed
like a threshing-machine.

v

Much of the loose talk which floated about regarding
the fire at the Houglums' consisted of vague allusions
and half-spoken guesses. No one seemed to know anything, yet all were curious. All approached the matter
in a roundabout way. As to the cause of the fire, one
guessed this, another that. . . . They had had an old
chimney at Houglums', said one. Yes, said another,
and now the evenings were getting chilly . . . Lizzie
had perhaps done her Saturday's baking . . . just a
spark would be enough. . . . Louis always sat up in
the evening, smoking . . . he might have thrown a
match—the Lord save us from the danger of fire! A
good thing that Louis and Lizzie were away when it
happened . . . they had at least escaped seeing their
house burn down. . . . Well now, had they really been
away? asked some one. Where would Lizzie have gone
that time of the night—she who never went any place?

Go? How you talk! Of course she must have been somewhere, you know that . . . or. . . . Shall I make you a cup of coffee? . . . Have you heard about the terrible accident at Dale's? Harold has lost his right ear . . . the doctor had to cut it clear off . . . he fell against the hay-rake . . . it happened last Saturday night. . . . The boy is disfigured for life. . . . Well —anyway, he won't have to go to war . . . the old folks can be glad of that!

. . . Last Saturday night, you say? Hm—how could that be? Was he out late? Is that so? Well now . . . fine weather for the corn. . . . Won't you have another cup? Most of this talk was among the women.

There was one fact in connection with the accident which the men never mentioned, not unless there happened to be only two present, and the one felt he could trust the other: How did it come that people got there too late to do anything? And—listen—where had the cars been that night? Yes, where had all the cars been? Tallakson's was gone when he ran to the shed to get his? So was Berg's? The same thing at Chris Nelson's —why, there wasn't a car to be found in the whole neighbourhood!

Where Louis and Lizzie had been during the fire no one ever found out, because, for certain reasons, no one cared to ask Louis point-blank. And, of course, it was nobody's business. Didn't a man have a perfect right to go wherever he pleased? A good thing he was away . . . for her sake, anyway . . . women are easily scared. . . . It was funny, though, doggone it if it wasn't! . . . They couldn't have been very far, though. . . . What was that you said?

But it was generally agreed that no serious harm had been done . . . anyway, not since the Houglums had happened to be away, because Louis had the house well insured . . . more than full value by a good margin. The neighbours soon knew all about the insurance: On Monday after the fire Tostein Hegg had made a special trip to town to find out about the insurance, and hadn't given up before he had the facts. In telling about it, Tostein stated emphatically that, though neither Louis nor Lizzie—and certainly not Lizzie—were his best friends, he would have taken up a subscription for them and himself canvassed the neighbourhood. . . . A misfortune like that is no fun for any man; but since Louis would get at least one-third more than the house actually was worth, Tostein had dropped the idea. He talked at great length about what he had intended to do . . . they must remember, he said, that old Tom Öien was a pretty decent sort of man!

The night after Tostein had made his great drive in the interest of the Liberty Loan Louis and Lizzie moved out of their bedroom and up into the hayloft. Lizzie suggested that they make the change . . . as long as the weather continued fine, it wouldn't hurt them to sleep in the hay. . . . That Tostein was a mean old fox . . . you could never tell what he was up to . . . she didn't just like the way he had looked at her when he left the house. . . . They better take bedding from the upstairs. "Now get a move on yourself so we can get this done!" she nagged Louis.

Neither of them had gone to sleep yet when the crowd came.

"There they are now—the skunks!" Lizzie whispered into Louis' ear, which opened wide to the terrible noises outside.

Unable to utter a word, he only groaned incoherently, from the throat down to the pit of his stomach, a long groan.

They heard car after car drive up and stop. . . . Would the procession never end? There must be at least a thousand. The sound of hurrying and scurrying feet came up to them, and the mutterings of low voices. . . . There some one swore loudly, after which followed much jeering and coarse laughter.

Lizzie thought she recognized at least some of the voices. A strange calmness had come upon her. She was in a high mood, and not more scared than *that!* She wanted to get up and see. She'd like to go out and have a talk with those fellows! she whispered into Louis' wide ear.

But he didn't hear a word of what she said; he lay there shaking, as though in a severe fit of ague, just hugging his wife. His helplessness was so great that she felt pity for him as she might have felt had he been her only child, suddenly very ill. He crushed her to him till she could hardly breathe. "Now, don't be so silly, Louis!" she crooned over him.

The hubbub of voices right outside the wall, the

hammering in of nails, the obscene comments on herself, made her forget Louis because now she must hear every word or her breath would leave her for good. And when a moment later the fire of the burning house began to roar, she became unmanageable. Tearing herself loose from his frantic embrace, she glided down from the ledge in the solid wall of hay where they were nesting. Behind her rose a low whining that fainted away in the dark.

In one of the boards was a big knothole; she knew exactly where to find it. Stealthily, catlike, she slid along the wall. She thrust one eye through the hole and watched her house burn down.

As she watched, her hands involuntarily felt around her waist till they found what they sought and her thumbs stuck in the belt. The eye in the hole glowed redder than the fire itself, smarting as though it had been squirted with strong brine. Otherwise she was cool and composed, the strange calm possessing her gave her a feeling of power; across her wrinkled, wizened face lay a faint smile. Not a word, not a sigh came over her parched lips.

Little by little as her house was turned to ashes, she felt herself being choked. . . . The ashes settled upon her, thicker and heavier, piling up in great heaps. And they were colder and clammier than the sleet on a late fall night. Suddenly she was freezing; her teeth chattered. Am I turning into cold ashes myself? The thought was ridiculous, but she had no time to follow it because she must keep her eye on those men in the yard.

She narrowed the lid, trying to force greater clarity of vision into her sight to focus it on the figures. But no matter how much light she screwed into the glowing eye, she could not recognize their faces—they were blacker than the shadows coming out of the womb of Darkness.

Drawn by some mysterious force, she stole over to the stairs. Faintly from up in the hay came low whimperings, hardly audible. For an instant she halted at the top of the stairs, then slipped down the steps. At the bottom she stopped to listen. Presently she glided through the door on the south side, facing the corn-crib . . . stood there. Had all of them escaped already? Straining her eyes in the direction of the crib she saw the outlines of a car close up against the crib . . . there was no one in it. Again she moved; like a shadow she glided over to the hogpen, followed the rail fence till she reached the corner of the crib. She was near the car now. Along the south wall of the crib grew a tall hedge of sunflowers. She disappeared in it. The fingers of her right hand groped searchingly along the stone foundation just back of her, found a loose object around which her hand closed convulsively.

—Now wait, wait! Tramping feet came hurrying toward her. Her lean body bent like the bow in the hands of a strong archer. She gripped the sharp edges of the stone till the blood oozed out.

"She'll be good and mad when she gets home in the morning . . . believe me! . . . Wonder how that darn fire could have started?" some one was speaking near her.

Her ears drank in every word. . . . That voice was not Tostein's!

"Just so they weren't in there!" This voice, too, was young, and so low and full of fear that she could hardly catch the words.

—That's that Dale boy! she thought.

The two black figures jumped into the car; a motor started to hum; two glaring, bright lights flung themselves down the road. Just as the car gathered speed, a stone shot through the darkness, striking first the ear of the man by the driver, then crashing through the windshield, breaking it into a thousand pieces which flew jingling down over the hood and the fenders. The motor didn't stop; the man at the wheel drove like one possessed. . . . What sort of deviltry was loose in the hogpen? The other man only groaned, holding his cut ear.

The yard was empty now. The harsh stench of smoke stuck in Lizzie's throat.

After circling about the heap of ashes, she remembered Louis, and went back into the loft to see about him. She laughed bitterly to herself. How scared he had been! Up in the hay she found a groaning, stinking heap that was breathing and had life, but was not a man, nor a human being, just an animal wallowing in its own filth. She sat down and sobbed, partly from anger, partly from pity. "Get yourself out of here, you dirty old ape, and change your clothes!" she croaked.

Before she could go on, her ear caught a whir of a car driving into the yard. "Hush! Lie still! Here they are again!"

Before Louis had time to think of what was happening she was down the stairs, had slipped out again, and had crossed the short space between the barn and the crib. Sliding swiftly and noiselessly into the crib and, peeping between the slats, she recognized Tallakson and Bratlien, her ears sucking in most of what they said. . . . By and by other neighbours arrived, among them Tostein Hegg. But when Lizzie heard Tostein say to Jim Olson that in his opinion this visitation came upon Lizzie Houglum as a just punishment for her greediness, there arose in her throat a cold, dry laugh that gave a rasping sound. She clenched her fists, muttering to herself: "That man's hide I'm going to have!"

Just as the first faint blush of light came into the eastern sky, the last car drove away. Satisfied that no one would be coming back, Lizzie went to the barn and called to Louis.

She continued to walk about inspecting things, trying to find out just how much damage had been done.

The deep glow of the Sabbath morning spread slowly over the silent prairies, flooding them with golden, rich day. From a hillside a prairie chicken cooed to her mate, he answering drowsily from his roost on another. Upon every straw and blade of grass the dew had laid itself heavily, in rows of sparkling crystals. Now and then a puff of wind, lolling across the yard, picked up particles of ashes and toyed them in the air, whiffing the odour of burnt wood far out on the prairie.

A glorious sun rode majestically up the high archway of the heavens. But Lizzie was not aware of it. She had gone back of the barn where the ground rose into a knoll, giving wide view and fair vision over the country round about. She saw the groves, and went from one to the other: there lived Bratlien; a little beyond, Tallakson; next to him John Henderson; then Tostein Hegg; to the west and the northwest lay the Dale farm; then Brun's—here she could see the houses; in the neighbourhood up north lived the Olsons and the Nelsons. All of them had been here during the night and had burnt the house over her head . . . had wanted to burn her, too. At each place she stopped long enough to unbosom herself of dark, hot wishes, soaked in hatred, which came rising within her like black flood waters. Having made the rounds, she turned and came back by the same road, her head shaking as if suffering with St. Vitus's dance, her eyes small and gleaming. But in her smouldering heart there was always more unsaid . . . always more . . . and then more.

She was jerked back to reality by the sound of long, low yelpings. Coming hurriedly around the corner of the barn she saw Louis, barefooted, in his underclothes, stand looking up at the two crucified figures on the wall. With a low, unearthly cry she snatched up a stick and struck him a hard blow from behind. "Now you go down to the creek and wash yourself—go, I tell you!" she hissed, pursuing him down the hill. The outburst seemed to give her relief; returning to the barn, she took the figures down, emptied the clothes, shook them out, then folded them up carefully.

For the next two weeks sleep fled from them. During the interminable stretch of darkness Louis lay tossing, fighting a terrible fear. . . . Since they had begun with arson, they'd not stop at murder! Suddenly he would break into tears, crying pitifully, and Lizzie would chase him out of bed.

With her it was not fear; she had more important things to think of. She was always the last to bed. Every night before coming up into the loft she placed the ax at the foot of the stairs. . . . Had the ax been there the other night, she'd have had one of them, at least . . . perhaps two . . . even more! . . . Every night she lay wide awake, analysing the slightest sound. She knew exactly where the ax was standing; in her thoughts she gripped the handle and felt her arm grow rich with strength . . . she hewed them down like weeds . . . one by one, in rows, and felt voluptuous pleasure—if they only would come again!

At times Louis feared her more than any other power, of man or God. In her was no pity. Sometimes the gleam in her eye and the expression of her face would make his blood run cold. He did not know where to flee from her because she was over him constantly; since there was no house for her to be in, she was always with him, always after him, demanding mad things: Wasn't he a man? she would ask, tauntingly. Weren't there guns and bullets to be had in town? And dynamite? Why did he stand there staring at her like a dead fish? If she were a man, in less than one week she'd have the whole of Greenfield Township blown into a thousand bits. . . . "Can't you see," she raved, "that they're trying to drive you off the farm so that they can have it themselves? Tostein wants it, so does that old fox Bratlien. It isn't your life they're after. What would they want with the life of an old dead fish? Oh, no, it's me they want to get because then they can scare you into nothingness and take the farm. . . . Shut your mouth, talking about the law! *Law?* There is no law. They rob and burn and hang—who cares about law? If I were married to a man, we'd now have some fun. . . . Hold your tongue and let me think!"

One day Louis went to town to see about the insurance money. To his astonishment, he was paid every cent. In an exalted mood he came home and counted out to Lizzie fifteen hundred dollars as her share of the money. She took it, snorting contemptuously: Must be some kind of deviltry about this? Junk, she s'posed? . . . Since he could pluck thousands out of the air, why hadn't he gone and got them long ago? . . . Did he have to wait for the neighbours to start the fire? She could have done that for him!

Because the season was so far advanced, the Houglums did not build that fall, but sold most of the poultry and moved into the chicken-coop—during the winter anyway, there wouldn't be much income from the chickens. Like most farmers thereabout, Louis kept a supply of lumber in his machine shed. Now he rebuilt the coop by nailing two-by-fours on the outside, laying paper across them, and siding on top. The inside he boarded up with shiplap; then he laid a double floor. When finished, that house, though not spacious, and rather low under the ceiling, was perhaps the warmest dwelling in all of Greenfield County.

VI

To the farming communities of the Middle West the spring of 1919 brought a strange infection, a peculiar distemper that lay hold of people's minds and finally worked itself out in an economic upheaval, the like of which that section of the country had not seen before. It came on with the mild weather, unnoticed, only a playful fancy in the minds of folk whose enthusiasm is easily kindled. With the lengthening days and the spring blooming into high summer the unrest heightened in intensity and widened into madness. The farmer riding on his cultivator beheld a new land, a fabulous goldened shore; and once he had caught the enchanted vision he stopped, bewildered because the realities which hitherto had guided him, had suddenly been swept away.

The years lying between the fall of 1914 and the spring of 1919 had seen no movement in farm land. There were no buyers and no farmer seemed anxious to sell. But in 1919 many boys, who had come of age during the war, and men mustered out of service, were looking for homes. Throughout the agricultural section great heaps of wealth had been accumulating—how could it be put to use? The banks were filled to overflowing with money and looking for profitable outlets. And in every little hamlet, from Dan to Beersheba, dealers in real estate sat watching developments, like prophets reading the signs of the time.

Signs and rumours there had been since the Armistice, but not until in the spring did the promises begin to be fulfilled. A shudder of wonder went through the community when a farm in the Greenfield settlement sold for $175 an acre; people could not believe it and sat up rubbing their eyes. A month later the same farm changed hands at $190, and two others were sold for $185 and $187, respectively. No one could tell where this madness would end. Golden clouds were rising on the horizon; folk saw them and wondered. . . .

While the spring work was on, and even more so after the crops were in, land-buyers began flocking into the settlements of southern Minnesota, like birds hungry from a long passage—coming up from Illinois, from Iowa, and from far-off Eastern states. They asked two questions: What was the quality of the soil on this farm, and what improvements did it have? Then they wrote out a check, and before one could wink an eye they were gone. By the time the corn was up, no less than seven farms in Greenfield Township had new owners, four of the farms having been sold twice in less than two months, two of them three times, and all seven were still offered for sale.

And the fever raged on. In wide-eyed wonder people looked at their possessions: was the land under their feet pure gold? It happened repeatedly that the man who had carved a home out of the wilderness got up and left his homestead as though it were a worn-out garment he had sold to the highest bidder. Nothing was any longer held sacred. In July a pastor in one of the most solid Norwegian communities in America wrote to a friend:

In these parts our church is about done for. For the last two days I've been knocking about in my Ford, counting the farms for sale. I find no less than forty. If you happen to have a few thousand salted away in an old sock, I advise you to put it on and come right up! I'd rather have you take the profit than see a stranger run away with it. We had better leave the ministry and go into real estate.

People walked about in a state of delirium. Every day brought new reports of fabulous sales.

That summer a great joy, a strange gladness, came into the little henhouse on the Houglum farm. Life was opening up new and unexpected possibilities, turning Lizzie's mind to brighter things.

One day a man drove into the yard and without any preliminaries offered them $190 cash for their farm provided they would give him the entire crop, and possession within two weeks.

Louis looked at Lizzie. But she refused to meet his eye. The man was making a fine offer, and since she would not say, Louis began to dicker with him: How could they let him have all the crop? They had to have food . . . they couldn't sell the bread out of their mouths and live on air . . . besides ——

"What are your terms, then?" the man asked.

"We aren't selling!" Lizzie spoke up. "Not yet, anyway."

"That's right, as Lizzie says," Louis echoed. "Besides, this farm should be worth more, and we'd have to have the crop, no two ways about that."

The man swore and drove off in a temper.

But they didn't mind that. Louis began to laugh, and to hear him laugh in this way was so funny that she had to join in. And there both of them stood, excited as two school children about to make their first date.

Two days later a man from the neighbourhood up north came to see the Houglums on important business. From the way he talked he couldn't be entirely sober. He had come to buy Louis out, he said. Would he consider two hundred per, and half the crop?

—Half the crop? Louis stared hard at the man, his mouth drivelling.

—Oh, well, the crop didn't matter, since Louis made a point of it. He had plenty to harvest at home. But next week his oldest son was getting married, and he s'posed it was up to the old man to provide a nest for the kids to coo in. Could they move out on short notice?

—They could not! Lizzie stated emphatically. They hadn't even thought of selling out . . . they'd have to think it over . . . he better come back later. . . . Could he pay cash?

—Cash? Well, he ought to be able to raise $40,000. The man that couldn't do that these days certainly wasn't much good!

Louis was about to speak, when Lizzie caught his eye and checked him. Her head was thrown back; her features softened under the broad smile spreading over her face; her voice sounded unusually kind:

"You drive over tomorrow night, and Louis and I will give you some kind of an answer. . . . Bring your wife with you . . . I used to know her."

That night Louis and Lizzie sat by the table figuring and arguing till long after their usual bedtime, she with a sheet of paper before her on which she had written several times the same sum—$40,000. On both faces lay a weird, unearthly expression. They laughed together uproariously and nagged each other by turns. Louis accused Lizzie of being crazy, and immediately Lizzie would say that Louis was crazier still—no mistake about that! Then both would go on laughing again. Never before had the henhouse witnessed such happiness.

Suddenly Lizzie made the important discovery that an additional five dollars per acre would give each of them an additional five hundred, and likewise, that ten would make a whole thousand more. This discovery she explained to Louis, and now they began to add and figure until the price was $225 an acre, which, as Lizzie pointed out, would make $22,500 for each.

"Ya, ya, ya, there you go!" Louis wasn't angry; there was a grin on his face.

Lizzie paid no attention. "When we get two hundred and thirty," she said with finality, "we'll let the old farm go!"

"You're plumb crazy! Why, if we get two hundred twenty . . . two hundred twenty . . . don't you see, that would give you twenty-two thousand dollars . . . doggone it! you oughtn't kick at that!"

"You're crazy yourself," she retorted, "that's what. Not a cent under two hundred thirty because that will bring you twenty-three thousand. . . . I'll stand for no more fooling . . . when I want to *give* you the money!"

"You can never get it, Lizzie!"

"Not unless I had more sense than you!"

"You're mad, that's what. I'll have to take you to Saint Peter. How can anyone be fool enough to pay forty-six thousand for a piece of land with no house?"

And now Lizzie became serious:

"I want you to promise me one thing: when the next buyer shows up, I'm to do the talking. If I'm not around, you call me . . . this farm is worth money . . . I know what I want for my half!"

The neighbour from the north did not return, which was fortunate, because only a few days later Tostein Hegg sold at two hundred and thirty-five, and his land, though it had better buildings, could not be compared in value to the Houglum farm. When she heard the news Lizzie felt so encouraged that she could have gone right over and thanked Tostein—for once in his life he had done a decent thing!

The next prospect was a real-estate dealer from Akron, and a more interesting man had never come to the farm. Talk flowed from his mouth in a steady stream; in all he said there was a laugh, yet you couldn't tell whether he was serious or only joking, because all the time he was so sober-faced.

He made an opening bid of one hundred and sixty-five an acre, then proceeded to raise it gradually, first by adding half-dollars, then dollars, finally whole five-dollars, keeping it up till he had reached two hundred, but there he rested for a little while. This farm, he declared, must be his, he'd die unless he got it; if there was no other way, he'd have to marry Lizzie—Louis would have to take his wife and get along as best he could! . . . Certainly he had to have the farm, that's what he had come here for. . . . Would they take two ten? A shame to offer such dowry, but if he got Lizzie —"Oh, but won't we have a jolly time, you and I? . . . No? Well, then you just don't appreciate what good courting's like . . . I was saying two ten, hoy there, old girl, come on!"

His amusing talk put Lizzie in fine spirits. . . . They had had that offer before, she informed him, only the other day . . . and cash, too.

"Two ten per, and all cash?" the man cried in dismay. "Well, well, *well*—now I never heard the beat!— Why didn't you add another ten and close the deal? . . . That's the way to do business. . . . There're no greater fools than us real estate men . . . that's what I keep telling my wife and she won't believe me. We're

crazy in the head; there's no worse madness than that
. . . forty-two thousand, and you turned that down!"

The man got up, evidently ready to leave. But just
as he was going he turned to Lizzie:

"Suppose, that just for fun I offered you two fifteen,
not that I'm crazy enough to do it, but suppose I did
—I merely ask, of course?"

"Then I'd say two thirty," she said; it was difficult
for her to get the words out, "and all cash!" Now let
him squirm! This was the greatest fun she had ever
had.

The man gave a deep, long groan, as if overcome by
a sudden pain. "Forty-six thousand dollars cash for a
handful of common dirt and this toothpick of a house!
There's something wrong with your head."

Louis had something in his throat and was coughing
violently: "Well—er—now—that is to say—Lizzie
means ——"

Lizzie cut him short:

"Louis means that we intend to get two forty when
we sell, but today you can have it for two thirty—since
you insist on getting me into the bargain." Her voice
was clear and ringing; the look in her eye held Louis.

Then the buyer turned around and did an odd thing:
he insisted on selling them a farm of a hundred and
sixty acres located about twenty miles north of their
place. He would let them have it as a gift, at two ten
per acre. "Yes, sir, honey," he turned to Lizzie,
"there's a present for you!" He had gone to the place
one day to ask for a cup of coffee, had found an old

couple milking cows, and in a moment of insanity had bought their farm at two twelve. He couldn't let the damn thing lie there rotting—would Lizzie do him the favour of taking it off his hands at two ten? . . . No? Well, that proved what kind of girl she was!

The man stayed and stayed, finally offering two hundred twenty-five an acre, damning himself as the biggest fool that ever wore shoes for not being able to get his eyes off Lizzie and her farm.

Lizzie smiled encouragingly, inviting him to go on courting. Unless he said the final word pretty soon, she'd have to look for another fellow . . . now she couldn't wait much longer!

Louis was touched; his eyes watered. He liked this man so well that he invited him to stay with them overnight . . . he could sleep in the haymow . . . perhaps they could agree in the morning . . . a deal like that couldn't be rushed through. . . . Wouldn't he stay?

The man left without buying.

But about a week later a man with no talk in his mouth came to look at the farm; he was well along in years and carried a cane. No, thank you, he said, they need not show him around, but might he have a spade? Lizzie found the tool, and after the man had gone off to the field, she called Louis, and both sat down to wait.

When he returned, Lizzie was still seated on the doorstep and Louis near by on the chopping-block, leaning his back against the wall. The man stuck the spade in the ground and said in a dry, cold voice that he would give $230. They could have the crop. But he'd have to get possession right away.

After the man's short speech there was a long silence. Louis' eyes lay steadily upon Lizzie's face like that of a devoted dog who watches every move of its master, and he had folded his hands.

—Yes, admitted Lizzie meditatively, feeling of the little knot of hair at the back of her head, they had talked of selling and would most likely sell, sometime, but not until they got a satisfactory price . . . this was the best farm on this side of the creek.

"What is your price, then?" the man asked, indifferently.

"Two fifty cash." There was no trace of excitement in her voice, only serenity.

"I'll make it two forty," spoke the man's dry voice, "but not a cent more."

Louis could not sit still; he arose and walked shakingly to the other corner of the house and leaned his elbow against the wall; his eyes were so blurred that he could not see clearly. At her calm, quiet refusal a shudder ran down his back and a faintness came over him . . . she was the terriblest person that ever lived!

Two weeks later they sold the farm to old Bratlien at $250 an acre. But after the price had been agreed on, and the division of the crops all settled, the deal almost floundered because the Houglums insisted on a cash payment . . . yes, all cash . . . they would not sell except for cash! At Bratlien's generous offer of half cash and the other half in a first mortgage at six per cent Lizzie just sniffed scornfully. Old Bratlien bristled with resentment. His honour had been questioned; his ability to pay, his integrity these people were not sure of. How ridiculous! They must know that he was good for this little patch of prairie . . . no, he would not deal with them . . . he would *not!* They'd never see him again. Bratlien drove off in great anger.

But as Louis and Lizzie remained adamantine and Bratlien had set his heart on adding this farm to his many others, there was nothing for him to do but to come to terms. The next day he returned in his Studebaker, telling them curtly to get in . . . they better go to town and have the papers drawn . . . perhaps he could borrow a few cents at the bank! The scorn in his voice was drowned in the humming of the motor.

V. The Winepress of the Wrath of God

I

LATE midsummer and a sky that blazed with heat from sunup to sundown. One day Bratlien went to Greenfield with the truck, and the Houglums made use of the chance to move themselves and their belongings to town. Not before they came to do the packing did they realize how much they had; but the granary had been full of junk—old clothes, shoes, bedding, tools of different descriptions, all of it unsalable, yet too good to burn; and so it had been packed into boxes, and now was loaded on the truck; together with the stove and the bed, the table and the two chairs, the big chest, and the bedclothes it made a loadful.

Today old Bratlien was in a high flow of good spirits; he laughed and joked and wouldn't leave Lizzie alone. He had to tease her about the cash she had made him dig up: which stocking did she keep it in—hey? In the left? . . . But he'd take his chances on the right! . . . How would she like to trade with him? He'd give her a new pair to boot . . . hey?

Both had been up early and had been working hard all morning; neither of them was in a mood for banter; Louis less so than she. As he climbed on top of the load and took a last look at the old place he felt depressed and worn out. As they drove down the yard his

271

eyes watered so that he could not see. The whole farm lay quiet and deserted. No life to be seen anywhere. Not a sound; not even a rooster crowed. The henhouse looked so squatty and forlorn. . . . Well, good-bye, old farm!

Lizzie, too, seemed out of sorts; you couldn't make her talk. Every once in a while Bratlien turned around shouting: "Are you there? If I had you insured I could make better time. . . . Hey! what was that?"

By and by Louis' mood brightened. He had nothing to feel sour about, he assured himself. . . . The place had brought much more than they had hoped . . . all cash, too . . . and the money was safe. . . . Now they were moving to town to take life easy and have some fun. . . . No more milking, and dirty chores, and hard work. . . . He'd miss the cows, though . . . well, one couldn't have everything . . . they had said good-bye and were through!

Once set in motion, Louis' thought picked up many problems: The seventeen hundred the auction had netted them would keep them for many years—as long as they lived . . . they wouldn't be needing many things . . . they had both stove and bed, table and chairs . . . in town they would not wear out many clothes. . . . Suddenly a broad grin lit up his face: smart of Lizzie to have insisted on getting all the fruit and the whole potato crop—leave it to her to make a bargain!

On the top of the chest Lizzie sat immovable, like

a statue, cold, indifferent; neither of the men could get a sound out of her.

The Houglums had indeed been fortunate in securing reasonably cheap living-quarters. Renting a house had been out of the question; besides, what would two old people do with a whole house? By sheer good luck Louis had found out about the two rooms above Jenkins' Drygoods & Groceries, at seven dollars a month, and had snapped up the chance at once; there they now moved with all their belongings.

The first day they worked hard, as though this were their last chance upon earth, Louis lugging the things upstairs, and Lizzie unpacking and arranging them. By Saturday night they were fairly well settled and the rooms had a cozy air. Of the boxes Louis had made several pieces of furniture: a kitchen table, a cupboard, a commode, and a washstand. Lizzie had draped the new furniture with white cheesecloth and made curtains of the same material.

The rooms made fine quarters. In the two front windows you could stand all day and look down upon Main Street. From early morning to late at night there was a steady stream af activity. They had much fun in picking out faces they knew; twice Louis had to run down and shake hands. People would stop right under the windows, and you could hear what they said. To both of them it gave a luxurious feeling of well-being to stand here, watching the world. Many times they had to laugh at what they heard—people talked so foolishly: There was Tostein Hegg who wouldn't go to

the place around the corner and have a glass of beer
Sam Johnson offered him, because . . . well . . . no,
not at this time of the day! . . . And there was Mrs.
Knapperud confiding to Mrs. Anderson that Hazel had
thrown Clarence overboard and now was going to
marry Roy Henderson, and Clarence so mad that he
threatened to blow them both into smithereens. In these
few days they had learned more about what was going
on in their old neighbourhood than in all the years they
had lived there. Here they stood like the gods to whose
judgment seats are brought all the deeds of men.

Before very long visitors came to see them, among
them some of the best people in town. One day the
Methodist minister and his wife called, he urging them
to attend his church and his wife inviting them to a
get-together lunch in the church parlours the next
evening.

The Houglums declined both.

Shortly after, two ladies, both very nicely dressed,
called on Lizzie. Louis, feeling embarrassed, went into
the other room, leaving the door open. The ladies told
Lizzie many useful things concerning their town and
its people, and were particularly enthusiastic about the
new movie theatre which had just opened up—the
Houglums must see it . . . the film running there now
was too killing for anything . . . some people didn't
like it, but that was because they had no sense of fun
. . . it was really grand!

They talked so much about the film that Louis made
up his mind to go, and begged Lizzie to go with him.

Neither of them had ever set foot inside a theatre and now was their chance to see what the world was like, and, hell! couldn't they afford it just for once?

Accordingly, at half past seven the same night, they both dressed up in their Sunday clothes, found themselves in the midst of a jostling crowd in the entrance of the new theatre. They were being carried forward by a seething sea of bright faces; there was much nudging of elbows, many funny remarks, and much loud laughter. Not a worry left in that whole crowd. The gay mood intoxicated Louis; he was young again, and in love; unconsciously he nodded to every eye that met his. But Lizzie could not so easily adjust herself to the strange surroundings. She gripped his arm hard, pressing her other arm rigidly to her side. With the jostling of the crowd her ten-year-old hat had been pushed a little over one ear.

At the ticket window Louis caused disturbance by holding back the crowd. It took him so long to get his pocket-book up, and the money out, and the change counted, and the purse put back safely, that the stream behind him grew impatient and pushed on, a strong voice calling out: "Say, colonel, this ain't no pie counter —get a move on you!"

Lizzie noticed how terribly recklessly people threw their money about; a hand would dig down into a pocket, toss money in at the window, and as carelessly sweep the change into the other hand. . . . This town must be all sin and wickedness. . . . No wonder that prices were so high, the way people took care of their money! . . . Now look at that couple, he with his arm around her, and she leaning up against him! Lizzie blushed hotly with shame.

The film was rather poorer than the ordinary run. A story of two married people deceiving each other: the husband was unfaithful to the wife and she to him; she stole money from him whenever she saw her chance, and yet they seemed to get along excellently—in fact, the worse the deceit grew, the better they got along, and the crowd was in one continuous snicker of delight. After the divorce—when the two had found new partners and were about to marry again, and all four having met at a restaurant, shook hands all around and drank to their mutual good health, pledging eternal friendship—a storm of applause roared through the house.

Louis soon lost himself in the story. At the conclusion of the scene in which the wife got up during the night and searched her husband's pockets, pilfering first a five-dollar and next a ten-dollar bill, which she hid in her stocking, he forgot himself entirely; he clapped his hands, shaking with laughter.

Enraged, Lizzie grabbed his arm and shook him, whispering hoarsely into his ear: hadn't he any more sense of decency than to sit here and enjoy himself over trashy rot like this? Her eyes blazed with indignation. She would have got up and left right then, but she saw no way out; they sat near the front in the middle of the row and the house was packed full. On the way home she was irate and spoke cutting words;

she told him plainly what kind of man he was who found pleasure in robbery and whoring . . . shame on him!

"All the same, Lizzie, you must admit that she was a doggone smart girl!"

—Smart? S'pose she got up during the night and helped herself to his money? Perhaps he'd call that smart, too?

"That would be different, you certainly can see that . . . we ain't going to get divorced!" Louis was still chuckling.

That night both took their belts off and counted the money; she first; then he: one couldn't be too careful! Each had $35,000. But in a small inside pocket of his belt Louis carried two one-thousand-dollar bills which he did not count and of whose existence Lizzie had not the faintest suspicion.

After going to bed he lay awake for hours, his thoughts circling about the woman in the film. He wished he could get acquainted with her . . . no doubt she knew more tricks . . . women are smart in such things. . . . He could have told her a funny story about an old shoe in the northeast corner of a hog-house. . . . The way she got up at night hunting through the pockets! Louis fell asleep wondering whether Lizzie had ever searched his overalls. . . .

To Louis, living in town was like living in fairyland itself. For more than three weeks he reveled in unstinted leisure and solid comfort. This was like Christ-

mas! What he had longed for all his life had come
to him: no work; no drudgery; no worry of any kind.
All he owned he carried with him always . . . and it
wasn't such a lousy trifle, either. It could, of course,
have been a great deal more if he had had sense enough
to begin saving earlier.

The best feature of his new existence was the absolute security, the sure safety, which he now enjoyed.
The constant fear he had been living in so long was
gone, completely swept away. . . . Here, if anywhere
on earth, he could feel safe. People everywhere . . .
the police, too . . . and the sheriff! . . . And he lived
directly above Jenkins' store . . . their bed stood right
above the cash register and the big safe. All the riches
of Jenkins' slept directly below him and Lizzie . . .
just the floor between them. . . . Nothing could happen inside the premises of old man Jenkins—good luck
had found him out at last!

At first Louis took a long afternoon nap every day;
even so he slept tolerably well at night unless the
weather was too unbearably hot. Most of the day he
spent down on the street, strolling about and getting
acquainted with people, or else in the store, where he
could sit for hours watching the clerks. . . . What
piles of money they took in! At every sale they'd press
certain keys on the cash register, turn a crank just like
on a grindstone, and the drawer would fly open with
a bang. . . . Wonder if they didn't steal a dime now
and then? Take that Mary Ann? If that girl was
strictly on the square, he'd eat his own shoes! She was

so darned quick in her movements, and she always had a sly smile. Sometimes he noticed how her hand, after coming out of the till, would slip into the pocket of her black apron. She didn't realize that he was an old thresher and could see a thing or two with only half an eye! . . . One day he could have sworn that he saw a flash of something bright between her fingers just as her hand went to her pocket; their eyes met, and he gave her an understanding smile to say that Mary Ann need not worry that he would tell tales out of school! None of his business what went on in the store, just so she didn't let herself get caught. . . . Don't you fear me, he smiled again; I know a thing or two myself!

While loafing in the store Louis would often meet old acquaintances from the country, with whom he would chat as long as he could get them to stay. When they had gone he would hurry upstairs to Lizzie and repeat to her, to the last detail, what this or that man had told him.

Town life, however pleasant, had one great drawback: it was terribly expensive. Neither Louis nor Lizzie could figure out why a pound of butter, for example, should cost a fortune. And take the milk: twelve cents a quart, yet so blue and thin that you could see bottom in many fathoms of water . . . Louis would like to know what kind of cows they had down here!

One day Lizzie went down to the store to get a few eggs and returned empty-handed, scandalized because the clerk waiting on her had asked fifty cents a dozen.

Lizzie turned her back on him . . . she wasn't going to stand for any highway robbery . . . last year at this time she had sold fresh eggs for forty-one cents, and now the war was over! Worse yet with the butter: last year she had got only fifty-three and now she had to pay sixty-seven!

But never mind, she'd get the best of them, they could keep their old butter. Lizzie began using the common substitutes on the market and invented new ones herself. Nut margarine made fairly good butter; in baking a cake you could nicely do without eggs, and sweetened water with the breakfast oatmeal was plenty good enough. In other ways, too, she tried to be as frugal as possible; now that they were not working, fried potatoes, roasted potato-cake coffee, good bread, and a thin spread of imitation butter had to do for supper. The noon meal presented greater difficulties: you couldn't be eating only bread all the time, either! When the cool weather set in, though, she'd be able to stretch a twenty-cent soup bone over four days—that she could see now.

But no matter how closely she pinched and skimped in the cooking and stinted herself in buying, the high cost of living gave her much worry. Money went for every turn they made; Louis had to have his tobacco; and there was not a blessed thing to sell; whatever was spent had to come right out of their pocket book. The money seemed to melt away between your fingers; you bought a box of matches or a spool of thread and it took cash. Though they had been here only four weeks it had cost them nearly fifty dollars.

"This can't go on, it just won't do!" Lizzie would say whenever she had been to the store.

"No, I guess that's right," Louis agreed, stirring uneasily.

II

Christmas was drawing near.

For the last three months and a half Louis had worked steadily as section hand at four dollars a day; by now he had earned a neat sum of money. But with the freezing up of the ground, work had stopped for this year. Again he loafed around at home, finding life exceedingly tiresome. The tedium of inactivity hung heavily upon him, especially now that he was left alone the whole spread of the day and during the long, lonely evenings.

Except for a few hours at night Lizzie had left him. After he had begun working on the section, staying away all day, the leisure and the loneliness in these strange surroundings irked her into boredom. What was she to do with herself? Here she sat like a caged bird. No one came to see her; there was not a soul in town that she might go to visit; and nothing whatever for her to do. She had patched and mended the winter clothes, her own and Louis', and that hadn't taken long.

She got up in the morning without any task to get up for; throughout the day she hung around, a grey, dull emptiness staring her in the face. All the while the days were lengthening instead of shortening. She would go to bed at night, not the least bit tired, but with a weariness that made her bones ache.

Often, as she sat here, her thoughts hied back to the farm, which only made matters worse. Out on the farm one could turn around! . . . Life pulsed and throbbed and fought lustily. Everywhere the sounds of beast and fowl, of cows and horses, of calves and pigs and cackling poultry—all screaming and battling madly to get to her first the moment they heard her voice. . . . And there was Flossie, the best milker they had ever had! Lizzie craned her neck to lean her head once more against Flossie's warm flank, and she heard the tail go switching about her ears. Unmindful of where she was, Lizzie listened for the cow's munching, and she looked for the soft, brown eyes of the beast. . . . At times she was overcome by an unearthly yearning for the life she had known so well and that she could confide in; then her muscles would twitch and her eyes get a faraway, hungry look. For hours she sat by the window above Jenkins' store and was oblivious to the life on the street below. Again she was out on the farm, mothering a struggling, hungry life. She heard a pig grunt brute satisfaction because she rubbed its back with the point of her shoe. She put her hand under a brooding hen to rob its nest and the mother snapped angrily till the blood oozed out. The pain gave Lizzie pleasure. . . . No, no; it was most fun of all to teach new-born calves how to drink; as the soft palate sucked her hand she knew voluptuous pleasure. As she came back to her window above Jenkins' store her sense of forsakenness deepened into profound gloom. She saw it clearly now: Out there she had lived close to the very life-force itself, had felt its pulse beats . . . in town she had been cast into a void of grey aloneness. Getting up from the window, unconsciously she chewed the knuckles of her left hand, walking aimlessly back and forth between the two little rooms. The feeling that she had been betrayed, that life at every turn of the road had tricked her and led her astray, was fast growing into hatred toward all mankind.

Or she might lock the door securely, bracing a chair against it for further protection; then she would sit down on the bed, remove her clothes so that she could get the belt off, and play with the bills. Usually her features would soften. Though the little fellows were all of the same denomination, she had favourites among them; some she loved more dearly than the others; she knew them individually and could tell how and when each one had come to her. . . . The five sleeping in this bed were her first-born; they were maturing now . . . had more substance. . . . Fine boys they were! When they first arrived they had been stubborn and naughty, with no tenderness in them . . . but under her heart, where they had lain these many years, they had softened—tears dimmed her eyes—yes, so they had! She laid them against her cheek; there was a silken tenderness in them; she could feel how fond they were of her and how they snuggled close to her.

. . . This one had come the winter after . . . Louis had had to go clear to Faribault for her; she remembered the occasion well because he had been worn and out of sorts after the long, cold drive, and had grumbled about the supper that night. . . . Here was one that had come all the way from St. Paul; the one lying next to him—it had a birthmark, a nick in the upper right-hand corner—was a Greenfield boy; Louis had got him at the State Bank . . . a love-child he was! . . . This one was a stranger from Minneapolis . . . must have come from a swell place, too . . . that was the reason why he refused to unbend to her like some of the others. . . . A war baby he was, that's what . . . during evil days he had come; perhaps that was the reason for his hardness? Lizzie felt a secret grudge whenever she had him out to nurse; as if for some purpose she would lay him aside until she got through with the others, then she would pick him up again and admonish: "You might just as well behave yourself! I've caught you at it—you know I have . . . now don't go trying any trick on me! . . . Did I hurt you? Oh, I didn't mean to . . . now come to Mother!" Before putting him back she'd lay the bill against her cheek, keeping it there until the thin paper felt warm and soft . . . then she nodded to herself, pleased, a bright look in her eye.

The remaining ones were newcomers, some out of Bratlien's bosom, others from St. Paul; some of them promised well but mostly they were mere strangers to her. . . . She'd have to give them better care! The resolve brought no peace of mind: somehow, deep down in her heart she knew already that she could never love them as dearly as some of the first-born—an old saying flashed upon her—for those "had been bought with a great price." . . . Yes, that was it: those early ones "had been bought with a price"!

One afternoon while Lizzie was playing with her secrets, a startling idea came to her: Each one of her boys was worth a whole thousand; there might be others of much higher value—of ten, fifty, one hundred thousand? A cold shiver ran through her . . . what magic could make one hundred thousand dollars dream away their lives in a piece of thin, velvety paper? There was black deviltry about it all. . . . And was it meant to be so? Take her own boys, now? Were they just meant to lie there? . . . Was that the reason some of them could not bend their ways to hers? There was a far-away expression on her face . . . how she hated life!

About one month after Louis had begun to work on the section, Mrs. Cadman, the doctor's wife, came to ask Lizzie whether she wouldn't come over to do the washing and cleaning, and perhaps also the ironing? She would pay her twenty-five cents an hour and board. Impossible these days to find capable help . . . she'd be delighted to have her come.

Perhaps, thought Lizzie, there might be other swell people in town who were in need of help. One day she went down to the store and inquired of Jenkins whether he knew of any such. Thus it came about that she found much more work than she was able to do. Sunday after Sunday she was washing dishes in the kitchen of a restaurant in the next block; besides getting a whole dollar, she was earning three meals both for herself and for Louis each Sunday. With both of them working they were now earning good money, and life was again endurable.

But all good things must come to an end sometime. Early in November the ground froze up; shortly after came a heavy snowfall; winter had set in, and that ended happiness for Louis.

From now on it was he who was locked up alone in the two upstairs rooms above Jenkins' store. And he had to prepare his own meals, which for him was the greatest trial he could think of. He swore as soon as he came near the stove, and would go into fits of desperation before getting the simplest meal cooked.

With long strides he tramped the streets until he knew the whole town by heart. At home he usually stayed by the front window. Tired of looking down on the people coming and going, he would put on his fur coat and visit one store after another. But of the stores he could only feel at home in Jenkins' Drygoods & Groceries. It was great fun to watch Mary Ann and the cash register! At train-time he was usually at the station to see the trains come and go, and the people rush and hustle. Where were they all bound for? Why were they always in such a hurry? Louis developed a grudge of envy against every man who seemed to be in a hurry.

By twilight-time he would be back at his rooms, sitting with his coat on, by the window. A chill was trying to get at his bones, working from his feet up. The room was like an ice box . . . wood eleven dollars a cord . . . coal twelve dollars a ton . . . Lizzie was making only ten dollars a week now. . . . His thoughts bore him back to the farm! Plenty of wood along the creek . . . enough to last man after man for generations. . . . And no want of milk and of butter . . . and eggs . . . and a rooster to cook on a Sunday . . . the spring chickens would make juicy mouthfuls by now . . . all that fresh milk, too!—He was too hungry to get up and start cooking supper.

What stung deeper than anything else was the loss of Jim and Fan. There was a gnawing at his heart and his eyes watered when he thought of his two horses. . . . If he could only spend another twilight hour with them, feeding them oats out of his hand! He remembered his old trick of going up into their stalls, holding the oat measure in one hand and feeding them out of the other. . . . Fan was especially clever; she could curl her soft, warm muzzle into the hollow of his hand and pick up the last kernel.

One afternoon his longing for his two friends became so unbearable that he set out to see them once more . . . he'd catch a ride . . . there'd be people going up that way this time of day!—He was more than a mile out of town before remembering that Jim

and Fan had been sold to an Irishman living far out
West on the prairie—Tom Morgan was his name . . .
yes, that was it . . . he must be sure not to forget the
man's name!

On his way home a mad wind cut his face savagely.
His eyes blurred and he wasn't so sure that he wasn't
crying. . . . God help him but this was a hard life!

III

Louis was spending as much of his time as he dared
downstairs in the store. He had asked Jenkins for the
privilege of tending the stove, which immediately had
been granted; and so he had brought a box over on
which he sat for hours trying to soak into his bones
as much heat as possible before dragging them to the
ice box upstairs.

One day while drowsing on the box, watching Mary
Ann through the corner of his left eye, he suddenly became aware of two men standing near him, absorbed
in eager talk. The tallness of the one was so great that
he had to bend himself into a horseshoe to reach comfortably the other's red face, perched on a rather stout,
squatty figure. Louis didn't know them, but he could
tell at once that they must be farmers. The air of
solemnity about them and the unearthly strangeness of
their talk made him sit straight up and look at them.
In the face of both men lay an inexpressibly sweet

kindness; though they were standing so close by that he could hear every word, it took him some time before he could get the drift of their conversation.

"Yes, it is wonderful," said the tall man, slowly, "that it has been given one in the synagogue of Satan to see the signs and interpret them. This time it is a learned professor, an unbeliever, one who scoffs and sneers, that has been forced to figure it out; do you know, I am thinking of the poor beast that Balaam rode."

"Yes," nodded the other, "and the Seventeenth will soon be upon us, the Lord be praised! All the newspapers are agreed on the date. 'Behold,' he quoted in a still rapture, 'behold, He cometh with the clouds and all the kindred of the earth shall wail because of Him. Even so. Amen!' But the wicked are smitten with blindness and can't see the approaching damnation before it's too late to repent. Only this child of perdition has had his eyes opened."

No longer able to hold back his curiosity, Louis asked what was to happen on the 17th. The weirdness of their talk was affecting him.

In sincere concern for his eternal welfare the strangers turned to him simultaneously:

"Ah, yes," said the tall man, bending the knot of his frame the other way, "you'll soon experience that; the Ancient of Days is returning to call you and me to judgment!"

"Yes, yes," the stout man broke in; "the time is at

hand; the end of all things is drawing near; soon we will see the heavens roll up like a scroll."

"That's so," agreed the tall man kindly; "the dissolution of all earthly things is upon us, and the wicked shall be broken to shivers like the vessels of a potter. On the seventeenth of this month the Four Horsemen are gathering; the signs are now so clear that a blind man has read them. How terrible"—his tone saddened noticeably—"that even now, after one of the children of darkness has had his eyes opened and is crying the truth from the housetops, that still the world refuses to listen. The Lord is hardening the hearts of the wicked in order that the Scriptures may be fulfilled."

Open-mouthed, Louis stood gaping, first at one, then at the other, finally at both together; that they weren't joking he could tell by their serious looks; they didn't appear more foolish than other people, and kinder human faces he had never looked into.

The stout man, seeing his bewilderment, began to speak admonishingly, in pleading tones, with an intense kindliness:

"Now, brother, you must hurry home and prepare yourself! Even in the eleventh hour labourers are hired for the Vineyard. There are not many minutes left now; the hour is getting late, the night cometh. I counsel thee to buy of me gold tried in the fire, that thou mayest be rich; and white raiment, that thou mayest be clothed, and the shame of thy nakedness do not appear; and anoint thine eyes with eye salve, that thou mayest see . . . behold, I stand at the door and knock!"

"Wha—wha—what am I to prepare for? There ain't no war now?" Louis stammered, uneasily shifting over to the other foot.

There was a benign smile on the tall man's face as he laid his hand on Louis's shoulder: "No, brother, now the war is over and we're nearing home. On the seventeenth of this month the world will be destroyed."

"Not destroyed, but rolled up like a scroll," corrected the other.

"Yes, that's it," agreed the tall man, amiably, "the last measure of God's wrath has been filled; His great patience with you and me has come to an end!"

"You must be crazy!" Louis burst out, right up into their eyes, unbelief and wonder written all over his face.

In warm, pleading earnestness the two faithful witnesses besought him to try to gain the crown of life ere it was too late, the one taking the words out of the mouth of the other, reminding him of death and the last day, of fire and brimstone, and the great horrors that would befall the unsuspecting world right before Christmas. As final evidence the tall man pulled a newspaper out of the pocket of his sheepskin coat, and read slowly, in an inspired voice, an article headed in black, bold type: END OF THE WORLD COMING ON THE SEVENTEENTH! That the world was coming to an end, and that the time for the catastrophe had been scientifically computed by a university professor, were the two concrete facts Louis gleaned from the reading. Doubt and dark unbelief were so clearly written on his face, that the two men left him as one of the many children to be killed with death. Here was no time to tarry; lest one be left behind he must get himself ready! The men walked away from him sorrowfully.

Their talk had disturbed Louis. His head was so full that he forgot his miserable loneliness in the cold rooms and the trials of making his supper out of thin coffee and fried potatoes.

Coming out of the store, he looked critically at the weather. There was an overcast sky, and grey, woolly, low-hanging clouds out of which an icy wind stung his face viciously. The weather was nasty, but nothing unusual for Minnesota this time of the year. He looked up and down the street, walked a few blocks, stopped and looked again; the houses hadn't moved any, as far as he could see; the trodden snow on the sidewalk was as mean and slippery as ever. People with their coat collars pulled high above their ears were hurrying by; he stared into each face that passed; they all seemed eager and happy, only anxious to get home. No indication of the old world tumbling down yet for a while.

He came up to the rooms, kept on his overcoat, and sat down, heavy with thought. . . . Didn't take much to scare the wits out of some people—gosh darn it! how those fellows had talked! How could a newspaper print such foolish things? The print was big enough for any fool to read. His thoughts strayed into a lone lane of soberness: It was a learned man who had figured it

out . . . one of the boys that foretell the eclipse of the
sun and moon years ahead, even to the last minute . . .
and who forecast the weather. For a long time he sat,
until the twilight had deepened into cold darkness.

Most of the time, though, they were wrong about
the weather . . . he'd undertake to forecast the
weather better than any prophet!

The idea cheered him so much that he got up and
cooked supper.

But Lizzie was no sooner through the door than he
asked her, eyeing her closely, if she had heard the news.

—What news?

—That Doomsday was coming?

—Huh! she snorted wrathfully; she was in no mood
for fooling; tonight the rooms were bitterly cold. She
hurried to undress.

—What did she think of it? Louis removed his fur
coat.

—Think of it? She had felt it in her bones that something like that must happen soon! . . . Would he ever
get ready and come to bed? Cold here as in an ice
box . . . no Doomsday could come too soon to suit
her!

Louis gave up; in the humour she was in tonight it
was useless to try talking to her . . . she might have
had a little feeling for a fellow who had to stay home
alone all day.

The next day Louis sat on the box by the stove,
watching old man Jenkins. As soon as he saw his chance
he went up to the desk and, assuming a shrewd air,

asked whether Jenkins had heard about this affair that
was going to take place on the 17th? He tried to give
a little chuckle, which, before he could get it out, stuck
in his throat; by the time he got it out, the chuckle had
changed into a cough.

Squinting up from his papers, the old man gave a
dry laugh that might mean anything: Yes, and a picnic
that would be! . . . Jenkins threw more observation
into his squint.

—What did he think of it? asked Louis, bluntly.

"Gosh if I know. If the thing is to happen, I suppose
the crash will have to fall some day. I would like to do
some real Christmas trading before it strikes here; I
have my store full of goods. . . . What can I sell you
today?"

Louis edged back to the box. . . . Old Jenkins was
a hard-fisted customer . . . no use to try him out on
such things . . . he needn't have joked about it
though; this was no laughing matter at all!

The problem absorbed him as his horsepower had in
olden times when it went on a strike: he couldn't rest
before he had located the source of the trouble. And
now his bachelor's life up in the cold rooms gave him
plenty of time for figuring. During the next few days
he would try to pick up a talk with any man who came
into the store and who seemed to have a minute to
spare. But instead of going right to the point he would
approach it from back alleys, beginning with the
weather, then casually working around to questions of
the sky: This promised to be some winter . . . the

coldest November on record . . . wonder what the reason could be? Perhaps this old world some day would freeze to death?

One day Jens Tröan, an old acquaintance from the country, a heavy framed giant of a man with a long flowing beard and hard glinting eyes—the most radical Non-Partisan Leaguer up that way—came into the store; Louis held him in high esteem, and at once began to sound him out.

Jens Tröan, it appeared, knew all about the coming cataclysm; a day or two ago he had read the story in *Skandinaven.*

At this information, which Jens gave in a deep voice, Louis felt cold shivers run down his back.

"Did you read it in Norwegian?"

"Course I read it in Norwegian—that's what I'm telling you."

"Just what did it say?"

Jens couldn't recall the exact words, but the sum and substance of it was that, on the morning of the seventeenth the Doomsday Cock would start crowing. A learned professor had figured out the hour.

After reading the article, Jens had dismissed the matter from his mind, but now that he was discussing it seriously with Louis, who showed much concern, he thought it more than likely that the last great smash-up could be expected almost any day. It would be a damned fine thing, too, he gleefully assured Louis, because then Big Bis and all the bloodsuckers would be swept away in one big swoop—just you let it come!

"Do you believe it?" asked Louis, deeply stirred.

"Course I believe it!" cried Jens, enthusiastically. "The profiteers must get it some time, and for once they will not throw the blame on us farmers!"

Utterly unable to understand such wild talk, Louis only stared at him; then observed, hesitatingly, that if there was to be a general shake-up, it might go hard on other people, too . . . on innocent fellows who never had done anybody any harm . . . "on you, too, Jens!"

—Oh, it was all the same to him, declared Jens; he didn't much care. He was getting old and worn out and couldn't last much longer, anyhow. The blood-suckers had sucked him dry. . . . He was done for, especially since his oldest boy got killed in the trenches in France . . . sacrificed on the altar of Big Bis! . . . The man's voice boomed deep, with an ominous rumbling sound. . . . Besides, he went on presently, he refused to believe that the farmer would be hard hit in that smash-up . . . he couldn't be made to suffer both here and in hell . . . oh, no, it would be the profiteers, and the idlers of the city, who whored on scarlet couches, and Big Bis, that would catch it this time—you just let the old cock crow!

So long did Louis' thoughts continue spinning around the problem that he had himself caught in a web he couldn't break through. In the grey, cold morning the problem was there to greet him, asking insistently what he intended to do about it; by evening it had grown even more vexatious. On going to bed he took it with him to keep him awake during dark, tossing hours; standing over the coffee-pot he forgot himself till he let the pot boil over, and said "Doggone it!" which he straightway felt that he ought not have said. . . . But why did some people take it so seriously and others not? . . . Terrible things had been prophesied concerning the Last Day—it sure would be no picnic! . . . The Last Day coming right in the dead of winter, and just now before Christmas . . . a queer time for starting a racket like that! . . . A dim impression from many, many years ago, from the time he was only a boy going to parochial school, began to hover before his eyes, "There shall be signs in the heavens and in the earth"; there had been something about the moon, too, but that he could not remember.

. . . Signs? It all depends on what you would call signs? No lack of black marks right now! This year winter had come earlier than he could remember . . . it was holding on with a beastly grip. . . . Anyone with eyes could see the wickedness those fellows had been blabbering about: for five years Europe had been turned into a slaughter-house . . . nations had gone mad butchering. What about that for a sign? And not a bit better in this country, when neighbours could burn down the house of another neighbour, right over his head, with the Law just folding its hands— don't talk about lack of signs! . . . Luxury and reckless spending wherever you turned your eyes . . .

when Roy Henderson the other day married Hazel Knapp—so people were telling—he had given her a fur coat that cost $500—plenty of signs, all right!

In his apocalyptic mood, Louis remembered the Bible, yes, that was it, the Bible would clear things up for him . . . now what in thunderation had Lizzie done with the Bible the day they moved? He rummaged through every conceivable hole before remembering that the Bible had burnt with the house . . . now he was in a fine fix: not a Norwegian Bible in all of Greenfield, with the 17th only a few days off!

Walking down Main Street toward the railway station one afternoon about four o'clock, he met a group of children on their way home from school, in a hubbub of excitement. Two came running ahead of the others, sobbing pitifully; a little way behind them, one alone, crying louder still. The rest were all tangled up in a fierce quarrel and, from the way it looked, would soon come to blows. Louis stopped to find out what was wrong, but the two in the lead flew past, sobbing harder than ever; the next whimpered broken-heartedly for his mother. The last ones in the group were two half-grown girls whose eyes blazed indignantly over the outrage they had witnessed. Seeing the old man stand there looking at them, they impulsively flew toward him, all out of breath, and talking fast, the one not heeding what the other was saying: Was it true that the world would be destroyed on the 17th? Could he tell them? Judith's mamma had said so—and

Judith had told Helen—and so Vivian and Helen had got so scared and begun to cry—and Harry and Spencer had had a fight 'cause Spencer's mother had said it would come true for sure—and Harry he said it was all a lie—and Spencer had got his nose just about knocked off—oh, it was awful! Was it true about the world?—could he tell them?

Glum-faced, Louis turned and walked to his rooms. . . . It wasn't only Jens Tröan, the newspapers, and two farmers that had gone crazy; the kids on the street were fighting about it . . . and it said so in *Skandinaven*—one better just stop and look out!

IV

That night Louis slept even worse than he had done since coming to town; he just lay there tossing, struggling with fearsome thoughts of death and impending doom. Toward morning he saw an idea come out of the icy blackness; he took it eagerly, turned again, and went right to sleep, never stirring until Lizzie had gone.

As soon as he had had his breakfast of oatmeal with sugar-water on it and a cup of strong potato coffee, he put on his fur coat, his winter mitts, and a pair of old, patched German socks . . . he better get himself off at once! His cap had no ear-protectors; they had been beyond mending when Lizzie patched the winter clothes, and so she had cut them off because the cap looked better without them.

Louis hurried downstairs, up Main Street, and took the road going into the Greenfield country. Old Reverend Christensen was there no more, but the new man —so Louis had heard—was a great preacher, particularly in the English language, and the purity of his Lutheranism was unquestioned. Last night as Louis lay there unable to sleep he had suddenly bethought himself: the minister ought to be able to solve the problem of the Last Day for him. Now he was on his way to seek enlightenment.

The day was cloudy; the air had a raw, nasty cut; the teeth of the strong east wind bit his face savagely. Across the flat prairie country the wind swept the snow into clouds which whirled and played in the air, and in passing him, always found his right cheek and ear. Across the road lay deep drifts. The crust was in a treacherous mood and enjoyed playing him mean tricks: if it bore him up under one foot, it would be sure to break down under the other; frequently he would go in up to his knees; then he had to stop for breath before he could pull himself out again. The walking was so heavy that before long his body was clammy with sweat. Contrary to what he had hoped, there were no rigs out today. When at last he had finished the seven-mile tramp and reached the parsonage he was so exhausted that he shook in every limb.

Fortunately, the pastor was at home and Louis was

shown directly into the study. A short, stocky man, rather stout, with a bald head, and cold grey eyes behind a pair of horn-rimmed spectacles, looked up from the study table as Louis entered.

—What could he do for him? asked the minister in a tone of official friendliness.

Still shaking, Louis hemmed and hawed, clearing his throat; he had lost the beginning of what he was going to say and so could not get started. And this man was so altogether different from Reverend Christensen.

"Do you take *Skandinaven?*" Louis asked, timidly, in Norwegian, dropping naturally into the speech of the settlement.

"No, indeed, I do not! I don't believe in taking a Norwegian newspaper, and thus helping to perpetuate a foreign-language press in America."

Louis was conscious of a cold draught from somewhere, and wondered if the window on the east could be shut tight; the wet shirt clinging to his body gave him a mean shudder—it was hard to keep his teeth from chattering. He looked helplessly at the man before him . . . there must be something wrong with a Norwegian minister who did not read *Skandinaven?*

"My dear man," the minister asked in the same colourless tone of official friendliness, "what can I do for you?"

"Can you speak Norwegian?" asked Louis, wearily, trying hard to hold on his teeth.

"I can—yes. But I've made it a point lately not to speak Norwegian to people who understand English.

And unless I am much mistaken you speak English easily; now, really, to be frank—don't you?"

Louis sat on the edge of his chair, slowly turning his cap, bottom down, on his knee, a light steam arising from it. The matter he had come to see the minister about slipped further and further away from him, seemed unreal, of no importance, and certainly out of place here. This man was so unlike Reverend Christensen . . . he had always spoken Norwegian, whether begging for the budget or for Foreign Missions. . . . This man had a jaw like old Jenkins . . . most likely he knew no more about what was going to happen on the 17th than an ordinary man did—and yet he was supposed to be a man of God!

Presently the minister began to speak, asking a lot of nonsensical questions about matters that didn't concern him in the least: Was Louis a member of the congregation out here? Did he intend to withdraw, now that he had sold and moved to town? Had he got a good price? How was he investing all that money? How much was he going to will to the church? Had he not been so tired, Louis would have got right up and left, but it felt so good to rest awhile longer.

When the minister had finished his round of questions a cold, dead silence fell on the draughty room. Louis was full of drowsiness and would have liked to close his eyes and drop off into a little sleep, just a wink; but over in the coldness were two sharp points pricking into him.

The pastor sat paging a book, reading a sentence here and there, occasionally looking up at the worn-out old man. Finally he asked, in a more human tone:

"Have you come to see me on business? Perhaps you have a confession that you want to make?"

Louis gave a disconcerted start:

—Business? Did the minister, too, speak of business?

"You may be carrying some secret sin that you wish to confess before God?"

"What?" Louis stared wide-eyed.

"You, who have lived so long in the same place and only concerned yourself with the things of this world, may be guilty of acts of both omission and commission that you dare not take with you to the grave?" the minister went on encouragingly.

"Hah?" It took Louis some time to recover from the shock so that he could speak: No, no, nothing of that kind! Living on the farm had been good . . . only play . . . them days had been good days . . . plenty to eat, all the milk they wanted . . . no lack of either food or fuel, and plenty of work all the time. . . . No, they had all been good neighbours, Louis went on, except, that is to say, some rough-neck boys —it happened two years ago, the war was still on— had set fire to his house. . . . Louis' teeth chattered with short, clicking sounds: But that was only some foolish boys. Likely as not they had been drunk, because he had found a few bottles and an empty keg. . . . Louis looked meditatively into his cap: Neither he nor

Lizzie had lifted a finger to strike back—that he could say before both God and man.

Suddenly the stout figure on the other side of the table rose, confronting Louis; he had placed both hands on the table and was leaning forward.

"So you're the disloyal citizen I've heard so much about?" The sharp eyes pierced through the glasses and stung Louis. "For your own good, I hope you've seen the grievous sin you did commit! How could you fall into the unspeakable iniquity of betraying your country during its hour of need!"

—Hah? Louis' mouth did not close right away. Not one word did he understand. He only saw an angry man facing him viciously. Gathering himself up quickly, he rose, asking in a low, stammering voice, what time it was. He must be going home! Without waiting for an answer, he stumbled through the door, out of the hall, down the icy steps, and started on the seven dead miles of empty road. He shook so violently that he could hardly stand up. A faint voice was calling from afar: "Run, run, run, run, doggone you!" Louis obeyed the voice and ran till the snow spurted about his ears. The last two miles he caught a ride, and got back more easily than he had hoped, only he was drunk with cold and could hardly stand on his feet.

The moment he was up in his rooms he tumbled into bed, so worn out that he could hardly cover himself up. . . . God have mercy, just so this thing didn't come before the 17th!

Even after he had got warm again, and though his bones lay dead with weariness, sleep would not come. Now it was easy to think; he saw each idea clearly. His thoughts pounded like the beating of a heavy surf: Never you fear but that professor had figured right . . . the world was standing on end already! . . . Could that man be a minister?—He wasn't like old Reverend Christensen . . . he was always kind . . . even when he asked for money and you said no. . . . And never, that Louis could remember, had he heard English speech come out of his mouth . . . but this fellow was too stuck up to say a Norwegian word, and he did not take *Skandinaven!* This man had not even begged money for Foreign Missions!

Pretty soon his thoughts turned into a different alley: What had become of Lizzie tonight? Must be eight o'clock already? . . . Since the Last Day was coming next week, they had enough to get along on . . . he had $37,000; then she must have——?

Like a blinding sheet of lightning the thought struck down: What about the money you have stolen from her? Answer that now, what about it? . . .

Louis was in a cold sweat and felt exactly the way he had on that night of terrors up in the hayloft. Now he jumped out of bed and began pacing the floor. The light from a street lamp flickering in at the window threw strange reflections on the wall; his own shadow crossing the light looked like a hovering ghost. Louis gave a low yelp, got out a match and lit the lamp, his hand shaking so violently that it was difficult for him to replace the chimney.

V

The previous night had been sparing in dealing out sleep to Louis. Tonight was still more close-fisted. Though his eyes burnt with a stinging smart and he tried, in sheer impotence, to cry, he could not get a drop of sleep. His thoughts travelled in a narrow circle, but whether coming or going they dragged with them the same problem: how could he get that one-thousand-dollar bill transferred to Lizzie's belt? Tomorrow was Saturday, the next day Sunday . . . after Sunday—only two days left! . . . Here he lay, with one thousand of her money in his possession . . . money that she knew nothing about . . . that account he'd have to settle before twelve o'clock Tuesday night!

Toward morning the problem was suddenly gone, not a trace of it left, and he lay there staring at a terrible picture: a huge threshing separator, running at full speed, standing at the top of a high bluff . . . round about, nothing but empty sky . . . an endless long line of human figures crawling up the bluff and right into the jaws of the separator . . . on the back of each stooping figure, printed in immense fiery letters, the one word THIEF. In the middle of the long line he recognized one, a man in an old fur coat, wearing a cap

with the earlaps cut off. From the straw-carrier, whose
top reached the clouds, came flying out, heads, arms,
feet, bellies—like dry, finely chopped straw. There
seemed to be no end to the line.

Louis was brought back to consciousness by an angry
outburst from Lizzie. "Oh!" she groaned. "Are you
trying to kill me? What's the matter with you, anyway?"—There Louis lay, all drenched with sweat, still
holding her in his arms.

After she had gone to her work Louis sat by the
stove, in utter dejection, like one sentenced to death
who has found out the hour of execution. His pipe and
tobacco lay on the table untouched. After a while he
got up and locked the door and, unbuttoning his clothes,
took out the belt. From the little pocket on the inside
he removed the two bills, held them in his gnarled hand,
for a long time lost in dark thought. . . . There were
only two . . . one of them belonged to her . . . that
bill he'd have to give back to her before Wednesday
morning!

The heat in the stove soon giving out, he went to
put on his fur coat and cap; but the sight of the coat
made the horrible dream-picture come back to him; he
was seized by a violent fit of shaking and had to sit
down.

All through the hours of the forenoon he struggled
with plans of how best he could pay her back the one
thousand, but only to have to give up one after another.
There was no way out! The longer he struggled, the
clearer he saw it: You couldn't fool Lizzie, and he

would sooner face Doomsday itself than confess to her that he had stolen one thousand dollars from her—it would mean the same thing! . . . No, by some hook or crook he must get the bill into her belt . . . though, some day, when she found it there? Well—that wasn't likely to happen before Wednesday.

Early in the afternoon he went downstairs and took his usual position by the stove. It was Saturday, the store crowded with people, and much fun to watch the trade. . . . None of these people seemed concerned about Wednesday.

Seeing no one he knew, Louis concentrated his attention on Mary Ann. The girl whisked about as nimbly as a squirrel, scattering bright smiles all around just as she turned the crank of the cash register. Once, when he saw a paper dollar disappear in her hand, he could have got right up and blessed her; the act gave him physical comfort. . . . Evidently he was going to have good company right from home! . . . She ought to be just a little more careful, though . . . he knew of a threshing rig, somewhere on a big bluff . . . with his own eyes he had seen what kind of grain was being threshed there! Not knowing what he did, he shook his head warningly. Mary Ann only smiled sweetly in return, and was gone quicker than he could wink an eye —what a girl she was!

Late in the day, Jens Tröan, tall, ponderous, in a big sheepskin coat, with heavy German socks that reached to his knees, lumbered into the store. Noticing Louis perched on the box, he pulled a newspaper out of his pocket and gave it to Louis: "Here you are. Read it yourself and make your own exegesis. Jorund, my woman, says the smash-up is sure to come soon. She can't get over having had her boy killed. Just let it come, I says to her, just let it break loose! To me personally it makes no difference when it comes. If I can live to see some of the Big Fellows roast in hell, I won't mind helping with the firing—no, sir!"

Louis was not listening to all this unholy talk; he had spread out the paper on his knee and was reading the piece about the *Coming of Doomsday*—first once, then again; by the time he had read the article the third time every word had photographed itself indelibly on the retina of his mind. . . . No longer could he doubt now! Here he had it written in Norwegian, as clearly as words could make it.

And he felt dizzy; a faintness was coming over him. . . . He'd better go out into the open air. Stuffing the paper into his pocket, he tottered through the door and out onto the street. Some one spoke right into his ear, in a strong, loud voice: "You'll have to confess to her —no other way out!" "Yes, yes," said a voice in the other ear, still louder, "but not before Tuesday night, because that'll be time enough!" . . . The first voice did not speak again.

With Doomsday steps he went upstairs, lit the lamp, got the fire started, and began cooking supper. The smell of the frying potatoes made him realize how hungry he was. Tonight he must have more to eat . . . just one more decent meal. . . . Why stint himself now?—Impulsively he snatched up his cap, ran down to the butcher shop, and bought half a pound of beef-steak, which he prepared, and ate to the last morsel.

But the night was empty of sleep. During the early part of it he kept awake purposely, till he was sure it was safe to touch Lizzie. Then he opened the small pocket in his belt, and by slow, intermittent movements, as though his hand stirred unconsciously, he took out one of the two bills and transferred it to his left hand. For a long time he lay quiet, listening to her breath come and go. By and by his right hand began to move—deftly, by spurts, more warily than hand had ever moved—till it lay on her hip . . . then moving upward on her body, slower than the crawl of the tiniest earthworm; it didn't move, really, only that one hour the hand was further away from the hip than it had been the hour before. . . . There it rested on one of the pockets under her nightdress! Louis bit his teeth together hard in order to stop the clicking sound. Suddenly she gave a low moan and turned around, facing him. After that, any further operation became impossible.

The excitement past, he sunk together in a limp heap. After a while his tired mind began tussling with a new scheme, and he thought he saw a ray of light in it. . . . He might try it, but not until Tuesday night . . . it was too dangerous! . . . By and by he lost himself in unconsciousness.

In the morning at the breakfast table he suggested casually that perhaps they better go to church today

. . Sunday was lonesomer than any other day of the week, and besides . . .

His suggestion irritated her; she had no time for foolishness! . . . Some one had to provide bread and butter for both of them. Why was he lazying about the house, days on end? He might go out in the country and find something to do . . . there'd be corn-shelling, or hauling . . . he could at least earn his own board . . . of her last week's wages she hadn't been able to save more than $3.45!

—Perhaps they had enough, Louis remarked, darkly.

—Huh-huh, so that was it? Did he know of any gold mine to go to? He was so restless at night . . . was he too lazy to sleep? . . . What was on his mind?

Louis stole a glance at her, his hand clutching the table. . . . No, he concluded, it was only her usual morning peevishness.

—Well, gosh almighty! he continued in a more belligerent mood, if the game was up by Wednesday, they had enough to get along on . . . he'd be glad to let her have a thousand . . . even two! He arose abruptly and showed her the article in *Skandinaven*.

As she read it, she gave mean, short, snorts: That wouldn't surprise her in the least, she said, scornfully . . . no, not in the least . . . she couldn't go on much longer, anyway! . . . She'd gladly quit the dishes and sing a few hallelujahs!

"You shouldn't make fun of such things!" Louis' face was very pale. He got up and moved his chair closer to the stove. "Very soon it might not be so

pleasant for some people . . . if you hain't got
you can have some of my money!" His tone car.
terrible earnestness; with his hand he had gripped
table, clutching it with all his might.

She looked so viciously at him that his eyes shied
away, a gleam of whiteness in them that came and
went. "Yes," he repeated and got red in his face: "I'll
let you have one of mine . . . you can give it back
in the spring when I begin working again."

"Do you know what I feel like doing with you?"
she said in a thin, high voice, drawing dangerously near
him.

"No," he answered humbly, "but you can have the
money—here . . ."

Before he could go any further she had hold of his
left ear and gave it a vicious twist; out of the other
ear came fat sounds of awful slaps, and his eyes saw
red stars.

Then the cry of a hoarse voice:

"I could just kill you dead . . . you fool!"

When at last he looked up she was gone. Unable
to stir, he just sat there. But he didn't feel angry; he
wasn't so sure that he did not laugh . . . anyway he
felt good all through.

. . . Easy enough for her to talk big—she wasn't
meeting doom with a thousand dollars stolen from another man's pocket. She was honest . . . she was fond
of screwing up the price in a deal, but she didn't cheat
. . . she would never think of taking money that belonged to another person . . . oh, no, she could face

Wednesday morning without blinking an eye! . . . To make her take the thousand dollars would be as impossible as to rake down stars from the sky.

Not knowing what else to do with himself, Louis put on his fur coat and went to the Methodist Church . . . he could at least idle away an hour there.

The speaker that day was an itinerant evangelist who travelled from place to place in order to help the local pastor quicken the spiritual life of the congregation. He had been conducting a series of revival meetings in Greenfield, and today, on the Third Sunday in Advent, he was closing the series. The man was a great speaker, possessing unusual spiritual power.

Today he preached on "The Three Paths that Leadeth to Destruction." The first was Drunkenness. . . . Annually thousands upon thousands were washed ashore upon the World Unknown, like splintered wreckage on uncharted coasts, leaving behind them widowed mothers and orphaned children. That was what King Alcohol did for humanity!

But greater still was the number travelling the Path of Adultery. For it was wider, looked so pleasant and so innocent. Originating secretly in the minds of the unchaste, adultery spread and spread, eating its way into the social organism like a deadly cancer, taking its bloody toll among boys and girls, among married and the unmarried. The speaker painted vivid scenes in strong colours; hunting down secret sins, he exposed them mercilessly.

These two divisions of the sermon had left Louis untouched. He had given only half an ear, and hardly that, to what the speaker was saying. The church was warm and cozy, with pleasant odours floating in the air. The frosty sheen of the wintry sun, breaking through the stained-glass windows, shed a soft brilliancy of many hues over the room. Out of the goldened pipes of the big organ had, only a moment ago, come low, sweet sounds which had brought him back to the country . . . to balmy spring evenings with the smell of dank earth bursting with growing vegetation . . . to the song of meadow larks . . . to a life filled with a great goodness. Sitting here was like lying on your back in a green meadow full of tenderness. . . . If that man up there only would shut his angry mouth, Louis could steal a little nap . . . now he was full of kind drowsiness. . . . As soon as the service was over he'd go home and fill himself up with sleep . . . he wouldn't stir a toe until tomorrow noon . . . perhaps not before——

. . . What was that? Louis dragged his body into a straight up-and-down position, rubbing thick sleep out of his eyes. Like the sound of a deep bassoon the speaker's words rang through the church:

"But the greed for gold is the wide gate that leads straight to perdition!"

And suddenly Louis was on his guard, listening with every nerve taut, craning forward to catch the meaning of the rhetorical phrases.

. . . The greed for gold, the speaker went on, was the broad highway to hell. There was no sin under the heavens that people would not commit for money. . . . For thirty paltry pieces of silver the Son of God was sold to be hanged on the cross. . . . For gold a man would barter his immortal soul as easily as he parted with a few head of cattle or an acre of land. . . . The greed for gold had changed Godlike man into a dirty swine. . . . Gold made man lie, steal, rob, and murder his fellow man; father betray son, and son his own father. . . . For gold husband and wife deceived one another, the wife stole from her husband and the husband from his wife. . . . Was it not the greed for gold and the lust after power that had caused the World War? . . . Never before in human history had the greed for gold raged more fiercely than now! The speaker closed with a peroration which threw a chill into the hearts of his hearers.

To deepen the impression of the great truths he had proclaimed he pulled a newspaper clipping out of his notes, bearing the caption "The Last Day Coming December 17th," and read it slowly, making only a few comments, his voice low, and uncanny with the intensity he put into it.

Suppose the prediction proved to be correct? Why shouldn't it be? They all knew that the End must come. Why not next Wednesday instead of one thousand or two thousand years hence? Wasn't it more likely to happen now? Had not the Master said that "In a little while ye shall see me"? If the End was near then, it must be nearer now!

Louis could not have told how he got out of the church, because he was not fully conscious before he reached the street, and started off in mad haste. He had to get away quick, away from the people, away from everybody. He was naked, and everybody stared at him with big eyes . . . at him only. And he began to run for his life.

VI

Louis followed Main Street until he reached the country road leading westward. There he turned and left town. On and on he hurried, in a fast walk that sometimes broke into a trot, with no thought of destination. A voice kept urging him: "Away! Away!" There was a thin, shrill note in that voice; it rose from under his feet and shrieked across the prairie.

The day was cold, clear, and so still that the white silences must have gone to sleep. The big sun pricked them with points of diamonds and of gold, but there was no sound. Louis' red, blurred eyes saw nothing of the dazzling splendour.

When he had walked for about three-quarters of an hour his ear caught the sound of hoofs and of iron-shod runners cutting through the snow; and he sent more speed into the muscles of his legs, then ran till he was drenched with sweat. But in spite of his efforts the sleigh gained on him . . . now it was very close. Drawing up beside him, it stopped, and the driver asked him to climb aboard and have a ride.

The voice had so much kind gruffness in it that Louis accepted the invitation. Instantly the horses were off again, the snow creaking under the runners.

"Where're you bound for?" asked the man.

"Hah?"

"Where are you going?"

"Well—you see ——" Louis lapsed into silence.

"Do you live out this way?"

"No. . . . I used to own a farm up in Greenfield Township."

"You live in town now, then?"

"Yes, oh yes—we're living in town."

"Are you going out in the country to work?"

"Hah? Well, that all depends."

—This is a queer old fellow! the man thought. He certainly has been through some kind of smash-up . . . he looks down and out, with not a hope left. . . . His boys may not have come back from Europe. The man studied Louis' face till he felt compelled to find out something about it.

"Are you a married man?"

"Yes." Louis didn't answer right away.

"Any of yours been across?"

"Hah?"

—Something wrong about this fellow, that's sure, the man thought . . . he seems to be in great pain.

For a while they drove in silence. Louis sat looking at the horses; one of them resembled Fan when she was young . . . this one was of about the same colour and build. A nameless longing that threatened to tear out his heart came over Louis—he must see Jim and Fan or he'd die. . . . They were out this way, some-where?

"Did you lose any of yours?" the man tried again.

"Any of mine—what do you mean?"

"Have you any that won't return?"

"I don't think so," said Louis, absently, in a tired voice . . . "I have too many as it is."

"What you mean?" asked the man, uneasily.

"You see," said Louis, confidentially, "I have one too many, and I see no possible way of getting rid of him . . . she won't listen to me."

The man whacked the horses with the lines and moved as far away from Louis as he could get . . . this fellow was hardly all there?

"How far might you be going?" he asked, cautiously.

Louis didn't answer right away. There was a twitch-ing around his mouth, the man noticed. "I'm looking for a man by the name of Morgan . . . Tom Morgan," he said in the same tired voice. "He should live out this way. . . . I don't suppose you happen to know him?"

At this information the man was much relieved. "Oh, that's it! Yes, I know Tom well. He lives only four miles from my place. . . . Do you know Tom?"

"No . . . oh no! . . . No, it's only a little errand."

The man drove as fast as the horses would go. The fear that his passenger was crazy deepened. Through the corner of his eye he kept watching him. . . . Good thing that he'd soon be rid of him!

At the side road leading up to his house the man stopped and told Louis to get out. "Four miles up the road you'll find Tom's place; it's the third farm on the left-hand side; there's a big red barn, you can't miss it. Be you going back today?"

—Hah? Louis said, and thanking him for the ride, he started off, never once looking back.

After an hour or so of hard tramping he reached the farm, went up to the house and rapped. No one answered. The entire farm lay deserted; not even a dog barked.

The goading fear of doom let go of Louis. A grin on his face, he started for the barn . . . just so they hadn't taken the horses! . . . He ran across the yard, tore the barn door open and, stopping on the threshold, peered in. He gave a low cry—there they stood, side by side, just as at home.

The next instant he had grabbed a tail in each hand, shaking them violently and talking in a choked voice:

"Well, well, Jim—boy, how are you, anyway? And you, Fan, old girl?"

At the sound of the voice of their old master the horses whinnied lustily; throwing their heads back and pulling at their halters, they rolled their eyes so that the whites showed. Their neighings set the quiet of the barn afire.

Louis went into Jim's stall first, petting the horse all over. But he couldn't stay there long. When Fan's turn came he slipped his arm about her neck, uttering low cries, half human and half that of a mother beast that has lost her young and then, unexpectedly, has found them. A dam somewhere within him had burst open, and now he couldn't stop the rushing flood. With his cheek pressed against Fanny's skinny neck he sobbed convulsively.

After a while Louis went in search of the oats and the feed-pan. Not since they had been sold had the two worn-out plugs been treated to such a banquet as the one they now got. Fan, of course, had to be hand-fed as in olden days. Her soft muzzle tickled him so that he broke into a good chuckle: "You haven't forgotten any of your old tricks yet, have you!"

After feeding them oats he brought them water, then went up into the hayloft and filled their mangers with the finest hay he could find. Later he cleaned their stalls and fetched dry bedding . . . tonight his old friends would sleep in a clean bed!

When he had looked after all their needs he could think of he took each beast by the tail and shook them tenderly, his voice low and blubbering: "Well, here's good-bye to you, boys! If things go bad with me, I know you'll be all right, never you worry!"

As Louis started on his eighteen miles back to town

the twilight was fast changing into deep dusk. The air was still, and laden with frost; but the intense cold was not noticeable because of the deep stillness. There was no moon to light up the tracks in the road, and the walking was heavy.

In saddened resignation Louis plodded on. . . . He was better prepared now than he had been earlier in the day . . . now he had bid them good-bye and was done! . . . Only tomorrow and the day after . . . then it would be over with.

. . . Yes—then it would be "over with." The words rose in the calm stillness; he heard them clearly, distinctly. His feet tramped to the rhythm of them: "Over with, over with," and they made it easier for him to walk. . . . But he didn't like the sound of those words. The night was dark; he was far out on an unknown road; the icy stillness was terribly awake—you could hear the faintest hint of a sound. The constant repetition annoyed him. Louis slowed up his gait, putting down each foot warily, as one walking across a creaky floor afraid of making noise. Still the words rang out so that you could hear them miles away. "Over with— over with!" they called as soon as he thought of moving his feet.

"All right!" he said aloud, trying to make his voice sound natural. "You don't need to go hollering all night; I heard you the first time. . . . Lizzie is going to get what she has coming, and more, too . . . so don't worry. . . . It isn't a full thousand, but that doesn't matter. I'll give her a whole thousand, even if she kills me!"

In order to get the two words out of his ear, he took up the idea he had seen last night and began to discuss it aloud with himself:

"Tuesday night I'll manage it so that we're up late. . . . I must keep the fire going till she comes, and I'll have lots to tell her from the store . . . perhaps I'll be making a trip out in the country tomorrow, and have news from there. . . . Before we go to bed I'll take off my belt and count the money. . . . I'll tell her about Mary Ann . . . then she'll get scared; she'll begin to count hers, too—just see if she won't. . . . She'll be sitting on one side of the table, I on the other . . . I'll be having all my piles in a row, then I'll get her to look around and I'll steal a bill over to one of her piles . . . I'll have to manage it somehow. . . . But not before Tuesday night!"

Suddenly Louis stopped dead, in a great refulgence. Before he could stop it, a shout had escaped out of his throat: "What an ass I am!" And he repeated it. "It's easy as pie: I'll—why, I'll tell her that I am carrying too many bills in one pocket . . . there is a bump on it that makes my skin itchy—that's why I can't sleep nights!" There Louis stood laughing, unable to move a foot. "Nothing to it: I'll just ask her to take care of a couple for me until I can get another pocket sewed on . . . doggone it! if I won't make her take *three!* What do I care as long as she gets hers?"

Louis felt so pleased that he sat down by the road-side to rest himself and to eat a few handfuls of snow.

VII

When Louis had covered about six miles of the road homeward, he had no more walking left in his feet; no urging them on would help. The last few nights had been stingy with sleep, and lately he had not taken much food—today there had been only a few spoonfuls of porridge.

Wearily he dragged himself over to the first light by the roadside, found a door, hesitated for a moment, then knocked timidly.

A man so tall that he had to reef in his height in order to look through the doorway came and opened. A kind voice asked him to step inside. Louis looked up into the face of that voice; just then he could not have moved a foot: here stood the man who first had told him of the End.

In the lighted room the man recognized him, too.

"Well, are you coming to see me? How are you getting along these days?"

—Not any too well, Louis admitted; but he was getting along. . . . Could he have a drink? He drank three glasses of water and sank down into a chair.

In the room were two other persons—the man's wife and a grown daughter; the girl was slim of build, with a pale, delicate face, and eyes of unearthly brilliancy. The two women sat on opposite sides of the table, each with a book open. They must have been reading just as Louis came in.

Beneath the clock shelf stood a wooden rocker over the back of which hung a scarf, embroidered with large bright-coloured garlands. Louis' eyes rested on the flowers; the strong colours seemed to revive him. The whole room was scrupulously clean and gave an air of coziness. His eyes travelled up the wall to the clock. As he read the hour, half past nine, he drew a heavy sigh that came from deep down.

"I'd better be moving on. . . . How far is it to town?"

"Twelve miles."

There was a pause; Louis sat as if he had not heard.

"Twelve, you say?" he repeated in a dull voice.

Again he sighed, and put both hands on his knees as old people often do preparatory to getting up from the chair.

The tall frame of the man swelled with kindness as he asked:

"You look very tired, Brother?"

"Kind of tired . . . yes, kind of."

"You can stop here until tomorrow; we've an extra bed; the night is cold."

"I'd better not." Louis shook his head ruefully. . . . "You see, she doesn't know where I am . . . and I must speak to her tonight . . . only two more days left now," he added meditatively.

In his eagerness the man stretched halfway across the floor to look Louis in the face; and he smiled with big childlike eyes.

"Have you, too, seen the signs? Do you believe now? Can it be possible?"

Louis nodded absently:

"Today I've been off to say good-bye. . . . Did you say twelve miles?"

The man raised himself into his full height, a light shining from his face:

"How did you come, Brother?" he cried.

"How did I come?" Louis repeated the question, looking at the man, with dull face.

"I mean, how did you find the Way?"

"Oh . . . I was walking along . . . I was very tired . . . then I saw the light . . . and I came." Louis' voice trailed off into a toneless weariness.

"Did you hear that, Mother?" cried the man, exultantly. "Did you hear that, Jane?—He was on the Way and saw the Light! When I found him a few days ago, he was groping about in darkness. But now he has been to Shiloh, and his eyes have been opened; in the last seconds of the eleventh hour he has received his sight. Can you understand it, Mother? A great miracle has happened right here in Greenfield. Let us rejoice with prayers and thanksgiving. Please give me the Book, Mother!"

Taking the Bible from her, he bent himself over, paging until he found the place, then began to read in a rapt voice that was sweet with joy:

"And I looked, and, lo, a Lamb stood on the Mount Sion, and with him an hundred forty and four thousand, having his Father's name written in their foreheads. And I heard a voice from heaven, as the voice of many waters, and as the voice of a great thunder: and I heard the voice of harpers harping with their harps: And they sung as it were a new song before the throne, and before the four beasts, and the elders: and no man could learn that song but the hundred and forty and four thousand, which were redeemed from the earth. These are they which were not defiled with women; for they are virgins. These are they which follow the Lamb whithersoever he goeth. These were redeemed from among men, being the firstfruits unto God and to the Lamb. And in their mouth was found no guile: for they are without fault before the throne of God.

And I saw another angel fly in the midst of heaven, having the everlasting gospel to preach unto them that dwell on the earth, and to every nation, and kindred, and tongue, and people, saying with a loud voice, Fear God, and give glory to him; for the hour of his judgment is come: and worship him that made heaven, and earth, and the sea, and the fountains of waters.

And there followed another angel, saying, Babylon is fallen, is fallen, that great city, because she made all nations drink of the wine of the wrath of her fornication.

And the third angel followed them, saying with a loud voice, If any man worship the beast and his image,

*and receive his mark in his forehead, or in his hand,
the same shall drink of the wine of the wrath of God,
which is poured out without mixture into the cup of
his indignation; and he shall be tormented with fire
and brimstone in the presence of the holy angels, and
in the presence of the Lamb: and the smoke of their
torment ascendeth up for ever and ever: and they have
no rest day or night, who worship the beast and his
image, and whosoever receiveth the mark of his name.*

*Here is the patience of the saints: here are they that
keep the commandments of God, and the faith of Jesus.*

*And I heard a voice from heaven saying unto me,
Write,*

*Blessed are the dead which die in the Lord from
henceforth: Yea, saith the Spirit, that they may rest
from their labours, and their works do follow them.*

*And I looked, and behold a white cloud, and upon
the cloud one sat like unto the Son of man, having on
his head a golden crown, and in his hand a sharp sickle. . . .*

*And another angel came out of the temple which is
in heaven, he also having a sharp sickle. And another
angel came out from the altar, which had power over
fire; and cried with a loud cry to him that had the sharp
sickle, saying, Thrust in thy sharp sickle, and gather
the clusters of the vine of the earth; for her grapes are
fully ripe. And the angel thrust in his sickle into the
earth, and gathered the vine of the earth, and cast it
into the great winepress of the wrath of God. And the
winepress was trodden without the city, and blood came*

*out of the winepress, even unto the horse bridles, by
the space of a thousand and six hundred furlongs."*

His reading had changed into an exalted song of
praise, his soul filling each picture with throbbing reality. And no sooner had he closed the book than he fell
on his knees by the chair from which he had arisen a
while ago and began pouring out his heart in supplica-
tions. His long ungainly frame contorted under the
waves of emotion that passed through it; his kind face
shone with the light of transfiguration. The prayer,
even more so than the reading had been, was the out-
pouring in spontaneous song of an enraptured soul.
First of all he gave thanks to God for His many tender
mercies, and for having called, even at this late hour,
one more unworthy servant to work in His Vineyard.
Now He must not let go of his hand before the tribulations were over and before he walked safely on the
streets of the New Jerusalem. There followed a pleading intercession for the ninety and nine who still were
astray in dry and desert places, far, far away from the
Green Pastures and the Sweet Waters of Love. He
closed with a humble petition for himself and his family that the Lord during the few hours that still remained would not forsake them! "Let the light of Thy
Countenance shine upon us," he continued in intense
fervour. "Let not the sharp prongs of fear press too
deeply into our faint hearts! Thou Who wast made into
the likeness of man and walked the way of the Cross
to the end, remember Thou how frail we are!"

As he closed, a deep silence fell on the room. For a while he remained kneeling, his eyes shut tight.

While he prayed the two women had folded their hands upon the table; now their heads rested on them. Suddenly the back of the girl arched, a surge swept through her lean body, and she broke into violent sobs, pitiful, heartrending sobs—the anguish of one who sees the last ray of hope vanish; yet, as with her father, there was in her despair an inexpressible sweetness.

Her father gathered himself up from the floor and hastened to her. Patting her head tenderly, he spoke low, kind words, meant only for her:

"Don't, don't, Jane! It breaks my heart to see you sorrow. I, too, have been young once. I know what it means to give up life. But I promise you that you'll go playing by the shores of the Crystal Sea! Just two more days, only two more, and you'll be in the arms of the Bridegroom!" His tall frame folded itself into a loop; dangerous twitchings passed through it, and he got up and rubbed his eyes.

Louis used the knuckles on his.

When the man had knelt down and had begun to pray, Louis dropped his cap on the floor and pushed his own chair over to the wall, his eyes staring wildly: This was awful to look at . . . a common farmer carrying on this way . . . worse than any preacher in church—he must have gone crazy! But as the man went on pleading with the unseen power that was near and alive, something loosened inside Louis, thawed out, and he felt easier. He was so tired that he could have

gone to sleep. . . . Pleasant to sit here and listen . . .
like lying on your back in a green meadow, closing your
eyes and just resting yourself. . . . When the man's
voice died Louis gave a start: what was this now—
rain blowing up again?

Not looking around at either of them, Louis got up
and went to the door. The man came after him, his
voice not quite steady yet:

"Are all your dear ones safe, too? I suppose you've
a family? Will you be bringing them along with you?"

"I've only my wife."

"Is she safe?"

"Aw . . . I guess she'll be all right . . . she works
every day," explained Louis in a dead voice.

"Listen to that, Mother! Jane, did you hear it?
There's a woman who isn't afraid! Still one more soul
from Greenfield—there will be many more from here
than we in our dark unbelief had thought!"

Again he turned to Louis:

"You must be a happy man now?"

"Hah?" Louis buttoned up his coat. "You see, Lizzie
is an honest woman . . . never was any crookedness
in her . . . no trick for her . . . oh, no!"

Louis said good-night and stumbled out into the
darkness, which now stood silent and impenetrable as
a stone wall.

As he came away from the house he walked right
against a huge embankment of snow, tottered backward, and lost his cap. He fumbled and groped about

in the snow till he found it, got to his feet, and was on his way again.

. . . Twelve miles, twelve miles! Good Lord—how could he make his feet go twelve more miles tonight! . . . If it wasn't for that one bill, he'd. . . . No, no, no! he must see her tonight!

. . . What was the sound over in the darkness?— that terrible humming and buzzing in the air . . . a roaring that grew louder and more ominous? Now that's that damned threshing-rig again. "Ouch! ouch!" it said at every gobful, just like his old rig when the boys threw wet bundles into it. . . . "Ouch!—ouch!" Awful how that machine roared! . . . Louis walked till the sweat flowed down his body—not even then could he stop.

After plodding on for a long time he came to a big grove on the right, close to the road. The trees were huge giants; they threw their black arms clear into the sky, up among the stars, and stirred without sound.

He stopped, puzzled, then walked to the end of the grove, a long stretch of road, but he could not get his bearings . . . this wasn't right: he hadn't passed these woods on his way out . . . he must have taken a wrong road!

He turned and began to run back. Though his legs groaned from weariness, he clenched his teeth and ran harder than ever. But when he had gone so far that he could see the light from the house he had come out of a while ago, he realized that there could be no other road . . . this must be right.

And turning for the second time he began to sniff loudly. Big tears ran down his face and into his open mouth. He dragged his feet after him, like a child that has grown tired and is giving up. A queer, unreasonable desire came over him: to fall on his knees and talk to some one, the way the tall man had done. . . . No, no! he must go on, and get home as soon as possible! . . . He must pay back that thousand dollars!

Reaching the grove the second time, Louis could not go any farther; he had to sit down to rest. Dragging himself over to the roadside, he sank down into the soft snow. He lay on his back—it felt good to lie here and just stretch. . . . The night must be turning bitter cold . . . an icy blanket was being wrapped around his bare body. But there was a pleasant drowsiness stealing upon him. . . . Well, doggone you! he heard an old man's tired voice calling: You can't be lying here much longer, that's sure. . . . Better get up now . . . Lizzie has been waiting a long time!

VIII

About eight o'clock in the evening Lizzie came away from her long day's work in the kitchen down at the restaurant. She had been on her feet since morning and her back ached as though it were broken. Her humour was not much better.

All day while standing over the dish-washing she had

felt depressed; her wizened face was so foreboding, her
manners so distant and unapproachable, that the woman
who worked with her, after the first friendly attempt
to make talk, had crawled into her own shell; during
the long hours they had exchanged only a few words.

She had not been able to get Louis out of her mind.
. . . A worse good-for-nothing dolt never lived. Every
day he was getting more hopeless in his good-for-noth-
ingness—she could trample him under her feet and spit
on him! . . . And now he had got this Doomsday
nonsense on his brain! A wicked chuckle escaped her.
As her mind struggled with the problem her bitterness
toward life became unbearable; in her throat stuck a
lump that threatened to choke her, and she coughed.
From her hard, drawn features all light had gone out;
only cold lifelessness remained.

But the occasional gleams in her eyes when she slung
stacks of dishes into the sink told of sparks still smouldering within the dried-up body. . . . If it wasn't for
him she could have managed nicely . . . then she'd
take a heated room, pay the rent in work, and put the
rest aside as clear profit. . . . Now she had to earn
the food for him, and provide clothes. . . . She wondered what he'd do for tobacco, and the gleam in her
eyes shone brighter.

On her way home she was still working with the
problem of what to do with him. She saw no way.
Only one thing was clear: she could not have him
hanging around all winter; on that point her mind was
made up. In the air she saw mean, cutting words, words

that would pierce the hide of any fool, and she garnered them in carefully . . . tonight she'd have a heart-to-heart talk with him!

Approaching the Jenkins Store, she glanced at the upstairs window; there was no light, only the panes gleaming with white frost in the darkness. . . . Could he have gone to bed already? she wondered, and her features wrinkled into a hard frown . . . that man will sleep himself sick—you see if he won't!

She stepped lightly up the stairs. The door was unlocked, a still surer sign that he had gone to bed already; she closed it with a bang that resounded through the whole building.

"Are you in bed already?" she called in a high voice.

There was no answer, only a faint echo from the far-off corners of the building.

"Where's the lamp?" she rasped, hoarsely.

Out of the black emptiness came not the faintest peep of sound.

"Louis!" her voice rose higher: "Louis!" She ran into the bedroom and, with the force of resilient steel prongs bent back and suddenly released, her gnarled fingers dug into the covers.

No one there. The quilts were damp from the raw cold in the room. And Lizzie felt a sharp point run through her, right below the heart. Slowly she turned from the bed, peering about in the dark, her eyes burning hotly. On the wall opposite flickered a faint glare, uneasily; in it stood a bent figure of huge dimensions, crouching low as if ready to spring at her . . . his arm was raised.

Staring hard at the figure, Lizzie gave a sharp, low cry. Suddenly she realized that it was her own shadow, and laughed bitterly at her own weakness. Deliberately she lit the lamp, but she had some trouble in getting the chimney on. Leaving the lamp burning on the table, she went back to the restaurant and inquired what time Louis had been there for supper.

By now the waiters had gone; the proprietor could not remember having seen Louis all day.

As she returned to her rooms there was a set expression on her face. Coldly, in a rational spirit, she went to work to solve the mystery. No detail escaped her: He couldn't be very far away . . . the door hadn't been locked . . . the key was still standing in the hole on the inside—another of his slovenly habits when he went out on short errands . . . she looked for his coat; it was gone. She felt of the stove; there couldn't have been heat in it for a long time. She was caught by a sound coming down the stovepipe, a low oo-ing sound with a moan in it; when she listened it seemed to die down, but started up again as soon as she let her breath go. She felt disgust with herself because she was so nervous tonight: he could just wait till she got her hands on him! . . . She went over to the bread box to examine the bread; the loaf had not been touched since this morning. Her brows knit themselves into knots: Never before had she known him to miss a meal . . . the fool couldn't have gone to the country without telling her, leaving the door unlocked and everything?

She had her coat on. As she looked about the rooms waves of uneasiness surged up in her, rising higher and higher, making bigger and shaggier the awful monster creeping upon her: What could that fool of a man have done with himself? Where could he be keeping himself this hour of the night?

Her eyes fell on two objects on the table and she drew a deep breath which gave her relief. Picking them up, she began to examine them critically: There he has gone off without his pipe! She looked into the package of tobacco; it was more than half full. . . . He couldn't have gone very far without his pipe.

An evil chuckle bubbled up in her throat: I'll just bet that old tomcat has gone to the movies—he has hinted about it before . . . well, if that man has no more sense than that! . . . Her hands closed in a tight grip, which immediately relaxed: no, he had certainly been out since this morning.

. . . This morning? Her face lit up: He must have gone to church. She grinned wickedly: Just like him to have gone to church . . . because when he got scared he'd stop at nothing. . . . Some one had perhaps invited him to dinner—these Yankees could be flush when they wanted to . . . he had stayed on and gone to church tonight too . . . he'd be home pretty soon. The annoying uneasiness prevented her disgust from breaking out anew.

With her coat still on she sat down to wait. There

had been no fire in the stove since early morning; the room was like an ice box. Even with her coat on, Lizzie froze. Holding her breath to catch the least little sound only increased her shivers.

Thus she sat till the clock showed ten, but then her uneasiness drove her to her feet: her figuring hadn't come out right. . . . If he had gone to church tonight, too, he certainly should be home by now!—She went to the front window and began to thaw a hole through the thick layer of ice. After considerable effort she had cleared a small spot, but the blackness of the night was so solid that she could see nothing except the street lamps; around them lay a greyish-white fog, which made the lights look drowsy-eyed. The cold seeping in through the window soon drove her away.

Coming back into the room, she found her home-knit shawl which she tied around her neck. To avoid the draught from the wall she pulled the chair into the middle of the room and sat down. Unless he came pretty soon she'd go to bed! . . . Where could he be keeping himself this time of night? And with all that money about him . . . old good-for-nothing that he was! Suppose . . . ? On the horizon of her consciousness dark clouds were piling themselves up into threatening banks; out of them blew a chill so piercing that Lizzie lost sight of the punishment she was going to administer to him when he came home.

By and by the uneasiness made her get up. She tied the shawl on better, put on her mittens, locked the door, and went out.

Down on the street she hesitated. The night was still and full of a cold that burnt her face. No life. No sound. Only dead silence that fell heavily upon her. She walked to the end of Main Street, crossed over to the other side, and came back; then she turned down Jackson Avenue as far as the depot. Reaching the Greenfield Coal Co., she stopped and peered into the alley, walking a few steps down among the coal sheds. The silent buildings gave her a sinister look, demanding to know why she was prowling around here. The half-empty coal-bins stared menacingly at her. Warily she retraced her steps, walking backward . . . did she see something stir in that bin? A shadow move her way? . . . When she turned into Jackson Avenue she began to run, never stopping until she reached her room. She was out of breath from running, yet she shivered.

She stepped into the room, closed the door, and listened: Had some one been here? Did she hear retreating steps? She seemed to hear words that had just been spoken. The lamp burnt with a dim light; most of the rooms lay in deep shadows, the inner one in complete darkness. It was colder now than when she had left. The clock told half past ten; the ticking of it stuck pin-holes through the silence.

All of a sudden the misgivings she had striven to keep down broke full and clear through the surface of her consciousness: Something must have happened to him! . . . This didn't look right . . . Louis out this time of night, and with all that money. . . . They had fooled him out, had killed him in order to rob him!

. . . Perhaps they had spied on him when he sat here alone counting . . . he was always so careless, went talking and blabbering to everybody . . . how could people help finding out!

. . . If they had got him, they'd soon have her, too —in town you were never safe. One after another she recalled the stories she had heard since she had come here: about assaults, robberies, and murders. Such things happened in broad daylight, on the open street, in private homes . . . even in guarded banks; and at night robberies took place in the thick of the city as though there was no Law in the land. . . . Now that the bloodhounds had tasted spoil, they'd be out after her!

Once the barriers were broken through, black, nameless terrors poured into her heart. She shook so hard that she had to hold on to the chair. But she didn't have time to think of herself; like a top her mind spun: I must find him first! Unless they had spied on him when he took off his belt, they would hardly find his money . . . they can't find it before they take his underwear off. . . . I ought to start right away to hunt for him . . . down among those sheds, in the empty coal-bins—he must be there somewhere . . . they can't have taken him far. . . . Like a drunken man who doesn't know where he is going she shuffled back and forth between the two rooms, but always near the door. . . . She found the ax and placed it by the door casing—tonight she better be on her guard.

The night grew heavy with fearfulness. The cold

of the winter gripped the buildings and cracked Doomsday cracks through every corner; you could hear the
reports far out on the prairie. The street lamp peering
in through Lizzie's window had a wicked eye; when it
looked at the wall there was a leer in it. A wind must
be coming up; Lizzie could hear it every time she
came near the stove, a whoo-ing and a oo-ing down
the pipe. In the shadows and on the stairs padded slow
feet; they shuffled about in the dark, waiting for her
to blow out the lamp.

Shortly before one o'clock she stopped abruptly.
Hist! There was some one at the door below the stairs.
Her frame bent taut in listening and her nerves stif-
fened into steel springs. She tried to scream, but there
was no sound left in her throat; her face was green
with pallour. . . . There it was again! She heard the
street door push open. Some one mounted the first step
and was feeling his way to the second . . . then she
heard nothing for a while. . . . He must be listening!
. . . There he was again! No, there was more than
one . . . two, at least. Like a shadow Lizzie glided
across the floor, no sound in her step, as swiftly as the
thought that shot through her mind: here they have
come! She grabbed hold of the door knob to turn the
key; the key was gone; she had left it on the table
when she came in. Now it was too late to get it; they
were halfway up the stairs already . . . there was a
whole gang of them! . . . O my God! she groaned.
Grasping the door knob tighter, she braced a foot

against each door casing and strained till sparks flew out of her eyes and her ears filled with deafening roars.

Her whole body drank sound. Higher and higher they came, step by step . . . they were dragging something after them; she heard it knock against the stairs. They were not walking, they crawled on all fours.

. . . Now they were clear up, fumbling and groping for the lock. There was a rasping sound on the other side of the door. The knob gave a twist and a hard jerk. Lizzie heard deep moanings come out of a dark cavern . . . felt another twist and more frantic jerkings. For the space of many hours, so it seemed to her, all was still as in a grave . . . then a huge bulk, that must weigh tons, sank in a heap right up against the door . . . there was another unearthly groan, and all was stiller than death itself.

Lizzie held on till her mouth filled with the taste of rank blood. The room was getting dark. Turning her head, she saw that the lamp was going out. Then she gave a terrible cry which went through the whole building and came back in a faint echo that died slowly.

Her back and arms were giving out; all strength had leaked out of them; she must rest herself or she couldn't hold out. Warily she let go of the knob with one hand; with the other she untied her scarf, threw a loop in it which she slipped around the knob—there now!

Hanging on to the scarf she lowered herself to the floor, and tried to listen through the opening at the bottom of the door. No sound; only an icy breath out of the black stillness . . . they were waiting for the room to get dark!

Thus she sat for a long time. The lamp had died, but she didn't notice it. She was getting drunk from the dead cold that flowed into her body. She did not notice that, either, because it was so pleasant and nice, and so warm.

Suddenly the door at the bottom of the stairs creaked open, then slammed. Lizzie crammed the last ounces of consciousness into her listening. . . . There it slammed again . . . more were coming . . . this gallivanter up here was only standing guard! She tried to raise herself and to hang on harder . . . where was the ax? . . . Now they were coming thick and fast—slow, padding, sneaking feet . . . slam-slam went the door.

. . . Still they were coming, an army of men with black faces, each with a scythe on his shoulder. Lizzie thought it strange that they should bring scythes when she was using the ax—there she recognized the face of Steve Berg. . . . "My goodness! if you ain't here, too! Now you just wait!"

She lost sight of Steve, and broke into a laugh that wouldn't stop; she had to hold on to her sides or the breath would go out of her. It was the funniest thing she had ever seen: There Louis stood in his shirt sleeves at the bottom of the stairs, snapping his fingers in the air; with each snap he gave a sharp, short whistle, and out of the stairway and into the street bounded a black-faced man with a long scythe dangling down his back. Snap-whiz, snap-whiz, and out popped the men, just like that!

Lizzie was warm and comfortable, and full of good fun. . . . Now that Louis had snapped all these black faces out of the house, she would take out her belt to see if her money was all right: Three, five, eight, ten . . . now, how was that? She had never had so many in one pocket. . . . Wait a minute: what had become of that high-toned fellow from Minneapolis? . . . Just a little imitation of a spank he'd have today . . . see how he cuddled up to her!

. . . Now she was sitting on the bed at home out on the farm. In the doorway stood Louis, grinning, with his pipe in his mouth and an old bushel basket under his arm. She was good and mad at him: Did you ever see such a man—lugging that old basket into the bedroom! . . . Couldn't he see that she had just swept? . . . Louis only laughed and laughed, till you couldn't see his eyes, and then he began throwing funny paper balls at her, picking them out of the basket and snapping them on his thumb. Pretty soon they were popping out of the basket like grasshoppers. She opened one, and it was a new one-thousand-dollar bill. Every last one of them was a brand-new one-thousand-dollar bill, and they flicked about her ears thicker than specks in a cloud of spring dust. . . . "Wait a minute! wait a minute!" cried Louis in a boyish voice, drawing the last "wait" out into a mile, "till I get you another basketful! You're going to have all you want, doggone it if you ain't!"

IX

Not until three days afterward were Louis and Lizzie found. Mrs. Cadman was the first to discover the tragedy. When Lizzie failed to show up as usual on Wednesday and did not appear Thursday morning, either, Mrs. Cadman went to see what could be the matter. But halfway up the stairs she became so frightened that she almost tumbled headfirst down the steps. A pair of feet with German socks on stuck out across the stairs. She had run herself out of breath when she reached her husband's office. She begged him to hurry over to the Houglums' . . . he must be quick . . . a drunken man was sleeping on the stairs . . . he looked dead, oh, it was an awful sight. . . . He must bring Lizzie home with him . . . if she couldn't get Lizzie to help with the work, there'd be no Christmas at their house! Mrs. Cadman wrung her hands and looked at her husband in utter dismay.

"Now, now, Evelyn, don't take it so hard! I'll get the old girl for you, and don't worry!" The doctor put his arm around her waist tenderly. "You go home, Evelyn, and wrap my Christmas present while I run up and see her!"

An hour later the doctor, quite shaken up, stepped into the store and asked to speak to Jenkins privately. He told him that there were two corpses upstairs and that he better call the coroner at once. "Really, one of the worst cases I've seen," confided the doctor. "The old couple have gone to work and just frozen to death. For the life of me I can't see how it could have happened. He is lying outside in the hall, and she inside the door with the ax in her hand. It's neither murder nor suicide. There is no sign of violence of any kind. You come and see if you can figure it out."

Mr. Jenkins grew excited. He implored the doctor to keep quiet. There were still a few days left until Christmas. If this matter got out, it might ruin his trade. What would he do with all these goods on his hands?

x

The undertaker did not come till it was almost night. It was the most unpleasant business he had ever had. The room was dark and full of frost, and the stench fearful. He worked with swift, sure strokes. The belts were cut and thrown in with the clothes. The doctor had given explicit orders that everything they had on must be burnt, because there might be danger of influenza—it had appeared in the East already.

After all the people had left the store the smoke from a small bonfire back of Jenkins' Drygoods & Groceries curled itself lazily up through the frosty air of the cold star-night. The paper which had been wrapped around the clothes and the clothes themselves gave a cheerful flame. The belts went more slowly. But gradually they too changed into slender columns of blue smoke which mingled with the calm, deep night and was gone.

THE END

DATE DUE